English Poetic Diction

FROM

Chaucer to Wordsworth

English Poetic Diction

FROM

Chaucer to Wordsworth

ARTHUR SHERBO

MICHIGAN STATE UNIVERSITY PRESS

1975

Contents

For Winona and in memory of Paul

Acknowledgments

I am grateful to Michigan State University for research grants that made it possible to have some clerical assistance; to the Ford Foundation, administered at Michigan State University by Dr. Ralph Smuckler, Dean of International Programs, for a grant that enabled me to travel to Cambridge, England; and especially to Dr. Alan M. Hollingsworth, Chairman of the Department of English at Michigan State University, for arranging a research leave in which I was able to finish this book. The staffs of the Michigan State University and Cambridge University libraries accorded me every courtesy. Miss Lorraine Hart, Associate Office Manager of the Department of English at Michigan State University, and Miss Rosemary Graham, formerly of the Cambridge University Library and now a graduate student at Leeds University, both of whom typed portions of my manuscript, helped to create order out of chaos. The Master and Fellows of Corpus Christi College, Cambridge, graciously elected me a Visiting Scholar of their College and by their hospitality made my final months of research and writing more pleasurable than one could reasonably expect.

Prolegomena

Dr. Johnson's well-known dictum that before Dryden's time there was "no poetical diction: no system of words at once refined from the grossness of domestick use and free from the harshness of terms appropriated to particular arts" is not one of his happiest utterances. He was, of course, thinking about what his century termed low or mean words and also about remote words "to which we are nearly strangers," so that upon their occurrence, "they draw that attention to themselves which they should transmit to things," and to this extent he is partially right. But when he continued that "those happy combinations of words which distinguish poetry from prose had been rarely attempted; we had few elegances or flowers of speech," he was overlooking a considerable body of English poetry.[1] But, like so many of his contemporaries, he was primarily concerned in these statements with distinguishing between the language of prose and that of poetry, and not so much with discriminating between good and bad poetic language.

For example, in 1762, more than fifteen years before Johnson's *Lives* of the poets, James Beattie[2] distinguished seven characteristics of what he termed the "English poetical dialect": (1) a few Greek and Latin idioms (quenched of hope), (2) words with additional syllables (dispart), (3) ancient words (featly), (4) uncommon words (cates), (5) abbreviated words (o'er), (6) compound epithets (rosy-finger'd), and (7) nouns transformed into verbs and participles (to hym, cavern'd). Like Johnson, Beattie was concerned with discriminating between the language of prose and, to use his own term, "the language of poetry" and he looked upon some words, "because they rarely occur in prose, and frequently in verse" as "poetical."[3] But poetical words, he realized, could be abused. Thus, for compound epithets, Beattie suggested that they be "used sparingly; and those only used, which the practice of popular authors has rendered familiar to the ear, and which are in themselves peculiarly emphatical and harmonious."[4] And thus, too, for those expressions which walk the tightrope between obsoleteness and poeti- calness, since here "the practice of Milton, Dryden, or Pope, may therefore, in almost all cases, be admitted as good authority for the use of a poetical word."[5] Here, also, however, Beattie felt obliged to enter a caveat, for no matter how excellent Pope's translation of Homer,

> sometimes, for the sake of his numbers, or for fear of giving offence by too close an imitation of Homer's simplicity, [he] employed tropes and figures too quaint or too solemn for the occasion. And the finical style is in part charac- terised by the writer's dislike of literal expressions, and affectedly substituting in their stead unnecessary tropes and figures. With these authors a man's only child must always be his *only hope,* a country-maid becomes a *rural beauty,* or perhaps a *nymph of the groves;* if flattery sing at all, it must be a *syren song;* the shepherd's flute dwindles into an *oaten reed,* and his crook is exalted into a *scepter;* the *silver lillies* rise from their *golden beds,* and *languish* to the *complaining* gale. A young woman, though a good Christian, cannot make herself agreeable without *sacrificing to the Graces;* nor hope to do any execu- tion among the *gentle swains,* till a whole legion of *Cupids,* armed with *flames* and *darts,* and other weapons, begin to discharge from her eyes their formida- ble artillery. For the sake of variety, or of the verse, some of these figures may now and then find a place in a poem; but in prose, unless very sparingly used, they favour of affectation.[6]

By "finical style," Beattie meant what today we would call one aspect of poetic diction and what Pope in *Peri Bathous, or The Art of Sinking in Poetry,* described as consisting of "the most curious, affected, mincing Metaphors." Beattie tolerated its occasional presence in a poem, a tolerance based upon the now outmoded view that the poet is servant to the needs of variety and versification, but he objected to its indiscriminate use in prose. All this is very well, if one is concerned, as Beattie was, with distin- guishing between the language of prose and that of poetry; for present purposes it is enough that Beattie catalogued most of the characteristics of poetic diction. Similar eighteenth-century conceptions of the art of poetry prompted Beattie to observe that poets sometimes reject words that are "untuneable and harsh" or too long or too short for their measure, and "hence another use of figurative language [is] that it contributes to poetical harmony. Thus, *to press the plain* is frequently used to signify *to be slain in battle; liquid plain* is put for *ocean, blue serene* for *sky,* and *sylvan reign* for *country life.* "[7]

One further observation is necessary. Beattie made much of the appropriateness or lack of appropriateness of the language given particular characters in drama and demonstrated his point with an example, choosing this speech by Desdemona,

> My mother had a maid call'd Barbara;
> She was in love, and he she loved proved mad,
> And did forsake her. She had a song of willow;
> An old thing it was, but it express'd her fortune,
> And she died singing it. That song to-night
> Will not go from my mind; I have much to do,
> But to go hang my head all at one side,
> And sing it like poor Barbara.[8]

His appended footnote reads

> Othello, act 4, scene 3. This charming passage, translated into the *finical style,* which, whatever be the subject or speaker, must always be descriptive, enigmatical, and full of figures, would perhaps run thus:
>
> > Even now, sad Memory to my thought recals
> > The nymph Dione, who, with pious care,
> > My much-loved mother, in my vernal years,
> > Attended: blooming was the maiden's form,
> > And on her brow Discretion sat, and on
> > Her rosy cheek a thousand Graces play'd.
> > O luckless was the day, when Cupid's dart,
> > Shot from a gentle swain's alluring eye,
> > First thrill'd with pleasing pangs her throbbing breast!
> > That gentle swain, ah! gentle now no more,
> > (Horrid to tell!), by sudden phrensy driven,
> > Ran howling to the wild: blood-tinctured fire
> > Glared from his haggard eyeballs, and on high
> > The hand of Horror raised his ragged hair,
> > And cold sweat bathed his agonizing frame.
> > What didst thou then, Dione! ill-star'd maid!

3

> What couldst thou do! – From morn to dewy eve,
> From Eve till rosy-finger'd Morn appear'd,
> In a sad song, a song of ancient days,
> Warbling her wild woe to the pitying winds,
> She sat; the weeping willow was her theme,
> And well the theme accorded with her woe;
> Till Fate suppress'd at length th' unfinish'd lay.
> Thus on Meander's flowery mantled side
> The dying cygnet sings, and singing dies.

> I hope my young readers are all wiser; but I believe there was a time, when I should have been tempted to prefer this flashy tinsel to Shakespeare's fine gold. I do not say, that in themselves these lines are all bad, though several of them are; and in some sorts of composition the greater part might perhaps be pardonable; but I say, that, considered in relation to the character and circumstances of Desdemona, they are all unnatural, and therefore not poetical.[9]

Beattie's complacence and his suggestion that the lines are not all bad, "though several of them are," and that "in some sorts of composition the greater part might perhaps be pardonable" indicate the distance that separates his view from ours, for there are not, in our eyes, *any* compositions in which the passage as a whole could be considered anything but bad. Its only merit lies in its parodic intent, but Beattie, intending the lines as parody because they do not fit Desdemona and her circumstances, did not see that they are bad under any circumstances.[10]

The existence of poetic diction as an undesirable phenomenon in eighteenth-century poetry is further attested to by the fact that it is ridiculed by poets, critics, and even novelists. John Dennis thought very little of "Mr. Pope's translation of Homer," upon which he wrote some *Remarks* in 1717. Of the line in the *Iliad*, "Conven'd to Council all the Grecian Train" (1. 75), he found it in his heart to write: "The Grecian *Train*, for Grecian *Army*, is something odd, and pretty near to Burlesque. And 'tis rather to be taken Notice of, because I believe he has made use of the same Word in the same sense, an Hundred times.[11] One would swear by his translation, that AGAMEMNON was nothing but some *Exchange-Alley* Stock Jobber, who had the Honour to command a Company of *Train Bands*."[12] Dennis, it is clear, objected to the word because of its frequency of use and because it had a "low" association. In 1696 Dennis had pounced on Richard Blackmore's epic, *Prince Arthur*, in some pamphlet *Remarks on a Book Entitled, Prince Arthur, An Heroick Poem*, regretfully writing at one juncture, "I

4

design'd particularily to have examined the difference between a Poetick and a Prosaick Diction," a task which he had had to forego, but a statement which is further evidence of the awareness of "Poetick" diction on the part of the critics.[13] Pope himself ridicules one aspect of poetic diction in *The Art of Sinking in Poetry*. There he defines periphrase as "another great Aid to *Prolixity;* being a difus'd circumlocutory Manner of expressing a known Idea, which should be so misteriously couch'd, as to give the Reader the Pleasure of guessing what it is that the Author can possibly mean; and a Surprize when he finds it," and gives an example from Richard Blackmore's *Job*. But Joseph Spence later pointed to somewhat the same fault in Pope's version of the *Odyssey,* singling out as "unnecessary Ornaments" such expressions as "A Store of flying Fates" for "a Quiver full of Arrows," and "the Sable Wave of offer'd Wine" for "a Libation." Indeed, in a number of his strictures on the *Odyssey* translation, Spence was concerned to point out and condemn what we would call poetic diction, objecting, for one example only, to the couplet, "Spread his broad Sails, and *plough the liquid way,* / Soon as the Morn *unveils her Saffron Ray.* "[14] To return to Pope, few faults were ridiculed by him of which he himself is not guilty, and usually in his translations of Homer.

John Gay was almost surely glancing at poetic diction when, in a song in *The Beggar's Opera,* he wrote

> Virgins are like the fair Flower in its Lustre,
> Which in the Garden enamels the Ground;
> Near it the Bees in Play flutter and cluster,
> And gaudy Butterflies frolick around
> > [act 1, scene 7],

and then followed the flower's progress to Covent Garden where eventually it "Rots, stinks, and dies, and is trod under feet." Later in the century Charles Churchill wrote caustically of those "Fops" among "the Scribbling tribe, / Who make it all their business to *describe,* " and then proceeded to parody their efforts:

> Let *liquid* Gold emblaze the Sun at noon,
> With *borrow'd* beams let Silver pale the Moon,
> Let surges *hoarse* lash the resounding shore,
> Let Streams *Meander,* and let Torrents *roar,*
> Let them breed up the *melancholy* breeze
> To *sigh with sighing, sob with sobbing* trees,

5

> Let Vales *embroid'ry* wear, let Flow'rs be *ting'd*
> With various *tints,* let Clouds be *lac'd* or *fring'd.*[15]

Tobias Smollett made tender fun of one of his characters in *The Expedition of Humphry Clinker* (1771) and of the diction of poetry descriptive of nature when he had Lydia Melford, in a letter to Letty Willis, dated April 21, write from Hot Wells,

> this is a charming romantic place. The air is so pure; the Downs so agreeable; the furze in full blossom; the ground *enamelled* with daisies, and primroses, and cowslips; all the trees bursting into leaves, and the hedges already *clothed with their vernal livery;* the mountains covered with flocks of sheep, and tender bleating *wanton lambkins* playing, frisking and skipping from side to side; the groves *resound* with the notes of black-bird, thrush, and linnet; and all night long sweet *Philomel pours* forth her ravishing delightful song [my italics].

Soon after the publication of *Humphry Clinker,* John Aikin wrote

> it is at least certain that supineness and servile imitation have prevailed to a greater degree in the description of nature, than in any other part of poetry. The effect of this has been, that descriptive poetry has degenerated into a kind of phraseology, consisting of combinations of words which have been so long coupled together, that, like the hero and his epithet in Homer, they are become inseparable companions. It is amusing, under some of the most common heads of description, in a poetical dictionary, to observe the wonderful sameness of thoughts and expressions in passages culled from a dozen different authors. An ordinary versifier seems no more able to conceive of the Morn without rosy fingers and dewy locks, or Spring without flowers and showers, loves and groves, than of any of the heathen deities without their usual attributes.[16]

Quite obviously, the stock diction of poetry of natural description was still flourishing in the third quarter of the eighteenth century and still attracting adverse critical attention.

Aikin's point about the poetical dictionaries is well taken and helps partially to account for the currency of certain words and phrases, a currency that goes back to the earliest days of some of these florilegia. The best known of these earlier poetical dictionaries is Joshua Poole's.[17] The meat of his collection is the alphabetical listing of those "choicest epithets and phrases," culled from a variety of sources, listed by Poole, including DuBartas, Ben Jonson, Drayton, May's *Lucan,* Quarles, Sandys's *Ovid,* "Horace Translated," *The Faerie Queen,* Shakespeare, Orlando Furioso, Chapman's *Homer,* "Comedies and Tragedies, many," Sidney, Daniel, "Virgil Translated," some works in prose, and a number of other poets. "Cowper's Hill" seems the work of latest date in the list. Most of the words used and to be used in the poetry descriptive of nature are in the alphabetical list, and one finds that Aegypt is corny (as well as reedy and swarthy), amber is unctious (and gummy), apples are pendent, birds are painted, eagles and horses (and princes) are generous, dew is pearly, fish are finny, right through to Zephyrus which is described as balmy, spicy, flowry, and in twelve other choice epithets. Some words, such as wave and wind, are described by some fifty epithets and phrases. A more modest but revealing example of the poetic diction in the collection can be seen in this complete entry:

> Mead, Meadow, v. [ide] Plains: Motly, smiling, verdant, enflower'd, fragrant, herby, grassy-paved, embroyder'd, diaper'd, enamell'd, tufted, dazied, levell'd, fertil, fruitful, sportive, gamesome, green-plush'd, checker'd, gaudy, painted, fair-clothed, wide-skirted, flower-enamell'd, flowry-mantled, greenmantled, soft-coated, pleasant, spacious, flower-spangled, green-breasted, stream-embroidered.

Virtually the gamut of personification by articles of dress is run, with embroidery, diapers, plush, clothes, skirts, mantles, and spangles. Here, then, is one of the ways, and doubtless an important one, in which much poetic diction was transmitted. The aspiring young poet not only had some two hundred pages of this alphabetical guide to fall back upon, but he also had about four hundred pages of quotation, arranged in alphabetical order under subject, in which he could see the epithets and phrases in various poetical contexts.

Modern students of poetic diction are in relatively close agreement in their definition of the phenomenon, most of them favoring some term such as stock diction, vocabulary, or phraseology. Other terms used are conventional, artificial, and stereotyped. Although the concept of frequency is at least implicit in some of the words used to describe poetic diction, some scholars have taken the added precaution of stressing its repetitive nature. Here, to anticipate briefly, it must be understood that the method of forming new adjectives by adding the -y suffix to nouns, one of the characteristics of poetic diction, may result in an adjective that appears only once or twice in a poet or even in a century, yet that coinage belongs to poetic diction because of its method of formation. Actually, only the most far-fetched

7

products of this method are not encountered again and again. Most of these same students of poetic diction are agreed on its elements: periphrases, adjectives formed by adding the -y suffix to a noun, Latinisms, and a vaguer but important category of favored or recurring words. Some add archaisms or compound epithets, but in this study only the four listed above are considered.

Again, with one or two dissenting voices, poetic diction is considered, for the most part, bad. Geoffrey Tillotson defines poetic diction as "the sum of the favourite words used by a single poet or a single set of poets." "These," he continues, "which may well figure in prose, strike us with particular force in the writings of the poets concerned because they appear frequently. They are necessary because the poets rely on them for the effects they wish to make and to make often." After listing a number of these "recurrent favourites" in the poetry written in the period "from Elizabethan times till into the nineteenth century, with a concentration in, say, the years 1650–1750," Tillotson makes a distinction between the use and abuse of poetic diction. "This sort of diction is sometimes dubbed 'stock,' but it is only that for poets who fail to rise to occasions. Each time a word is used by a good poet it is a partly new thing; the good poet is a voice, and only the bad poet that mindless thing, an echo—to adapt Goethe's useful distinction between genius and talent."[18] Two points need to be made here. While it is true of course that poetic diction spans centuries, it is curious that Tillotson should think of poetic diction in terms of "a single poet or a single set of poets," for it is found in poets of all kinds, even of violently opposing schools of poetry—as, for instance, in the poetry of Pope and of the Warton brothers and Collins. But I cannot agree that each time "a word is used by a good poet, it is a partly new thing."

One of the earliest modern studies of poetic diction is that of Myra Reynolds.[19] Miss Reynolds's chief preoccupations are with attitudes toward nature, how they came into being, and what expression they were given in English poetry. As part of her analysis of the treatment of nature in poetry up to about 1700, she states that the poets of this period, beginning in 1621 with Waller's first couplets,[20] tend to turn away from "the grand and mysterious" in nature in favor of "the gentler forms of outdoor life."[21] However, this feeling toward gentle nature is largely superficial and hence manifests itself in "idyllic descriptions [which] are to the last degree artificial and unreal."[22] The details—i.e., the poetic diction—in these descriptions are standardized, with great frequency of "limpid" or "lucid" bodies of water; "shady" or "flowery" or "verdant" meads, dales, vales, and woods; breezes that are "gentle" or "whisper" or "fan" the field.[23] Miss Reynolds writes that

> By universal consent certain words and phrases seem to have been stamped as reputable, national, and present, and to have formed the authorized storehouse of poetical supplies. If one writer hit out a good word or phrase, it became common property like air or sunshine, and other writers did not waste their time beating the bush for a different form of words. Frequently words in the accepted diction may be traced to some Latin author, but the point to be noted here is that whatever the origin of the word, its use is incessant.[24]

Many of these items of poetic diction are listed, the formation of -y adjectives from nouns is glanced at, and the indebtedness of the poets of this period to Latin writers is acknowledged. In short, one has here the beginnings of a study of one aspect of poetic diction, that which is used in the description of nature.

Miss Reynolds detects the beginning of a new attitude toward nature, an attitude finding expression "during the two decades before the publication of [Thomson's *Winter*] in 1726,"[25] and follows its fortunes in that period, and also in the periods from 1726 to 1730, 1730 to 1756, and finally from 1756 to 1798. What she has failed sufficiently to observe is that some of the poetic effects she most admires in the treatment of nature in the poetry of these later periods are conveyed in that poetic diction she had condemned in the earlier period. Thus, she can write of Thomson's line describing stars "That more than deck, that animate the sky" that it seems "a turning away from the old artificial conception."[26] If the conception is new, the verbs deck and animate, as used by Thomson, are part of an old poetic diction. The same can be said of "a surprisingly large number of such words as 'effulgent,' 'refulgent,' 'effusion,' 'diffusion,' 'suffusion,' 'profusion,' from the roots 'fundo' and 'fulgeo' with their idea of liberal pouring out."[27] While Miss Reynolds finally acknowledges that Thomson is still strongly influenced by the old diction, she is impelled to defend his large use of Latinized words as hardly belonging "to any received poetic diction."[28] The point to make here is that the very practice of using Latinized words is part of the received poetic diction, even if the words she gives as examples were not in widespread use before Thomson. She lists bibulous, concoctive, gelid, hyperborean, incult, irriguous, luculent, ovarious, relucent, and turgent. None is to be found in Dryden's *Virgil* or Pope's *Iliad,* but irriguous has its precedent in Milton's *Paradise Lost* (4. 255) and in Virgil; gelid too comes from Virgil.[29] It is an easy step from Milton's "lucent orb" (*Paradise Lost* 3. 589) to relucent; and Virgil has three uses of *reluceo*. Hyperborean occurs in what Tillotson conceives to be a seminal work in the formation and transmission of poetic diction, Joshua Sylvester's translation of DuBartas (1. 5. 635), and in the poems of William Drummond, of Hawthornden.[30] Turgent is a medical term, which places it *hors de combat*, although it is to be found in Thomas Creech's translation of Lucretius, 1714, Book 4, 1. 1054;[31] incult may be a recollection of Virgil also, for *incultus* appears five times in his poetry. Concoctive is listed in the *OED* as used by Thomson for the first time in the secondary sense of "Tending to ripen or mature by heat." In its primary meaning of "Pertaining to digestion (of food); digestive" it had been used by Milton in *Paradise Lost* (5. 437, "concoctive heat"); ovarious is first exemplified in the *OED* by Thomson's use of it; bibulous, meaning absorbent of moisture, was used in 1675 by Evelyn, and there is no earlier use of the word in the *OED*. Twice in the *Georgics* (1. 114 and 2. 348) Virgil uses biblulus in the sense in which it appears in Thomson. Miss Reynolds's remarks on Parnell,[32] John Brown,[33] William Julius Mickle,[34] and Michael Bruce[35] are also vitiated by her failure to note the ubiquitous presence of the old poetic diction in the poems and lines she admires.

Poetic diction found a champion in C. V. Deane in his examination of nature poetry in the eighteenth century, for it is his belief that "the adoption of stock diction generally imparts an easy movement to verse" and that "the existence of a stock diction that could be drawn on at will may be considered a poetical asset; the performer was free to play whatever new tunes he wished when the technique of his instrument was so secure."[36] Much of what Deane goes on to suggest is based on his assumptions that eighteenth-century poets writing nature poetry deliberately used stock diction to set off their striking original phrases and that "an artificial style, if artistically managed, is capable of yielding effects of absolute poetic merit."[37] As a result, he can write that Virgil, for him one of the great sources of poetic diction, whose *liquidi fontes* he quotes as one example, "used such phrases (which occur far less frequently in the *Ecloques* than in the translations or original pastorals of eighteenth-century writers) not out of poverty of descriptive vocabulary but of set purpose, as being conducive to the pastoral atmosphere of agreeable semi-reality."[38] Unfortunately, although he examines or discusses the nature poetry of a number of eighteenth-century authors, most prominently Pope, Ambrose Philips, John Philips, and William Shenstone, his examples fail to reveal exactly what he includes in the term poetic diction. Indeed, it may be suspected that much of what is characterized as poetic diction by others would not be so characterized by him. Thus, he praises four lines in Pope's *Windsor-Forest* for their fidelity to the actual look of the forest at one particular place,

> Ev'n the wild Heath displays her Purple Dies;
> And 'midst the Desart fruitful Fields arise,
> That crown'd with tufted Trees and springing Corn,
> Like verdant Isles the sable Waste adorn
>
> [11. 25–28]

but says nothing about the presence of "Purple Dies," the old coronation figure in fields that are "crown'd with tufted Trees" (probably meant to recall the "tufted trees" of Milton's *L'Allegro,* 1. 78), "verdant Isles," and "sable Waste."[39] Of Goldsmith's *The Deserted Village,* he can write that the "style is perfectly suited to the matter expressed; simple and direct enough to permit the convincing reproduction of rural scenes and characters, yet capable of spreading an agreeable haze over the whole—in which a line like
> No cheerful murmurs fluctuate in the gale
with its conventional elements [murmurs?, gale?], does not in the least strike as inappropriate."[40] This impressionistic criticism has little to do with the poetic diction in Goldsmith's poem. Thus, train, one of the words Tillotson sees as so frequent in the diction because of its fitness for "the rime position,"[41] appears nine times—eight times in the rhyme position.[42] The -y adjectives are also present: glassy brook, weedy way, bloomy flush of life, plashy spring. Latinate diction appears in the decent church, cumbrous pomp, daily care, contiguous pride. There are three uses of the coronation figure (11. 85, 99, 351). Also part of poetic diction are deep and main for ocean, a "pensive plain," "fair tribes," and a "grassy-vested green" with a neighboring "warbling grove." These, at least, are what I would consider the most prominent items of poetic diction in the poem. Possibly they are not enough in number or cumulative effect to disturb a reader who is not especially looking for them, but their presence cannot be ignored in any consideration of Goldsmith's use of what Deane calls stock diction.

For Bernard Groom, "poetic diction," which he distinguishes by quotation marks to avoid confusion with "the diction of poetry" (his term but my quotation marks) is used when he means "to imply a charge of convention or of mechanical repetition."[43] But he, too, is aware of and makes distinctions. "For example," he writes on the heels of his definition, "the phrase 'amorous descant'—almost a cliché in the middle of the eighteenth century—is 'poetic diction' in the sonnet by Gray which Wordsworth ana-

11

lyses in his Preface, but it belongs to the diction of poetry in Milton's beautiful description of the nightingale (*Paradise Lost* 4. 603), where it originated. The expression, though often abused, remains intact in its earliest setting."[44] I do not know the frequency with which "amorous descant" occurs in eighteenth-century English poetry, nor does Groom give evidence for his statement, but it would have to appear in enough different poets over a period of time for it to be included in what I term poetic diction. And I am not so sure that Gray's *considered* use of the phrase, with its conscious evocation of a Miltonic frame of reference, does not thereby disqualify it from being termed poetic diction.[45] The *OED* quotes Gascoigne's *Complaint of Philomene*, "To hear the descant of the nightingale" (1. 6) and thereby suggests a possible source for Milton's linking the nightingale and descant although the word is applicable to any singing bird.[46] But the only example in the *OED*, other than Gray's, of "amorous descant" comes in Charles Churchill's *The Prophecy of Famine—A Scots Pastoral* (1763), a satiric poem. Since Gray's sonnet was not published until well after *The Prophecy*, Churchill was almost surely glancing at Milton's use of the phrase. However, Churchill is parodying the kind of description of evening, the "blissful bower," and "the Rites / Mysterious of connubial love" celebrated by Milton. Churchill's Eve is a cook-maid named Lardella; his Adam *and* his nightingale is the "youth, turn'd swain, and skill'd in rustic lays, / Fast by her [Lardella's] side his am'rous descant plays" (11. 21–22). Surely Gray's and Churchill's use of "amorous descant" cannot properly be termed poetic diction. And so, too, with other poets who use and call attention to some item of stock diction for reasons other than lack of originality.

Tillotson's *Augustan Poetic Diction*[47] starts out with quotation of lines from a play and five poems to exemplify the view that the question of poetic diction "hardly arises" in the "greatest poetry of the ages of Dryden and Pope." The lines quoted are from Dryden's *Aureng-Zebe* (the first four lines of the famous "When I consider life" passage in 4. 1), Swift's *Verses on the Death of Dr. Swift* (1. 228, "The Dean is dead, *(and what is Trumps?)*," Pope's *Epilogue to the Satires* (2. 208–9, "Yes, I am proud," etc.), Johnson's *London* (11. 177–79, "SLOW RISES WORTH," etc.), and Gray's *Elegy*, the last four lines. Although the question of poetic diction *does* arise in the greatest poetry of the ages of Dryden and Pope, there is little reason that it should arise in the lines chosen if simply because one has a character in a play speaking the first lines, an imagined speaker in Swift's poem, the "poet" in Pope's poem, and Thales and somebody or other speaking the lines in Johnson's and in Gray's poems. This conclusion is hardly an original one; John Arthos, for example, had written that

12

It is also to be noted that before Dryden poets did not make much use of this language [poetic diction] in poems of character, like *The Testament of Cressid,* and even Shakespeare and Corneille employed it only sparely in their plays. Nor is it found much in the pastoral poetry written in the style of Theocritus. This is partly explained, I think, by the form of such poems, made up of many short speeches, many of them concerned with personal affairs, and by the fact that this vocabulary is properly descriptive and didactic and not very well suited to most lyric or dramatic purposes.[48]

Since much satiric poetry is cast in monologue or dialogue form, one would not expect, and correctly, to find much poetic diction used. This holds equally true for most prologues and epilogues, as well as for many songs in the plays of the period. However, sometimes the implied dramatic speaker in a poem will suddenly go from an unadorned style to an ornamental one when he turns from narration to description. One remarkable example occurs in Matthew Green's *The Spleen,* where the speaker, up to this point quite innocent of poetic diction, describes the house he would like to have.

> And may my humble dwelling stand
> Upon some chosen spot of land;
> A pond before full to the brim,
> Where cows may cool, and geese may swim,
> Behind, a green like velvet neat,
> Soft to the eye, and to the feet,
> Where od'rous plants in evening fair,
> Breathe all around *ambrosial air,*
> From Eurus, foe to kitchen-ground,
> Fenc'd by *a slope with bushes crown'd,*
> Fit dwelling for *the feather'd throng,*
> Who pay their quit-rents with a song,
> With op'ning views of hill and dale,
> Which sense and fancy too regale,
> Where the half-cirque, with vision bounds,
> Like amphitheatre surrounds,
> And *woods impervious to the breeze*
> Thick phalanx of embodied trees,
> From hills thro' plains in dusk array
> Extended far repel the day.
> Here stillness, height, and solemn shade
> Invite, and contemplation aid:
> Here *nymphs* from hollow oaks relate

13

The dark decrees and will of fate,
And dreams beneath the spreading beech
Inspire, and docile fancy teach,
While soft as *breezy breath of wind,*
Impulses rustle thro' the mind:
Here Dryads, scorning Phoebus ray,
While Pan melodious pipes away,
In measur'd motions frisk about,
'Till old Silenus puts them out:
There see the clover, pea, and bean,
Vie in variety of green,
Fresh pastures speckl'd o'er with sheep,
Brown fields their sallow sabbaths keep,
Plump Ceres golden tresses wear,
And *poppy-topknots deck her hair,*
And *silver streams* thro' meadows stray,
And Naiads on the margin play,
And lesser nymphs on side of hills
From play-thing *urns pour down the rills.*
                    [11. 646–88; italics mine]

Note also the nymphs and Dryads, Pan and old Silenus, and Ceres and the Naiads in the passage. Curiously enough, poetic diction does not offend here, almost surely because it exists cheek by jowl with somewhat less poetic language, so that the old coronation figure in "a slope with bushes crown'd" does not obtrude too much because it is a slope with bushes and the whole serves to fence in a "kitchen-ground." So, too, with "the feather'd throng, / Who pay their quit-rents with a song," for that "quit-rents" is enough to offset anything vestigially objectionable about "the feather'd throng." And so, for still another example, in the lines "Plump Ceres golden tresses wear, / And Poppy-topknots deck her hair," where the possible objection to deck is more than obviated by Ceres's plumpness and those "Poppy-topknots." Here, further, is one passage in which the use of poetic diction for the purpose of decoration is justified, but it is actually the mixture of the decorative and the homely that gives the passage its charm. The speaker then resumes his normal narrative tone, and the little idyll is over.[49]

If Tillotson means that the question of poetic diction does not arise anywhere in the play and the four poems in question, one may disagree, especially as regards *London* and the *Elegy.* In the *Elegy,* Gray has "the genial current of the soul" (1. 52), "the cool sequester'd vale of life" (1. 75), the verb "deck'd" (1. 79), "some hoary-headed Swain" (1. 97), and "trem-

14

bling hope" (1. 128), a by no means inevitable translation of Petrarch's "paventosa speme" from which, Gray's note informs us, he took the phrase.[50] In *London,* Johnson has a "silver flood," "verdant osiers," the "laureat tribe," a golden "pile" that "aspires," and a "shining train." Tillotson had written earlier that "there is no 'diction' in the satires [of Pope], although there are touches in the *Dunciad* since they help the mock heroics."[51] This dictum can be extended to the satires of other poets of the period, always with the same proviso that poetic diction may be used for parodic or mock-heroic effects. One would not, then, really look for the greatest concentration of poetic diction in the genres represented by the five passages quoted but rather in epic, pastoral and georgic—as Tillotson of course recognizes.[52]

Dryden was forty-five years old when *Aureng-Zebe* was published; Gray was thirty-five when the *Elegy* came out, although he may have begun it some nine years earlier; Johnson was twenty-nine in 1738 when *London* appeared, and Pope and Swift were old men when the *Epilogue to the Satires, II,* and *Verses on Death of Dr. Swift* were published. But it is in the poetry of the young, the apprentice poets, that one will find the greatest concentration of poetic diction, although even this admits of two exceptions. The poetry of the downright poor, or at best mediocre, poet is full of poetic diction irrespective of the poet's age. And the largest concentration of poetic diction resides in Dryden's *Virgil* and Pope's *Homer,* even though both had more than served their poetic apprenticeship, the former finishing his translation only three years before his death. The young Pope wrote his *Pastorals, Windsor-Forest,* and the *Messiah,* as well as translations from Ovid, Statius, and Homer; Swift wrote Pindaric odes as a fledgling poet; Johnson's earliest poetry is composed largely of school exercises, translations from Virgil, Horace, and Homer. Gray's early poetry, including his translations, contains more poetic diction than his later poems, but then he was, as he described himself, "a shrimp of an author" and wrote but little. Dryden's *Annus Mirabilis,* his longest early poem, also offends somewhat in the matter of poetic diction. Miss Reynolds finds that "as a rule, such significant poetry as appeared during the transition period [between Pope and Wordsworth] was the work of men who had spent much of their youth in the country or in country villages; it was practically their earliest poetic venture, and usually the work of their youth," lists the obvious exceptions to this general rule, and then cites John Armstrong, John Dyer, James Thomson, Mark Akenside, Allen Ramsay, William Pattison, William Julius Mickle, Michael Bruce, and James Beattie in evidence of the truth of her premise.[53] In short, it is largely true, if somewhat anticlimactic, to state that

15

most young poets offended in the matter of poetic diction, especially when they wrote poetry descriptive of nature or translated other poets. All this is very well, but, as has been noted, Miss Reynolds does not sufficiently take into account the fact that the early work of the poets she names is full of that poetic diction already in use for at least a century.

For most of the critics examined, then, poetic diction is marked by frequency of appearance, by longevity, and almost inevitably by the lack of poetic excellence that results from staleness. Sometimes certain conjunctions or collocations of words are almost formulaic, especially in epics, a phenomenon which finds its warrant in Homer. Possible examples are rich repast, heaps on heaps, or headlong falls. Sometimes it is a nice question whether a word, or more usually a phrase, traceable to a source in, say, Homer or Virgil, is not to be considered as used for its allusive quality rather than condemned as poetic diction because of the frequency with which it had already been used. Thus, knowledge that sylvan scenes, and the phrase appears frequently in English poetry, comes from Virgil's *tum silvis scæna coruscis desuper imminet (Aeneid* 1. 164) might conceivably in some of its earliest appearances in English poetry save it from the charge of being poetic diction, but by the time that it had gone through many hands its possible allusive or associative value would be almost nil. What is more, the adjective sylvan, by virtue of the readiness of poets to abuse it, is almost always suspect; sometimes, however, it is saved by its appearance with an unlikely noun. Pastoral poetry also has its almost formulaic phrases: shady grot (or cave), chrystal (or silver) stream, verdant mead. If any of these had any associative value, it was soon lost. Both pastoral and epic formulas, because they *are* formulas, defy specific identification in the reader's mind, for it is impossible to ascertain which of so many contexts should be recalled or was intended by the poet. Hence, whatever specific allusive quality these formulas may have had tends to be lost with their frequent repetition. It is another matter, of course, when a writer of mock-epic or mock-georgic poetry uses these formulas solely to enhance the mock-epic or mock-georgic tone of his poem, for he need not have any specific epic or georgic in mind.[54]

Perhaps the most difficult problem confronting a student of poetic diction is determining the reasons why a line of poetry or a passage that contains one or more items of poetic diction is still somehow saved from being bad. The answer surely lies in the context in which the usually offending words or phrases are imbedded, as in the lines from *The Spleen* quoted on pages 13–14. Deane offers another, more widely encompassing explanation, for he writes that he is trying "to establish the view that there is nothing inherently vicious in the prevalence of a markedly conventional verse-vocabulary, and that an artificial style, if artistically managed, is capable of yielding effects of absolute poetic merit."[55] R. D. Havens had earlier written that "our ancestors" used "nature in poetry, as in painting and architecture, for purely decorative purposes; as they conventionalized leaves and flowers for ornamental borders and the capitals of columns, so they conventionalized the landscapes with which they adorned their poems."[56] Other critics are quite willing to defend the use of one or another bit of poetic diction in the work of Milton, Spenser, or Wordsworth simply because they are great poets, while the same words or phrases are condemned in the work of lesser poets.[57] Still other critics do not find poetic diction exceptionable at all. Thus, James R. Sutherland admits that "at its best—in Pope or Gay, for instance—eighteenth-century poetic diction seems to me wholly delightful, and perfectly adapted to its purpose."[58] Since no examples are adduced and there is no explanation of the "purpose" of poetic diction, one can only quarrel with Sutherland's taste. An even more extreme and unacceptable view is that of Bonamy Dobrée, who states that "if read with an alert mind and an imagining eye, such phrases as 'the finny tribe' or 'the feathered kind' cease to wear the air of a tiresome affectation, and enrich the poem to the limit of the reader's recognition of what the poet is talking about. But the poet of these days [1700–1740] could assume in his reader at least a fairly expert acquaintance with country life."[59] This is criticism in its most apologetic guise, exculpating the bad poet with the good because both commit the same sins. Tillotson, too, can write that "it is true to say that the good poets of the eighteenth century use language, including the poetic diction, with a scrupulousness far in advance, say, of Shelley's use of language," adducing as example a passage in Thomson's *Winter* (ll. 256–64), which is marred for me by the presence of "the bleating kind."[60] This phrase is a lapse from the scrupulous use of poetic language attributed to eighteenth-century poets, albeit Tillotson claims that it is "anything but an unthinking substitute for 'sheep.' Thomson is saying: we think of sheep as creatures who bleat, but they are silent enough in the snow; it is the dumb eye [Thomson's "Eye the bleak heaven . . . / With looks of dumb despair"] and not the voice that tells us of their despair." Perhaps so, but I think Thomson is getting more than his due in such an interpretation.[61] To determine the justice of a number of such critical judgments as Tillotson's remark on Thomson's "bleating kind," one should have a great deal more information, largely as to the frequency with which certain words and phrases were used in the course of English poetry from Chaucer to Thomson.

It is hoped that this attempt to trace the origins of this diction and to chart its progress in English poetry from Chaucer to Wordsworth will result in a greater understanding not only of the phenomenon itself but of the history of English poetry in general.

NOTES AND REFERENCES

1. Samuel Johnson, *Lives of the English Poets,* ed. G. B. Hill (Oxford: Clarendon Press, 1905), vol. 1, p. 420.

2. James Beattie, *An Essay on Poetry and Music as They Affect the Mind,* 1776.

3. Ibid., p. 229, 1778 ed.

4. Ibid., p. 240

5. Ibid., pp. 246–47.

6. Ibid., pp. 258–59.

7. Ibid., p. 255.

8. Ibid., p. 268.

9. Ibid., pp. 268–69.

10. Ibid.; see pp. 304–5 for his further reliance on poetic diction as he translated a short passage from Tasso into English.

11. If anything, the estimate is low. And Dryden used the word 89 times in his translation of the *Aeneid.*

12. John Dennis, *Critical Works,* ed. E. N. Hooker (Baltimore: Johns Hopkins University Press, 1943), vol. 2, p. 131.

13. Ibid., vol. 1, pp. 47–48; for "train" as a favorite word in the period, see Geoffrey Tillotson, *Augustan Poetic Diction* (London: The Athalone Press, 1964), hereafter shortened to *APD.*

14. Joseph Spence, *An Essay on Mr. Pope's Odyssey in Five Dialogues,* 2nd ed. 1737, pp. 75 and 8 respectively.

15. Charles Churchill, *Gotham,* 1764, Bk. 2, 11. 41–48. In *The Prophecy of Famine,* 1763, Churchill has parodied the diction and conventions of pastoral poetry. See page 12 here for one example.

16. John Aikin, *An Essay on the Application of Natural History to Poetry,* 1777; quoted in John Arthos, *The Language of Natural Description in Eighteenth Century Poetry* (Ann Arbor: University of Michigan Press, 1949), p. 9.

17. Joshua Poole, *The English Parnassus: or A Help to English Poesie. Containing a Collection of all the Rhyming Monosyllables, The Choicest Epithets and Phrases. With some General Forms upon all Occasions, Subjects, and Themes, Alphabetically Digested* (London, 1677). This second edition is fuller than the first, published in 1657; there were no other editions.

18. Tillotson, *APD,* pp. 49–50.

19. Myra Reynolds, *The Treatment of Nature in English Poetry Between Pope and Wordsworth* (Chicago: University of Chicago Press, 1909).

20. Ibid., p. 1.

21. Ibid., p. 24.

22. Ibid.

23. Ibid., p. 26.

24. Ibid., p. 39.

25. Ibid., p. 58.

26. Ibid., p. 89

27. Ibid., p. 92; cf. Tillotson, *APD,* p. 33, on Virgil's fondness for "fundo."

28. Reynolds, *Treatment of Nature,* pp. 99–100.

29. Tillotson, *APD,* p. 35.

30. The *OED,* my source, also finds it in a prose work dated 1633.

31. The editions of *The Seasons* from 1728–1738 contained one use of the word, "Turgent in every pore / The gummy moisture shines," in *Spring,* but it was dropped in the 1744 edition. However, Thomson used it in *Autumn* (1. 693, "the turgent film"). See *The Complete Poetical Works of James Thomson,* edited by J. Logie Robertson (Oxford: Oxford University Press, 1951), pp. 21–22, for the revision of the lines in *Spring.*

32. Reynolds, *Treatment of Nature,* p. 69.

33. Ibid., p. 148

34. Ibid., pp. 154, 343.

35. Ibid., p. 162.

36. C. V. Deane, *Aspects of Eighteenth-Century Nature Poetry* (Oxford: Basil Blackwell, 1935), pp. 4, 5.

37. Ibid., pp. 13, 18.

38. Ibid., p. 36

39. See James Sutherland, *A Preface to Eighteenth-Century Poetry* (Oxford: Oxford University Press, 1963), pp. 118–19, on this passage.

40. Deane, *Aspects of Eighteenth-Century Nature Poetry,* p. 53.

41. Tillotson, *APD,* p. 36; and see Dennis, *Critical Works,* p. 8.

42. With village (1. 17), trade's unfeeling (1. 63), busy (1. 81), harmless (1. 135), vagrant (1. 149), lowly (1. 252), gorgeous (1. 320), loveliest (1. 337), persuasive (1. 433).

43. Bernard Groom, *The Diction of Poetry from Spenser to Bridges* (Toronto: University of Toronto Press, 1955).

44. Ibid., p. 4. I discuss Arthos's *Language of Natural Description* on pp. 51–2, 63–64.

45. See, for example only, Joseph Foladare, "Gray's 'Frail Memorial' to West," *PMLA* 75 (1960):61–65, on the allusive quality in the sonnet.

46. Samuel Johnson's *Dictionary* has no "amorous descant" except Milton's.

47. The genesis of *Augustan Poetic Diction* is this: *On the Poetry of Pope* (Oxford: Clarendon Press, 1938), chap. 1, "Correctness," part 3, "Language"; an essay in *Essays and Studies by Members of the English Association,* vol. 25, 1939; a reprint of the "Essays and Studies" essay in *Essays in Criticism and Research,* 1942; and finally *Augustan Studies,* 1961, of which *Augustan Poetic Diction,* 1964, reprints only the first four chapters minus the appendix in the fourth. Tillotson's definition of poetic diction is quoted on page 8 here.

48. Arthos, *Language of Natural Description,* pp. 16–17.

49. See Patricia Meyer Spacks, *The Varied God, A Critical Study of Thomson's "The Seasons"* (Berkeley and Los Angeles: University of California Press, 1959), p. 105, for a different view on the passage in Green.

50. See Tillotson, *APD,* p. 28, on "trembling"; also *On the Poetry of Pope,* p. 69.

51. Tillotson, *On the Poetry of Pope,* p. 89.

52. Tillotson, *APD*, p. 28; the work of other modern students of poetic diction appear on pages 16–18, *passim*. See, for example, the discussion of the work of H. C. Wyld in Chapter 2.

53. Reynolds, *Treatment of Nature*, pp. 329–31.

54. See Arthur Sherbo, "Virgil, Dryden, Gay and Matters Trivial," *PMLA* 85 (1970):-1063–71.

55. Deane, *Aspects of Eighteenth-Century Nature Poetry*, p. 18.

56. R. D. Havens, *The Influence of Milton on English Poetry* (Cambridge, Mass.: Harvard University Press, 1922), p. 138.

57. Among these critics are Miss Reynolds and Bernard Groom; see pp. 9 and 10.

58. James R. Sutherland, "Wordsworth and Pope," in *Proceedings of the British Academy, 1944*, p. 49.

59. In the *Oxford History of English Literature* (1949), vol. 7, p. 162.

60. Tillotson, *Augustan Studies*, p. 42.

61. See also p. 159.

Chapter 1.

Some Origins of Poetic Diction

Reuben Brower, in an examination of "Dryden's Poetic Diction and Virgil," admitted initially that "there will never be any simple explanation for the origin of the so-called poetic diction which adorns—and mars—much English verse in the late seventeenth and in the eighteenth century"; he then went on to demonstrate that "the poetic diction which Dryden and his contemporaries innocently bequeathed to the eighteenth century may thus be traced in part to the 'best of poets' [Virgil]."[1] His method seemed simplicity itself: identification of the source in Virgil for a number of examples of poetic diction in Dryden's poetry before 1697, the year of his translation of Virgil's works. Possibly other students of Greek and Latin classics may find precedents for some passages in Virgil that Brower claims as Dryden's models. Possibly not. But it should be obvious that the further back in literary time one goes in his search for the origins of poetic diction the more confident he can feel that he is getting to the *fons et origo* of that phenomenon. Behind Virgil's epic are Homer's epics; behind the *Pastorals* and *Georgics* are the pastoral poems of Theocritus.[2] Ovid's *Metamorphoses*, not entirely divorced from the epic by any means, were written some two decades after Virgil's death; Statius's *Thebaid* is heavily indebted to the *Aeneid;* Lucan's *Bellum Civile,* better known as *Pharsalia,* also figures in

21

the transmission of that poetic diction found in the epic. Tillyard was of the opinion that "to the creation of the English epic [I would add English epic diction] certain classical writings served as a permanent background. They were five poems and one prose work (with a possible second)."[3] The poems are Homer's two epics, the *Aeneid*, the *Pharsalia*, and the *Thebaid*, plus Xenophon's *Cyropedia* and possibly the *Aethiopica* of Heliodorus. The *Cyropedia* was translated by Francis Digby and John Norris in 1685; the *Aethiopica*, by "a Person of Quality" and N. Tate in 1686. Both are prose and had no bearing on the history of poetic diction. To these should be added Ovid's *Metamorphoses*, since it too shares in that diction that became associated with the epic, especially as it evolved by way of English translations.

It needs no Dr. Johnson *redivivus* to remind us that the classical writers of Greece and Rome, simply by virtue of being first on the scene, invented not only plots and characters but also a poetic language which has been imitated ever since. Thus, when Homer described a hero as godlike, a fall from a chariot as headlong, a meadow as flowery, a lion as tawny, and various cities as sandy, rocky, or grassy, while he may have had some literary and topographical precedents unknown to us, he may be considered as inventing the images so far as the course of English poetic diction is concerned. Some, if not all, of these descriptive words in the contexts in which they appear again and again may seem inevitable; but the truth is, of course, that none is, and a ready and frequent recourse to them by later poets is evidence of the tenacious hold that a reservoir of words, phrases, and images can have on the poetaster, the budding poet, and even the mature poet—the last especially when, as was true in the eighteenth century, he was observing the rule that certain genres had their own vocabularies or diction. Since relatively few of the classically educated Englishmen of the seventeenth and eighteenth centuries read Homer in Greek, their reliance was on translations, some of them translations of translations, i.e., an English version of a French translation of the *Iliad*. And as more and more translations appeared, there arose a tradition of rendering certain passages in either the identical or very similar language. So it was with Homer's successors and imitators. Virgil's *Aeneid* would be a far different epic than it is if Homer had not written before him; Statius's *Thebaid* owes much to Virgil, who owes much to Homer. Translators of Virgil owe much to translators of Homer; translators of Statius and Lucan owe much to translators of Homer and Virgil. And, of course, original efforts at the writing of epics, or poems attempting to achieve an epic tone, were directly and extensively influenced by the existence of this traditional body of diction.

According to more than one student of Augustan poetic diction the greatest concentration of this diction is to be found in the poetry of natural description. In discussing "The Ideal Landscape," Ernst Robert Curtius writes that "from Homer's landscapes later generations took certain motifs which became permanent elements in a long chain of tradition: the place of heart's desire, beautiful with perpetual spring, as the scene of a blessed life after death; the lovely miniature landscape which combines tree, spring, and grass; the wood with various species of trees; the carpet of flowers."[4] He continues, of those "places where man delights to sit and rest": "What are the requisites of such a spot? Above all, shade—of great importance to the man of the South. A tree, then, or a group of trees; a spring or brook for refreshment; a grassy bank for a seat. A grotto can serve the purpose too." But men do more than merely sit under these trees.

To write poetry under trees. . . , on the grass, by a spring—in the Hellenistic period, this came to rank as a poetical motif in itself. But it demands a sociological framework: an occupation which obliges him who follows it to live outdoors, or at least in the country, far from towns. He must have time and occasion for composing poetry, and must possess some sort of primitive musical instrument. The shepherd has all of these at his disposition. He has ample leisure. His tutelary deity is the spirit of the flocks, Pan, inventor of the shepherd's pipe of seven reeds. Beautiful shepherds (Anchises, Endymion, Ganymede) had been deemed worthy to be loved by gods. The Sicilian shepherd Daphnis, who scorned the love of a goddess for the sake of a mortal woman, had already been celebrated by Stesichorus in the seventh century. But Theocritus of Syracuse (first half of the third century) is the true originator of pastoral poetry. Of all the antique poetical genres, it has had, after the epic, the greatest influence. There are several reasons for this. The shepherd's life is found everywhere at all periods. It is a basic form of human existence; and through the story of the Nativity in Luke's gospel it made its way into the Christian tradition too. It has—and this is very important—a correlative scenery: pastoral Sicily, later Arcadia. But it also has a personnel of its own, which has its own social structure and thus constitutes a social microcosm: neatherds (whence the name bucolic), goatherds, shepherdesses, etc. Finally, the shepherd's world is linked to nature and to love. One can say that for two millenniums it draws to itself the majority of erotic motifs. The Roman love elegy had a life span of but a few decades. It was little capable of development or renewal. But Arcadia was forever being rediscovered. This was possible

23

because the stock of pastoral motifs was bound to no genre and to no poetic form. It found its way into the Greek romance (Longus) and from thence into the Renaissance. From the romance, pastoral poetry could return to the eclogue or pass to the drama (Tasso's *Aminta;* Guarini's *Pastor Fido*). The pastoral world is as extensive as the knightly world. In the medieval *pastourelle* the two worlds meet. Yes, in the pastoral world all worlds "embrace one another."[5]

Tracing the development of the *locus amoenus* (the pleasance), Curtius quotes what he considers the earliest example of this theme in Latin poetry, "Petronius, *carm.* 131," and adds its translation into English by J. W. and A. M. Duff. While this English translation is itself interesting as a whole as a proof of the longevity of poetic diction, the last line, "Bird and river, breeze and woodland, flower and shade brought ravishment," is of especial importance as it enumerates the "six charms of landscape" that occur again and again in natural description.[6] Awareness of the fact that "the man of the South" sought shade simply because he could not stand the extreme heat of the sun, and that poets in lands where the sun is eagerly welcomed in its more infrequent appearances—much of England, for example—were quite mechanically following a tradition, makes it easy to account for the shade in the ideal landscapes of poetry written in more temperate climates. Surely, too, when Milton writes of the Garden of Eden, his *locus amoenus,*

> How from that sapphire fount the crisped brooks,
> Rolling on orient pearl and sands of gold,
> With mazy error under pendant shades
> Ran nectar, visiting each plant, and fed
> Flowers worthy of Paradise . . .
> [*Paradise Lost* 4. 237–41]

his "pendant shades" are rather only a concession to tradition than "not merely convenient hanging trees but also a proleptic suggestion of the horrid shadows that impend."[7] One might further suggest that "pendant shades" and "horrid shadows" are entirely different things and that when Milton wanted to be quite explicit he could write of "horrid shade" (*Paradise Lost* 9. 185). But the point is that the necessity for shade in the pleasance is merely traditional. Joseph Warton, discussing the influence of Theocritus upon most "succeeding painter[s] of rural beauty" concluded that "a set of hereditary objects has been continued from one poet to another, without any propriety either as to age or climate,"[8] repeating the

24

charge in much the same words soon after in his *Essay on the Genius and Writings of Pope*.

Homer, who may be considered the ancestor of Western poetry, rarely pauses to describe the face of nature; he is a describer, rather, of objects, but on two occasions in the *Odyssey* he forgets himself momentarily; once to describe nature untouched by man—the cave of Calypso—and once to describe nature manipulated by man—the gardens of Alcinous. George Chapman put a marginal note by each passage in his translation, "descriptio specus Calypso" and "hortus Alcinoi memorabilis," and Pope elected to translate the gardens of Alcinous passage for his *Guardian* essay on pastoral (No. 173, Sept. 29, 1713). Pope evidently thought well enough of that early translation to incorporate it verbatim when he came to translate the seventh book of the *Odyssey*, and perhaps it was no accident that he undertook the translation of that book and the fifth, which contains the description of the cave of Calypso, rather than entrust it to Elijah Fenton or William Broome. The existence of the early translation of the gardens of Alcinous passage suggests that Pope would have therefore pre-empted the seventh book for himself. Robert Fagles has conjectured that there was probably an "imaginative affiliation" in Pope's mind between his grotto at Twickenham and Calypso's cave, good reason for him to have elected to translate the fifth book.[9]

Pope devotes fifteen lines to his description of Calypso's cave. Chapman had given it thirteen lines; both Thomas Hobbes and John Ogilby had contented themselves with ten. Only Hobbes's version is free of poetic diction. Chapman uses the old coronation figure, "With odorous Cypresse, Pines, and Poplars crownd" (1. 88), closely followed incidentally, by Ogilby, "With Poplar, Alder, and tall Cypress crown'd" (p. 65), both using round as the rhyme word. Chapman has "silver streames and medowes all enflowrd" (1. 96) and flowers that "deckt the soft breasts of each fragrant Mead" (1. 98). Ogilby is guilty of some "verdant Branches" (p. 65) but of nothing else in this passage. Pope, more than any of his predecessors, avails himself of the poetic diction ready to hand. The "various sylvan scene" of the first line of his description borrows "sylvan scene" from any one of a number of possible sources, Milton and Dryden included, but ultimately deriving from Virgil (*Georgics* 1. 164), while various is what Tillotson terms one of the "recurrent favourites" of Augustan poetic diction.[10] And in the rest of the passage (11. 81–94) Pope rings in "groves of living green" and a "loquacious crow," possibly a reminiscence of Dryden's "loquacious frogs" (*Georgics* 1. 521 and 3. 654), if not of his "loquacious nest" of young

25

swallows (*Aeneid* 12. 694) whose mother "now hawks aloft now skims along the flood" (1. 693). Not only is Pope's crow without precedent in the earlier translations, but the action he gives it and the other birds, "And scream aloft, and skim the deeps below," not in his original, is obviously taken from Dryden's line. Pope also has "depending vines," four "limpid" fountains that "from the clefts distill" (every one of which "pours a sev'ral rill"), "mazy windings," and "bloomy meads" "crown'd with vivid greens." Pope remembered a couplet in his pastoral, *Summer,* "Where dancing Sun-beams on the Water's play'd, / And verdant Alders form'd a quiv'ring Shade" (11. 3–4) in the lines, "Poplars and alders ever quiv'ring play'd, / And nodding cypress form'd a fragrant shade" (11. 82–83), and may have had Milton's "glowing violet" (*Lycidas,* 1. 145) in mind when he described the violets around Calypso's cave as "glowing."

Pope's inclusion of purple to describe grapes, his green groves, and his "vivid greens" with which the meads are crowned are not to be found in Homer's Greek or in Hobbes or Chapman. Hobbes's account is colorless; Chapman offers "blue Violets"; Ogilby has "purpling Clusters" of grapes. Now, while purple was a much-abused word[11] and, while it takes no painter's eye to see green, vivid or not, in a landscape, Pope, in the gardens of Alcinous passage, has been praised for his eye for color. Brower writes that "the glowing, luscious quality of the picture is nearly all Pope's; every one of the words for colour, all the suggested 'tactile values' are his, too."[12] The colors and the objects they describe are a "green enclosure," a "reddening apple" that ripens to "gold," the "blue fig," the "deeper red" of the pomegranate, "purple" grapes and "ever green" herbs. There are no colors in Homer's Greek in this passage; none in Chapman or Ogilby. Hobbes has only "green beds of herbs." So far as color is concerned, Pope is clearly more interested in that aspect of the description of nature than his predecessors in the translation of this passage. But here, too, as in the cave of Calypso passage, Pope depends more heavily on poetic diction than do his predecessors. Hobbes, as might be expected, employs no poetic diction; Chapman has the Gods deck the Court of Alcinous (1. 180); Ogilby has "blushing Fruit," "yielding Branches," and "silver fountains" (p. 90). Pope's trees "confess'd the fruitful mold"; his olives are verdant and the spirit of the western gale is balmy; wine is a "liquid harvest," and grapes are in "autumn's richest purple dy'd." The order of the beds of various herbs is beauteous; and the two fountains, which the "whole prospect crown'd," to "various uses" bring their "various streams."

Robert Fagles also suggests a relationship between Pope's grotto at Twickenham and the Naiad's grotto in Book 13 of the *Odyssey,*[13] and again it is Pope who translates this book, not Fenton or Broome. And just as in the descriptions of the cave of Calypso and the gardens of Alcinous, it is Pope, rather than his predecessors, who has recourse to poetic diction. There is none in Chapman or Hobbes. Ogilby has nymphs plying "rocky Looms" and Gods using a gate for "Egress and Regress" (p. 180). Pope's version (11. 116–35) contains "Two craggy rocks projecting to the main" as well as waves which "in softer murmurs glide." The coronation figure is present in the olive tree which "crowns the pointed cliffs with shady boughs"; there are "massy beams" and bees "from the roof depend." Pope appends a note to this passage in his edition of the *Odyssey*, calling attention to Virgil's imitation of the "description of this haven" in *Aeneid*, 1. 159 ff., and he reprints Dryden's translation (1. 228–40). Interestingly enough, Dryden too succumbs to poetic diction, with briny waters, a sylvan scene, massy seats, and bearded anchors. All of which is to say that while Homer is responsible for a great deal of epic diction as it descends through Virgil and others, English poets found little in his descriptions of nature that they could add to their store of poetic diction. But, as will become increasingly more obvious, with each translation the dependence upon poetic diction became greater and greater.

Critical insistence that the literary genres had their own characteristic diction makes it relatively easy to account for that recurrence of word and phrase which gradually resulted in poetic diction. While it is far from accurate to suggest that there was not an appreciable degree of overlapping from the diction of one genre to that of another, it is observable that the critics were in substantial agreement on the requisites of an epic style.[14] Addison, writing of Milton's epic in *Spectator* 285, stated that the first requisites of "the language of an heroic poem" were perspicuity and sublimity and then added, in justification of his second requisite, that "it is not therefore sufficient, that the language of an epic poem be perspicuous, unless it be also sublime. To this end it ought to deviate from the common forms and ordinary phrases of speech. The judgment of a poet very much discovers itself in shunning the common roads of expression, without falling into such ways of speech as may seem stiff and unnatural; he must not swell into a false sublime, by endeavouring to avoid the other extream." One of the ways to achieve sublimity of language "is to make use of the idioms of other tongues," a practice necessary to rescue blank-verse epics "from falling into the flatness of prose." In a later essay on *Paradise Lost, Spectator* 321, Addison praises Milton for following Aristotle's "rule of lavishing all the ornaments of diction on the weak inactive parts of the fable, which are not supported by the beauty of sentiments and characters."

Blackmore, like others, had no doubt that the language of an epic should strive for sublimity, but he also wrote that "the judicious and happy choice of pure, proper and expressive words, and splendid and polite diction, give outward richness, elegance, and magnificence."[15] He, too, warned against "the vain pomp of the false sublime" as well as against "all odd and uncouth phrases, low language, and vulgar metaphors." And, like Addison before him and critics after him, he directed that "this shining and beautiful diction be employ'd to represent thoughts that are much greater and more sublime. If the sentiments are generous and majestick, it is but fit they should appear in a richer and more splendid dress; but when they are mean and common, their habit should be so too." Blackmore further insisted that there was also a "roughness in the true sublime" which obviated "exact and polish'd diction."

Another critic, Henry Pemberton, was moved in 1738 to write his observations on poetry by the publication of the very popular blank-verse epic *Leonidas,* by Richard Glover, in the preceding year. His statement about the origins of the diction of the epic, or what may be called epic poetic diction, is that

> In Homer we often find the commonest things expressed by their plain names. But when the first writers became ancient, and many of their words somewhat out of use; it being, as I suppose, observed, that under an unaccustomed name the disagreeable impression of the meanness of the image did not so strongly present itself, such less common words, and a more studied form of phrase became in fashion upon these occasions. However this reservedness may easily be carried to excess, and degenerate into an effeminate delicacy, lay writers under unsurmountable difficulties in expressing their thoughts, and introduce into a language the greatest poverty, of which the most judicious of the French writers in particular complain.[16]

Pemberton also makes a distinction which anticipates, at least in its broadest implications, much modern discussion of point of view, as that term is understood in the criticism of fiction. He writes that "for ornament the poet's own language may be enlivened with a greater pomp of expression than ought to be put in the mouth of any character."[17] For the most part, epic writers seem to have been aware of the necessity to observe this distinction. Pemberton, at pains throughout to distinguish between the language of poetry and of prose, concludes his discussion of "Of the language of poetry" by stating that "the sum of what has here been said amounts to this, that the perfection even of a figurative style consists in its being free from any luxuriant and ostentatious pomp of words, or any affectation of pleasing the ear unconnected with the principal office of speech, which is to convey our ideas with ease, clearness and force."[18] In exemplification of these qualities in Glover's epic, Pemberton quotes eight passages totaling seventy-five lines. Five of the eight passages are epic similes; three contain descriptions of nature.

Perhaps one passage chosen by Pemberton may serve as an example of the mingling of epic diction with the diction of poetry descriptive of nature.

> ——like the vast Atlantic, when no shore,
> No rock or promontory stops the sight
> Unbounded, as it wanders; but the moon,
> Resplendent eye of night, in fullest orb
> Throughout th' interminated surface throws
> Its rays abroad, and decks in snowy light
> The dancing billows.
>
> [Bk. 2. v. 239]

Here one has the personification of night, a periphrasis for moon, a Latinate word in interminated, the -y adjective in snowy (not a startling one), the verb to deck, and billows that dance. Other examples of the mingling of two kinds of diction will be seen in discussion of the translations by Dryden and Pope. Despite the lip service paid to the difference in the language of epic poetry as opposed to that of the pastoral, one need only to compare Pope's theory, as seen in his remarks on Homer's "expression" in the Preface to the *Iliad* translation and on pastoral in his *Discourse on Pastoral Poetry,* with his practice in the *Homer* and in his four *Pastorals,* to realize that Pope, for one, did not practice what he preached. Virtually every element of the diction used in poetry descriptive of nature is to be found in the translations of epics, both in the seventeenth and eighteenth centuries. And one will find most of that diction in Dryden's *Virgil* and Pope's *Homer.*

The immediate antecedents of Dryden's *Virgil* and Pope's *Homer* are, of course, earlier English translations of those works. These will be examined for their influence on the course of poetic diction later in this study. There were, however, other translations of epics or parts of epics that affected poetic diction as it was channeled into those two great reservoirs, Dryden's *Virgil* and Pope's *Homer.* One of the classical epics said to have been important in the creation of the English epic is Lucan's *Pharsalia,* of which there were two abortive translations in the sixteenth century, one by Barnabe Googe and the other by George Turberville, and two complete versions in the seventeenth, those by Sir Arthur Gorges in 1614 and by Thomas May. May translated the first three books in 1626 and the entire epic in 1629; subsequent editions in 1631, 1635, 1650, and 1659 are sufficient evidence of the work's popularity. Christopher Marlowe had translated the first book as early as 1593, and there are selections in Sir Francis Beaumont's *Bosworth-Field* (1629).[19] Nicholas Rowe's translation, first published in 1718, was highly praised by Dr. Johnson in his life of Rowe:

> The version of Lucan is one of the greatest productions of English poetry; for there is perhaps none that so completely exhibits the genius and spirit of the original. Lucan is distinguished by a kind of dictatorial or philosophic dignity rather, as Quintilian observes, declamatory than poetical; full of ambitious morality and pointed sentences, comprised in vigorous and animated lines. This character Rowe has very diligently and successfully preserved. His versification, which is such as his contemporaries practised without any attempt at innovation or improvement, seldom wants either melody or force. His author's sense is sometimes a little diluted by additional infusions, and sometimes weakened by too much expansion. But such faults are to be expected in all translations, from the constraint of measures and dissimilitude of languages. The *Pharsalia* of Rowe deserves more notice than it obtains, and as it is more read will be more esteemed. *(ad finem)*

Rowe's translation, like May's, proved popular, with some eight editions up to 1807. Pope, although he thought Rowe "amplified" too much, wrote to his friend Henry Cromwell on November 11, 1710, "I have (as I think I formerly told you) a very good opinion of *Rowe's* 9th book of *Lucan.*"[20] Perhaps it is worth noting that in the "Argument" to Book 9 in Rowe's version it is stated that "the Account of the Original of Serpents in Africk . . . with the Description of their various Kinds, and the several Deaths of the Soldiers by 'em, is perhaps the most poetical Part of this whole Work." John Hughes's "The Tenth Book of Lucan's Pharsalia Translated," which he left unfinished, appears in his *Poems on Several Occasions* (1735), and is some further slight evidence of the popularity of the poem. Hughes also translated a short passage from the fourth book. In 1719, Christopher Pitt, unaware that Rowe had already translated the work, "presented to the electors [of New College, Oxford], as the product of his private and voluntary studies, a compleat version of Lucan's poem."[21]

Lucan's appeal was at least twofold. The horrors of civil war, his central theme, was one which struck a responsive chord in Englishmen of the sixteenth and seventeenth centuries. And he was, in the words of the Revels editor of Marlowe's poems, a prodigious rhetorician, so that Quintilian, the chief authority for the Renaissance on classical rhetoric, while admiring his fire ("ardens") and his brilliance in sententious epigrams, thought him a better model for an orator than for a poet. There are no silences, no detached understated moments of a Vergilian kind, in Lucan's unfinished masterpieces; all is noise, hyperbole, *power*.

The same authority states that Marlowe's translation "is close to the original, not only in tone but in sense. Marlowe naturalized Lucan without, for the most part, losing his substance."[22] One can easily see why Marlowe was attracted to the fiery Lucan with his "noise, hyperbole, power."

Lucan is most often linked with Statius, especially in Dryden's critical writings. Thus, for one example, both are condemned for venturing their bold metaphors "too far," something which "our Virgil," often contrasted with one or the other, never does.[23] At another time, Dryden is animadverting on "a middle sort of readers," whom he further describes as "a company of warm young men who are not yet arrived so far as to discern the difference between fustian, or ostentatious sentences, and the true sublime . . . they would certainly set Virgil below Statius or Lucan."[24] Again, "as for hyperboles, I will neither quote Lucan nor Statius, men of an unbounded imagination, but who often wanted the poise of judgment. The divine Virgil was not liable to that exception."[25] Besides these comparisons with Virgil there are various pejorative remarks upon the language of these two poets. The most extended criticism of Lucan's style comes in *Of Heroic Plays: An Essay.* Dryden writes of Lucan, "who followed too much the truth of history, crowded sentences together, was too full of points, and too often offered at somewhat which had more the sting of an epigram than of the dignity and state of an heroic poem . . . he treats you more like a philosopher than a poet [*vide* the remark that Lucretius "was so much an atheist that he forgot sometimes to be a poet"]. . . . In one word, he walks soberly afoot, when he might fly."[26] Shelley, in his *Defence of Poetry,* characterizes Lucan as a "mock-bird" rather than a real poet. Although Dryden has some qualified praise for Statius, he more often criticizes him adversely, accusing him of "bluster," as well as of the other faults already noted.[27] The name of Silius Italicus, it is of interest to note, occurs only once in the corpus of Dryden's criticism; and there, while he is described as "a worse writer" than Lucan, he is adjudged more properly a writer of epic than Lucan, who is rather "among historians in verse."[28] Dryden, incidentally, does not mention the translation of Silius Italicus by Thomas Ross, published in 1661. Whatever praise Dryden mustered up for Lucan, Statius, and Silius Italicus was far overshadowed by his love and admiration for Virgil. Perhaps because it is so apposite, Bolingbroke's comment in a letter to Pope, dated February 18, 1724, may be quoted here, for he writes that "Claudian, nay Lucan who was so much elder, had not certainly the Diction of Virgil; but if Virgil had not writ, both these, and Silius Italicus and several others, who came between them, or after them, would have writ wòrse."

The degree to which epic diction had been virtually codified by the beginning of the Restoration can be seen in Thomas Ross's translation of Silius Italicus's *Punica* under the title *The Second Punic War between Hannibal and the Romans,* published in 1661, with a "Continuation from the Triumph of Scipio, to the Death of Hannibal" added to a second edition in 1672. Ross, as tutor to James Scott, later the Duke of Monmouth, Charles II's illegitimate son, is better known to historians than to literary scholars. Indeed, neither Dryden nor Pope, both of whom knew the *Punica,* ever refer to his English translator; and Addison, who translated a number of passages from that epic in his *Remarks on Several Parts of Italy* (1705), seems to have been equally unaware of Ross's translation, for he did not use it, although he used existing translations of other Latin poets in the same work.[29] Perhaps it would be well, therefore, to document the degree to which poetic diction was entrenched by 1661 by considering Harington's *Ariosto* (1591), Edward Fairfax's *Tasso* (1600), Sir Edward Gorges's and Thomas May's translations of Lucan's *Pharsalia* (1614 and 1629),[30] and Sir Richard Fanshawe's *Camoens* (1655) as forerunners of the poetic diction in Ross's translation of Silius Italicus. Translations of Virgil and Homer published earlier than 1661 would also, of course, have a part in the lines of descent, but they are reserved for separate treatment.[31]

First, it may be of some interest to note that a number of words in the growing reservoir of poetic diction occur in all six translations: glittering, vital, watery. Here, and in what follows, it is to be assumed that with but rare exception these words appear in familiar contexts, at least their familiarity increases from 1591 to 1661.[32] Five of the translations contain: craggy, crew, crystal, cut, deck (verb), devote[d], headlong, massy, train; four have adverse, augment, band, dire, distain, flinty, hoary, liquid, pitchy, shaggy, and thunderbolt[s] of war (i.e., mighty warriors); three have aetherial, airy, animate, aspire, athwart, crown (verb), curl (of waves), downy, embrew, flowery, frothy, generous (of noble birth), grisly, glut (with blood), infest, mow (of battle), pendent, profound (as noun), roll (of rivers or waves), sable, servile, sway, vault[ed] (of sky or earth), welkin, yielding. All of the above appear in Ross's translation, with the exception of flinty, shaggy, downy, flowery, athwart, grisly, pendent, profound, and welkin. As a further, slight indication of the persistence of this vocabulary it should be noted that Nicholas Rowe's translation of the *Pharsalia* (1718; I used the second edition, 1722) contains all the words listed above in the various groupings except crew, augment, flinty, pitchy, shaggy, thunderbolts, airy, curl, downy, flowery, frothy, mow, profound, welkin, yielding. Thus, out of a list of forty-five words of poetic diction all but nine are to be found in Ross's translation and all but fifteen in Rowe's.

Such a comparison only tells part of the story. While these translators coincide in a number of their usages, each, sometimes with one other of this group of six—Rowe, coming after Dryden's *Virgil,* can be now omitted—has added something of his own to the growing store. Harington's translation of the *Orlando Furioso* has relatively little to offer outside of the words that figure in the previous lists, but he includes, among his Latinisms, exalted, grateful, infuse, pompous, and rebate. Of Latinisms, Fairfax contributes horrid, pompous, respire, undistinguished, and verdant; Gorges has prevent, spoils, coinquinate *(rara avis),* cumbrous, express (reveal), infuse, invest (a city); May has auspicious, curious, involve, meridian, unctuous, effuse, express, missile (adj.), voluminous; Fanshawe has auspicious, circumfused, congregated, erudiates, irrefragable, meridian, obsequious, reverberated (adj.), verdant, and vocal. Ross, coming after the other five, has ambient, conscious, constipated (pressed close together), delicious, distinguish, dubious, elate, expire, fallacious, fervent, frequent, horrid, ingeminate, intercept, invest, involve, lautious, missile (adj.), obvious, onerate, opimus, perplex, perspicuous, promiscuous, provoke, sagacious, social, spoils, and unctuous—carrying on with a vengeance the tradition of using words in their Latin root meaning. Most of the Latinisms of these translators, with certain easily guessed-at exceptions—coinquinate, lautious, opimus, and others—find their way into Dryden's and Pope's translations. Many of them, it bears constant repetition, had appeared in pre-1661 translators of Homer, Virgil, and Ovid. The metaphor of a body of water that begins as a trickle and grows into a veritable torrent, suggested earlier, is also worth repeating.

But there was more than just Latinisms in these six translations. The -y adjective was used conspicuously, beginning with Harington's drossy and scaly and Fairfax's fleecy—I discount those that figure in the lists above—going on to Gorges's fenny, fleecy, steepy, brisky, cliffy, flaggy, frosty, globy, gloomy, hugy, icy, lithy, moisty, snaky, snowy, and swarthy; May's papery, piny, showery, snaky, and wavy; Fanshawe's briny, dewy, dusky, leavy, milky, pearly, rosy, ruddy, spicy, spiny, and spongy; and Ross's briny, dewy, fishy, gloomy, milky, mossy, scaly, snowy, sooty, and woody.

33

Certain words also crop up in these translations, words whose recurrent use in epics *and* in the poetry of natural description strongly suggests that generic vocabularies were less strict than precept would have one believe. Harington has his feathered foules, his swains, his azure sky, and his gaudy flowers. Fairfax is fond of azure, using it with sky, heavens, beam, flood, night's mantle, and the face of heaven. He antedates Milton with his shadows brown. For him the sun "with his beams enamel'd every green" (Bk. 1, st. 35) and birds are feather'd fellows. Shades are horrid; night is sable, but also has a starry veil; air, deep, and sky are all yielding. Most of Gorges's -y adjectives, listed above, have their place in the vocabulary of poetry of natural description; this is also true of May's and of others'. Where Fairfax has sylvan pinfolds, May has a wanton sylvan, the rarer use of the word as a noun. For Fanshawe, the sky is azure, as are the towers of heaven; the main is briny; rustics are swains; flowers are "inameld" and also "imbost" (Bk. 9, st. 21); the ocean is the humid realm or element; trees have leavy locks; Thetys's silver flood curls; weeds are spongy. Ross's seas and main are briny; night is dewy; the shore is fishy; a boar's bristles are horrid; caves are mossy; waters purl; a snake's back is scaly. With the serpent's scaly back, it may be pointed out, as one example of the tenacity of poetic diction, that it occurs at least as early as Spenser's *Virgil's Gnat* (1. 305) and at least as late as Wordsworth's translation of the second book of the *Aeneid* (1. 291), a period of some two hundred and twenty-five years. Scaly, as applied to serpents or dragons, appears also in Harington's *Ariosto,* in Drayton, Sylvester, Phineas Fletcher's *Locusts,* Sandys's *Ovid,* Vicars's *Aeneid,* Ogilby's *Virgil,* Denham's *Destruction of Troy,* Howard's *Achilleis,* Ogilby's *Homer* (in both epics), and in the Pitt-Warton *Virgil*—as well, one can be sure, in many other works.

Besides the Latinisms, the -y adjectives, and parts of the diction of the poetry of natural description, later poets could have gone to these six translations for much else, for single words—Harington's rebate, Fairfax's tribute (used of a river), Gorges's cumbrous, May's unctuous, Fanshawe's serene (as a verb), Ross's missile (as an adjective)—as well as for phrases and images. Something of this possible borrowing, or conscious or unconscious recollection, can be adumbrated in a table devoted solely to certain resemblances between Ross's *Silius Italicus* and Dryden's *Virgil.* It should, of course, be obvious by now that neither Ross nor any other poet or translator is to be considered as a probable source for the poetic diction in Dryden's *Virgil* other than when there is coincidence on something other than commonplaces. Thus, in Table 1, the first word, abodes, is such a commonplace, even when coupled with blest or dark, that Dryden could

34

have remembered it, if it needed an act of remembrance, from many places. Remote abodes are rarer; and, although the conjunction of the two words would not tax any poet, there is a somewhat greater possibility of influence. Pope, incidentally, has remote abodes also. In the table, references under Ross are to book and page; references under Dryden are to line numbers in the *Pastorals* (P), the *Georgics* (G), and the *Aeneid* (A).

TABLE 1

Similarities Between Ross and Dryden

Term	Ross	Dryden
blest abodes	2. 53; 9. 253	A. 2. 393; 10. 8
dark abodes	13. 387	13 times
remote abodes	3. 70	A. 1. 492
aspire (smoke)	4. 100	fire A. 2. 1031: flames G. 4. 554
aspiring (rocks)	1. 22	vines G. 2. 301
augment (fear)	2. 34	A. 4. 675; 7. 796; 9. 662
band (youthful)	3. 72	A. 4. 124
briny main	17. 488	A. 5. 186; 10. 307
briny sea	15. 449	P. 10. 7; G. IV. 339
dewy night	5. 124; 13. 369	A. 11. 306
dire contagion	12. 326; 14. 414	G. 3. 710
dire presages	6. 183	A. 4. 661
a dubious fight	15. 451	A. 10. 899
an easy conquest	4. 115	A. 2. 517; 9. 243
expire (breathe out)	12. 327	A. 8. 335; 10. 795; 4. 286; 12. 455
fallacious	2. 34	A. 2. 116; 11. 1060
fishy shore	14. 401	fishy food A. 4. 373
gloomy night	15. 443	A. 2. 1001; 4. 173; 6. 208
humid shade	3. 64	A. 4. 505
infest (attack)	3. 72; 4. 112	A. 3. 512; 8. 75; 12. 397; G. 1. 199; G. 4. 358
liquid air	13. 362	A. 3. 571; A. 6. 757; 9. 636; G. 1. 557; 3. 378;
liquid plain	3. 74	4. 21
massie gold	4. 93	A. 1. 223
pitchy cloud	6. 164; 12. 347	A. 9. 55
provoke war	3. 69	A. 3. 748; A. 4. 170
rend the air	1. 19, 28; 2. 49; 5. 131	A. 5. 569; 7. 616; 10. 123. 793
		A. 7. 554; G. 1. 557

scour the field	2. 31; 9. 251	A. 2. 480; 8. 5; 11. 776; 12. 502; G. 3. 307
smoaking waves	1. 8	smoking billows A. 3. 375
spoil (a lion's)	2. 38	A. 2. 982
thunderbolt (a warrior)	15. 445; 17. 493	A. 6. 1159
a num'rous train	13. 367	A. 1. 697; 3. 445; 5. 380; 6. 549; 12. 654
vital breath	13. 378	A. 4. 486; 5. 946; 6. 769; 7. 1059; G. 4. 699
wat'ry plain	14. 406	G. 2. 625
yielding air	1. 14; 3. 86; 6. 162; 13. 365	A. 9. 1006; G. 4. 26, 666

Both use the coronation figure—i.e., to crown—in a metaphoric sense with goblets, cups, tables (or board), hills, or mountains. Both also use dire as an epithet: Ross with Antiphates, Cannae, Charybdis, Cocytus, and Eumenides; Dryden with Ulysses, Calaeno, and Tisiphone. Many of the terms in Table 1 will be found in Pope's *Iliad,* some coincidences between it and Ross's translation that do not appear in Dryden's *Virgil* being: social bands, frequent (full), headlong rage, missile (as adjective, used of weapons), and intercept the skies (cut off the sight of; three times in the *Iliad*).

To proceed to the possible influence of translations of other epics, Pope has left us more than one statement about his early reading; in one he wrote, "I have often mentioned my great reading period to you [Spence] (from about thirteen or fourteen to about twenty-one). In it I went through all the best critics, almost all the English, French, and Latin poets of any name, the minor poets, Homer and some of the greater Greek poets in the original, and Tasso and Ariosto in translations. I even then liked Tasso more than Ariosto, as I do still [March 1743], and Statius, of all the Latin poets by much, next to Virgil."[33] Pope himself noted his use of Ariosto in the fifth Canto of *The Rape of the Lock* and referred to Ariosto's and Tasso's use of allegory in the prefatory note to *The Temple of Fame* (Twickenham edition, 2. 251); his references to Tasso are more numerous and always laudatory. For example, in his *Discourse on Pastoral Poetry,* he states forthrightly that "Tasso in his *Aminta* has as far excell'd all the Pastoral writers, as in his *Gierusalemme* he has outdone the Epic Poets of his country" (*TE* 1. 31). From this expressed preference one would properly conclude that although he knew Ariosto in Harington's translation, there is little in the earlier writer that Pope could not have come upon and remembered from more favored works, including Fairfax's *Tasso*. Thus, Harington's poetic diction includes words and phrases such as azure skie, christall streame, craggie rocks, crew (some nineteen uses), to deck, an innumerable train. He has his "feathered fowles" and "fishes [that] cut the liquid stream"; he, too, describes gold as massy, and vital is coupled with "sprites" (spirits), blood, and humor. Possibly the most remarkable words are Latinisms, for he has the juice of herbs "infus'd" into a wound (Bk. 19, st. 19) and he has a knight who does "his swords edge rebate" (Bk. 45, st. 67). Pope uses infuse in similar fashion five times in the *Iliad* (4. 250; 5. 506, 1112; 2. 983; 19. 369), but he could more easily have gone to Ogilby's *Iliad* or Dryden's *Virgil* for it, and he has the point of a dart rebated at *Iliad* 2. 304. Ogilby uses rebate in its literal sense five times in his *Iliad* translation, and Pope could have encountered it, used in a metaphoric sense, in Dryden's *Palamon and Arcite* 3. 502 and in its literal sense of to reduce the effect or force of a blow or stroke in Dryden's version of the twelfth book of Ovid's *Metamorphoses* l. 231. Pope almost surely owed nothing to Ariosto's sixteenth-century translator in the matter of poetic diction. Dryden again, however, may have been an intermediary between Harington and Pope: for Dryden praised Harington, linking him with Fairfax and Spenser as descendants of Chaucer and ancestors of Waller and Denham.[34]

Since Pope admired Tasso as much as he did, and since Tasso's epic is more squarely in "the traditions of Western heroic thought"[35] stemming from Homer, there is greater likelihood that his diction in the *Homer* owes something, directly or indirectly, to Fairfax's translation.[36] One might start with the Twickenham editor's note on line 170 of *Eloisa to Abelard,* "And breathes a browner horror on the woods"; the note reads: *"Brown* shadows are found in English poetry as early as Fairfax's *Tasso* XX. 123, 1. 1." The note might have included the presence of brown shadows in at least three other passages in Tasso's epic—3. 56; 6. 1; and 14. 37—heightening the possibility that Pope got them there, although he might just as well have taken them from line 134 of *Il Penseroso.* But use them he did, as witness the "brown Shade" of *Iliad* 10. 547 and the four in the *Odyssey,* all in books translated by him and with none in those translated by Broome or Fenton.[37] Further similarities in poetic diction exist between the two translations, for where Fairfax has "God the Lord Armipotent" (3. 70) Pope has "Mars armipotent" and "th' Armipotent or the God of Light."[38] Fairfax's "cleave the yielding deep" (15. 12) has its exact counterpart in the *Odyssey* (9. 210) and a close one in "cleave the hoary deep" (9. 116). Sheep are the shepherd's

37

"fleecy charge" for Fairfax (19. 47); they are the sheep dog's for Pope (10. 211). Fairfax describes a pagan warrior grisly like Pluto (18. 87); Pope calls Pluto "the grisly God" (9. 209). Both translators, like their predecessors and followers, are fond of headlong, as adjective and adverb, and they coincide in "headlong fury" (Fairfax 7. 113; Pope 9. 143 and 16. 840), as well as in the more common headlong falls. Fairfax's "horrid shades" (12. 29) is an ancestor of the same phrase in Milton's famous line in *Comus*, "By grots and caverns shag'd with horrid shades" (429), which Pope changed slightly for line 20 of *Eloisa to Abelard*, "Ye grots and caverns shagg'd with horrid thorn." But Pope also has his "horrid shade" in the *Odyssey* (9. 219), as does his colleague Fenton (19. 503). Both translators are fond of the "not half so . . ." gambit; both combine it with dreadful, loud, and swift.[39] Fairfax's "massy substance" (2. 28) appears in Pope's *Iliad* (12. 546); his "steepy hills" (8. 51) become "a steepy Mound" in Pope (16. 446); his use of respire meaning to breathe (20. 87) is followed by Pope (11. 424, 933; 16. 63). Fairfax describes "How to sea his tribute Nilus pays" (15. 16); Milton describes how two rivers meeting "joined their tribute to the sea" (*Paradise Regained* 3. 258); Pope has the river Scamander complain that his "choak'd Streams" cannot "roll their wonted Tribute to the Deep" (21. 235–36). There are further similarities in the use of azure (skies, flood), craggy (rock, stone), distain (with blood), doubtful (of the issue of a battle), embrue (with blood), glittering (rays, helms, weapons, arms), inglorious (deaths and falls), sable (of night), smoke (of a horse), thunderbolt of war (warrior), train, vital (blood), and yielding (air). Fairfax even has "feather'd fellows" (birds, of course, 16. 13) and the sun as an enameling agent (1. 35); Pope has "the feather'd Race" (22. 338) and uses "enamel" once in the *Iliad* at 15. 507.

The editors of the Twickenham *Homer*, it may be recalled, list Camoens as one of the epic writers whose work was in the tradition of Western heroic poetry. Fanshawe translated the Portuguese epic in 1655, giving it the title *The Lusiads*. Pope refers twice to Camoens in *The Dunciad* (*TE* 5. 205, 340n.) but never mentions his English translator. But Fanshawe, who had already translated the popular fourth book of the *Aeneid* in 1648, had inherited a body of epic diction and used it in *The Lusiads*. And hence one has craggy rocks and mountains, doubtful war, arms and squadrons that glitter, seas profound, sable (night, cloud, wings of endless Night), vital breath, yielding air, a warrior described as a thunderbolt of war (Canto 10, st. 15), vocal trumpets, congregated clouds, and a few unusual Latinisms —erudiates (from *erudio*, to polish, educate, instruct) circumfuse, irrefragable, and reverberated (of arrows). Of these last Latinisms, Pope has only circumfuse in his *Homer* (*Iliad* 5. 967; 14. 390, 402).[40] Fanshawe also has disembogues (5. 10), the Ganges paying "Silver Tribute" to the sea (10. 120), and a fairly unusual use of serene as a verb meaning "To make (the sky, air) clear, bright, and transparent. Also, to clear *from* (cloud)," in the phrase "serenes the skye" (9. 24). Only once in the canon of Pope's poetry, and that once in the *Iliad,* does serene appear as a verb in words descriptive of Jove, "a Smile serenes his awful Brow" (15. 178).[41] While Pope may, of course, have read Fanshawe's translation, the absence of any reference to it and the lack of any strikingly original parallels to it—with the possible exception of serenes—lead to the conclusion that his was part of the cumulative influence upon Pope's epic diction rather than a direct contributor to it.

Pope, like Dryden before him, had the translations of Marlowe, Gorges, and May, principally the latter two, as further repositories of epic diction. By the time Rowe had published his translation of the *Pharsalia,* Pope had almost finished the translation of the *Iliad,* and hence there can be little influence of the former on the latter, although it might be a nice point to determine the possible influence of the early volumes of Pope's *Iliad* on Rowe's work. No evidence exists that Pope knew either Marlowe's or Gorges's translations, but Tillotson, in his capacity as editor of *The Rape of the Lock* and *The Temple of Fame* sees parallels to May's translation in three places in Pope.[42] Editors and critics of Pope's poetry, from Joseph Warton and Gilbert Wakefield to the editors of the Twickenham edition have seen parallels to Lucan's work in Pope's *Pastorals, Windsor-Forest. The Rape of the Lock, The Temple of Fame, Elegy to the Memory of An Unfortunate Lady, Essay on Man,* and *The Dunciad.* Among these, another bit of poetic diction, the "headlong Streams" of Pope's *Summer* may have come from Lucan's "De rupe pependit / abscisa fixus torrens," according to Wakefield (*TE* 1. 79 n.). Pope quotes Lucan twice in the notes to his *Homer* (*TE* 8. 434 and 10. 60), links him with Statius in the preface to the *Iliad* (7. 4), and sums his work up in a note on the *Odyssey:* "If the Poet [Homer] had follow'd the natural order of the action, he, like *Lucan,* would not have wrote an Epic Poem, but an History in verse" (*TE* 9. 304 n.), a clear echo of Dryden's opinion.[43]

The editors of the first two volumes of the Twickenham *Pope* point out parallels between passages in *An Essay of Criticism* and *The Rape of the Lock* and Addison's translation of parts of Lucan in his *Remarks on Several Parts of Italy,* first published in 1705 (*TE* 1. 245 n.; 2. 164 n.), giving rise to the possibility that Pope recollected other parts of Addison's translations from Lucan. Actually, Addison translated only a total of seventy-four lines, mostly from the first two books but with passages from Books 3 (8 lines), 6 (2 lines), and 7 (12 lines), and there was not much poetic diction in these short passages.[44] In the passage from Book 8, Addison has the line, "And one promiscuous ruine cover all" (p. 173), which may be somewhere in the remote background of the last line of Book 4 of *The Dunciad*. He has his wat'ry veins (also stores, moons, marshes), hoary mountains, woody realms, Latium "crown'd" with cities, an aspiring nation, and a rather unusual use of the verb erect in "No land like Italy erects the sight" (p. 192). Pope has "promiscuous death" in the *Odyssey* (9. 65), but no parallel use of "erect"; the others are commonplaces.

Of the translations of part or the whole of Lucan's poem, Thomas May's would seem to be the most promising supplementary source for the transmission of poetic diction to Pope's *Homer*. Some part of May's diction comes from Gorges, whose fondness for -y adjectives (brusky, cliffy, flaggy, globy, hugy, lithy, and moisty) and whose occasional Latinisms (coinquinate, express, infuse, infest, invest, prevent) added to his use of a number of other words or phrases of epic diction (devoted, distain, doubtful, headlong, massy, spoils, sway) deserve a place in the history of poetic diction. So, too, with Marlowe's translation of Book 1 which, since it is in blank verse, is not rich in those monosyllabic words of epic diction (train, band, crew, breed, tribe) so convenient as rhyme words. But Marlowe, writing in 1593, is relatively early on the scene as far as epic diction is concerned, and his translation runs to only 694 lines. May's, then, as the latest translation of Lucan, except for the few lines by Addison, was the official or definitive version of the *Pharsalia*. It was in his translation that Pope could find, what he could find elsewhere as well of course: adverse fleets, auspicious birds, warlike bands, craggy hills, temples and chariots decked with bays or laurels, devoted foes, dire used as an epithet, swords distained or glutted with blood, a doubtful fight, glittering swords, the air involved with clouds, massy stones, ponderous spears, the sea profound, sylvan as a noun, missile weapons, vital parts, and a number of other words and phrases that he would use in exactly the same way or with slight variation in his own translations.

One other translation should be mentioned if only to be disposed of. There is almost no poetic diction in the King James Bible. The number of noun plus -y suffix adjectives is very small; Latinate diction is most infrequent. While rivers are floods, the sea is the deep, a rock is flinty, and fowl are feathered, most of what constitutes poetic diction is absent. Weapons glitter as they do in epics; the heads of the old are described as hoary (as is frost once, again no innovation); but the uses of to crown and to deck in their figurative senses are few. Crystal is used only as a stone, and ruddy, with four appearances, is never used with a following noun. Deliciously is used only twice, both times to mean pleasantly, its Latinate sense, but it— with exalt and curious and one use of decently—is among the very few Latin words so used. Whatever influence the King James version had upon poets was certainly not in the matter of poetic diction.

NOTES AND REFERENCES

1. *PQ* 18 (1939):211–17.
2. English translations of Theocritus are discussed in Chapter 6.
3. E. M. W. Tillyard, *The English Epic and Its Background* (London: Chatto and Windus, 1954), p. 19.
4. Curtius, *European Literature and the Latin Middle Ages,* tr. Willard R. Trask (New York: Harper Torchbook, 1963), p. 186.
5. Ibid., p. 187.
6. Ibid., pp. 195–97.
7. Alastair Fowler's note on that line in the Longmans *Milton* (London: Longmans and Green, 1968). Fowler also directs attention to his note on *Paradise Lost* 8. 653, where he discusses shade and shadow further.
8. Dedication to his and Christopher Pitt's translation of Virgil's *Works,* 1753, 1. iii.
9. Twickenham *Homer* 7. ccxxiv-vi. Joseph Spence called Pope's description of Calypso's cave "an exact and beautiful Draught" in his *Essay on Mr. Pope's Odyssey in Five Dialogues* (2nd ed., 1737, p. 64).
10. Tillotson, *APD,* p. 49.
11. See Arthur Johnston, " 'The Purple year' in Pope and Gray," *RES* N.S. 14 (1963):- 389–93.
12. Reuben Brower, *Alexander Pope: The Poetry of Allusion* (Oxford: Clarendon Press, 1959), pp. 50–51.
13. Twickenham *Homer* 7. ccxxiv.
14. Most of what English critics writing on his matter had to say is gathered in H. T. Swedenberg's *Theory of the Epic in England, 1650–1800* (Berkeley and Los Angeles: University of California Press, 1944), to which I am indebted for what follows.
15. Blackmore, *Essays Upon Several Subjects,* 2 vols., 1716; quoted in Swedenberg, *Theory of the Epic,* pp. 351–54, passim.
16. Pemberton, *Observations, on Poetry, Especially the Epic (Occasioned by the Late Poem upon Leonidas),* p. 87.
17. Ibid., p. 139; the same point was made in much the same language in the "Reflections on Didactic Poetry," which made up part of the Christopher Pitt-Joseph Warton translation of Virgil (1753).

18. Pemberton, *Observations,* p. 102.

19. For Googe and Turberville, see C. H. Conley, *The First English Translations of the Classics* (New Haven: Yale University Press, 1927), p. 50.

20. Rowe's translation of the ninth Book was published in the sixth part of Tonson's *Poetical Miscellanies* (1709); he also published part of the second and sixth books before the entire translation came out.

21. Johnson, *Lives,* 3: 217.

22. Millar Maclure, ed. *Poems of Marlowe* (London, 1968), p. xxxv.

23. George Watson, ed., *Of Dramatic Poesy and Other Critical Essays,* 2 vols. (London and New York: Everyman's Library, 1962), 2:204.

24. Ibid, 2:243.

25. Ibid, 1:201.

26. Ibid., 1. 160.

27. Ibid., 1. 277.

28. Ibid., 1. 95.

29. Addison's translation of a passage in the *Punica* is adduced as a parallel to a line in *The Rape of the Lock* (*TE* 2. 203 n.).

30. I have used May's 3rd ed., 1635.

31. See Chapters 6 and 7 *passim.*

32. Since these counts are the result of quite rapid reading, errors will be of omission rather than of commission.

33. Spence *Observations, Anecdotes, and Characters of Books and Men,* ed. James M. Osborn (Oxford: Clarendon Press, 1966), p. 20.

34. Watson, 2. 281; Dryden again praises Fairfax, calling him one of the "great masters in our language" and again links him with Spenser in the same preface to *Fables Ancient and Modern,* Watson, 2. 270.

35. *TE* 7. clxxxiii, Ariosto is omitted from a list which is made up of Milton, Camoens, Tasso, Statius, Lucan, and Virgil.

36. I discover no influence on Fairfax of Richard Carew's translation of the first five cantos of Tasso's epic (1594). Carew used words such as blacky, hugy, largy, shrilly, and straungy (from strange); Fairfax is singularly free from this sort of thing.

37. See 3. 97; 9. 126; 10. 298; and 17. 215.

38. *Iliad* 13. 384 and 20. 166. References will be to the *Iliad* unless noted as to the *Odyssey;* references to Tasso's epic are to book and stanza.

39. Fairfax 4. 3; 4. 3; 6. 40; Pope 227. 133; 14. 457; 15. 266.

40. I do not find erudiate in the *OED* which, incidentally, lists Young's *Night Thoughts* (1742) for the first use in poetry of reverberate, meaning driven or forced back.

41. *OED* gives J. Davies (1613) "serene the Heaven," Fanshawe, Bishop Ken, and David Mallet.

42. *TE* 2. 196 nn. and 277 n. In the last, *Temple of Fame* (283) the bees' "flow'ry Toils," a bit of poetic diction, is said to owe something to May's "flowery taskes" in the bee simile in Lucan's work.

43. G. G. Loane cites Quintilian 10. 1. 90 and Petronius 118 as antecedents for Dryden's opinion (*Notes and Queries,* Nov. 6, 1943, p. 273); Kinsley quotes as an English precedent the preface to Davenant's *Gondibert* (ed. *Poems of John Dryden,* Vol. 4, Oxford, Clarendon Press, 1958). James Welwood in the preface to Rowe's *Lucan* wrote that *"The*

Pharsalia is properly an Historical Heroick Poem, because the Subject is a known true Story," p. xviii of the 2nd ed., 1722.

44. The translations are on pp. 21, 64–66, 70, 95, 128, 173–74, 192, in vol. 2 of *The Miscellaneous Works of Joseph Addison,* ed. A. G. Guthkelch (London: G. Bell, 1914).

Chapter 2.

Chaucer to Spenser

Chaucer's poetry is almost innocent of poetic diction, which is quite understandable. As far back as 1913 Havens wrote "in proportion as the subjects of poems draw nearer to those of ordinary conversation, the language and style grow conversational, and . . . 'poetic diction' is employed only in passages which it is desirable to have as different as possible from prose."[1] Pemberton had made somewhat the same observation in the eighteenth century, remarking that it was when the poet himself spoke or paused to describe something that one got poetic diction rather than when someone in the poem was speaking.[2] One scholar has suggested that Chaucer had a part in the matter of one of the characteristics of poetic diction, the -y adjectives. Among others, he has "hugy okes," "teary eyn," "starry skie," and "waky nightes." The same scholar mentions Turberville, Warner, and Spenser as among "the later poets who affected—and hence perpetuated" this method of word formation, but the phenomenon is present in most English poets, early and late.[3] There is a handful of words, the frequency of whose use by many poets causes them to fall in the category of poetic diction, but their infrequent appearance in Chaucer saves them from being so considered. That flowery, for example, once with "mede," should be found three times in Chaucer's poetry is of little, if any, significance. Additionally, Chaucer is more an English poet, in the sense that his vocabulary is more largely native, less Latin, than that of the poets that followed him,

44

there being an increasingly larger dependence upon Latinisms in the next four to five centuries, at least of those Latinisms not in common, even everyday, use.

A little more than a century and a half after Chaucer's death appeared the collection of poems that has come to be known as Tottel's *Miscellany*, after its publisher, Richard Tottel. Chief among the poets represented were Henry Howard, Earl of Surrey, and the man with whom his name is invariably coupled, Sir Thomas Wyatt. In 1557, the date of publication of the collection, Surrey had been dead ten years and Wyatt fifteen, and it was not until that year that the former's translation of Books 2 and 4 of the *Aeneid* was published, also by Tottel. Hyder Rollins writes of Tottel's collection that "it is hardly possible to overestimate the influence of Tottel's *Miscellany* on sixteenth-century, and hence indirectly on later, English poetry . . . the appearance of new editions of the miscellany until 1587, when the magnificent outburst of Elizabethan lyricism had begun, kept its influence constant and potent."[4] Since almost all the poems in the *Miscellany* are love poems, there is virtually no influence on the poetic diction with which we are concerned. Love poetry has its own poetic diction, made up of ice (or snow) and flames, of the war of red and white, of love conceived in military terms, of the ladies' killing eyes, of sighs and complaints, and of the mythology of Venus and her blind son with his so potent arrows, but rarely does this special vocabulary coincide with that of other, nonlyric poets. Lips are ruddy, gold is massy, the sky is the welkin, and heads are hoary in the *Miscellany*, but that is almost the extent of coincidence. Latinisms are few and not unusual in their employment. Taken as a whole, then, Tottel's *Miscellany*, like so many of its imitators, and they were many, is of no importance in the history of poetic diction other than that of love poetry. And so it is, too, that many poets writing in the second half of the sixteenth century do not figure at all in that history, except to contribute or to repeat an occasional word or phrase.[5]

The Earl of Surrey may not, however, have been entirely without influence on epic poetic diction through his translations of the second and fourth books of the *Aeneid*. Whatever the merits of the translations, they commanded much respect because they were the first blank-verse poems in English; while it is impossible to say how much they influenced epic poetic diction, certain of Surrey's usages were to appear again and again in later translations of classical epics, in English attempts at epic poetry, and in mock epics. Prominent among these are words such as abode, as in "the proud abodes / Of Myrmidons" (2. 1043–44); distain, as in Hector's appearance, "distained with bloody dust," in Aeneas's dream (2. 346); "glit-

45

tering arms" (2. 534); headlong, as in Mercury's descent from Heaven, "with body headling bente" (4. 325); massy gold (2. 1016), and embrued, coupled with blood or gore (2. 214, 4. 261 and 887).[6] Twenty-five years after Surrey's translations, Richard Stanyhurst translated the first four books of the *Aeneid,* and his version serves admirably as one example of the popularity of the new -y adjectives, for he has bracky, browny,* crabby,* doggy, dolye (sad), drossy, flasshye,* frothy, fledgye,* downy (feathered), fledgie* (ready to fly), franckye (stalled), frostye, glimrye,* harshye, helly, hudgy (huge) plasshye,* plumy,* quaffye,* snarrye* (snarling), spumy,* swartye, tarry.[7]

Two years after the publication of Tottel's *Miscellany* and Surrey's translations another popular collection of poems appeared. The poems in the famous *Mirror for Magistrates,* unlike those in the *Miscellany,* were verse narratives in "the fall of princes" tradition and had a frankly didactic purpose. The first edition, 1559, was not distinguished poetically, but the second, appearing in 1563, included an *Induction* and the *Complaint of Henry Duke of Buckingham* by Thomas Sackville which far outshone the other poems in the collection. *A Mirror for Magistrates,* like Tottel's *Miscellany,* was enormously successful and went through a number of editions. The editors of the anthology *Poetry of the English Renaissance, 1509–1660,* echoing George Saintsbury, write that Sackville's *Induction* "is usually accounted the most considerable poem written in the period between Chaucer's *Canterbury* Tales and Spenser's *Fairy Queen.*"[8] Given the popularity of *A Mirror for Magistrates* and the fact that both Spenser and Joshua Sylvester praised Sackville—the former in Sonnet 12, dedicatory to *The Faerie Queene,* the latter in a poem dedicatory to his translation of DuBartas—it is highly likely that his contribution to the *Mirror* exerted some influence on later poets. Some of that influence probably was in the direction of poetic diction, and here it would be well to anticipate later discussion by pointing to the importance of both Spenser and Sylvester in the establishment and handing on of that body of diction. Sackville knew and admired the poetry of Wyatt and Surrey, mentioning them along with Chaucer in the stanzas that come after the *Complaint;* and one scholar states unreservedly that "Surrey's influence on Sackville is without question. The poet of the *Induction* knew well not only Surrey's poems in *Tottel's Miscellany* but also his translation of the *Aeneid"*[9] In any event, Sackville has a fondness for "hugy," for it appears three times in the *Induction* and once in the *Complaint* (st. 58, 65, 73, 181),[10] and he finds place for "raynie eyn" (tears, st. 177) as well as "cristall teares" (11). Alecto's hair is properly "snaky" (st. 170), and so too is the hair of the personified Debate (st. 58).

46

Hearts are "stelie" (st. 148), Charon is "grislie" as is the foot of the constellation, the Bear (st. 69). "Pluto god of Hell" is "grislie blacke" (st. 16), there is a "grislie lake" (st. 26), Hell is a vast, hideous hole with "grislie jawes" (st. 30),[11] and a boar is described (as was to become conventional) as "fomie" (st. 161). Sackville has a sword "with blood imbrued" (st. 56), war is clad in "glittering arms" (st. 56), night's "mantle" is "mistie" (st. 4), and the sky is "the welkyn" (st. 169). The *OED* credits Sackville with the first use of "devest," in the figurative sense of to strip, in the line "the roiall babes devested from their trone" (st. 109); his other remarkable use of a Latin word, the soon to be much overworked vital, comes in stanza 159, in which one can see how much can be accomplished in the description of nature without recourse to poetic diction:

> Mid night was come and everie vitall thing
> with swete sound slepe their wearie lims did rest
> the bestes were still the litle burdes that sing
> now sweteli slept beside their mothers brest
> the old and all were shrouded in their nest
> the waters calme the cruell seas did cesse
> the woods and feldes and all things held their peace.[12]

Later poets would write of vital blood, vital heat, vital powers; Sackville's "everie vitall [living] thing," with its joining of the Latin vital to the simple and seemingly unpoetical thing, achieves an effect that is denied the others. And he needed no periphrases; his "litle burdes that sing" and his "bestes" and his "woodes and feldes and all things" would have suffered poetic death had they been transmogrified into the elegant periphrases that were all too soon to become the vogue. Indeed, most poets up to the time of Sylvester's translation of DuBartas were quite happy to write of birds as birds or to use specific names.[13]

Part of the impetus given to verse narrative by *Mirror for Magistrates* was directed to translations from Ovid, with the *Metamorphoses* leading the way, and with Arthur Golding's influential version of 1565–67 as the most popular. Golding helped to perpetuate some items of poetic diction. Grisly, for example, he links with the constellation named the Bear, with the "Stygian lake," and with "grim Medusa" (2. 174, 3. 362, and 5. 304). He also has some "flakie clouds all grisly black" (3. 375). There are two quite conventional uses of ruddy to describe some aspect of morning, but a stone is "made ruddy" with Orpheus's blood (11. 19–20) and a "ruddie colour" results from a blow on the stomach (3. 606). Other -y adjectives include clammy, craggy, fenny, hoary, massy (three times with gold), pitchy, sedgy, and watery. Apollo speaks of his chief abode (1. 627); reference is made to the "heavenly cope" (2. 208); and an axe is "embrewed with blood" (2. 785). Water and bodies of water are predictably crystal, breath is vital, and the sky is the welkin. There are few Latinisms; Golding's version is often described as "rugged," a term that accurately suggests a highly individualized and Anglo-Saxon vocabulary.

Imitations of Ovid were also highly popular and much less laborious to turn out than translations. Thomas Lodge's *Scylla's Metamorphosis,* published in 1589, is one of the earlier and better of these imitations and may stand as an example of the kind of diction that was being employed. For one thing, the fondness for -y adjectives is seen in Lodge's "balmie breath" (of the winds) and "balmie deaw" (st. 9, 34); in "the watrie world" (st. 10, 111), "Neptune's watrie sound" (st. 30), "watrie realme" (st. 67), and "watrie bosome of the tide" (st. 112); a face is "palie" (st. 20), a river is "calmy" (st. 63, an adjective made from another adjective), cliffs are "chalky" (st. 66) and garlands are "mossie" (st. 127).[14] Water is "silver" or "crystal" (st. 10, 128), "meades" are with "flowres distained" (st. 37), grass is "yeelding" (st. 101), and there is a "beauteous traine" as well as a "holy" and "happy troope" (st. 95, 96). All of these, of course, were to become part of poetic diction; it only remained for them to be handled and rehandled enough times. Other poets of this last quarter of the sixteenth century, in lyric poetry, in narrative verse, and in translations were either picking up or coining—or resurrecting—words and phrases and conjunctions of words that were to prove useful to later poets; unfortunately, in too many instances, too useful.

Chaucer died in 1400, and while some poets after him and before Spenser, men like Wyatt and Surrey, for example, had much to do with the future course of English poetry, particularly lyric poetry, it was not until the publication in 1579 of Spenser's *Shepherd's Calendar* that there occurred something like a radically new departure in poetic diction. Spenser, according to Rubel, "in preparation for writing *The Shepheardes Calendar,* had steeped himself in the work both of Chaucer and of *Tottel's Miscellany* as well as reading all he could lay hold of in the works of other early poets,"[15] but for Rubel the more important parts of the diction of Spenser's first published work are the archaisms, the dialect words, the borrowings from the French, and other aspects that are not germane to present purposes. In any event, it is a curious phenomenon that English pastoral poetry and pastoral drama had not, up to this time, exerted any discoverable influence upon poetic diction, especially in the light of the setting and dramatis personae of these poems and plays. The answer lies, of course, in the fact that much pastoral literature is either didactic or satiric—or both. Thus, *Certayne Egloges of Alexander Barclay Priest,* published in 1515 and regarded as the first eclogues in English, treat of "the miseryes of Courtiers and Courts" (the first three), of "the behavour of Riche men agaynst Poetes," and of "the disputation of Citzens and men of the Countrey." What little description of nature there is is barren of poetic diction, with virtually no periphrases, -y adjectives, or unusual Latinisms.[16] Next in order of importance in the pastoral genre is Barnabe Googe whose eclogues appeared, with others of his poems, in 1563. He too had nothing to contribute to poetic diction, using largely the language of love poetry, but also using the eclogue as a vehicle for religious expression. Googe, along with Turberville, who in 1567 translated nine of Mantuan's ten eclogues into English, almost surely stimulated Spenser, who knew the work of both poets, to write his *Shepherd's Calendar.* And it is in *The Shepherd's Calendar* that one gets the first real clustering of items of poetic diction. Of the -y adjectives alone there are bushy, craggy, dreary, frosty, grassy, grisly, hoary, leany, mazy, moldy, stormy, vetchy, watery, weedy, wintery. Of these, the *OED* gives one prior use of leany, and that in a cookbook to describe meat, and one prior use of weedy, and that in a book of husbandry; there is no prior use of vetchy. Latinisms are fewer, but Spenser coins, or rather takes almost directly from Latin, his word "crumenall" in the lines, "The fatte Oxe . . . / Is now fast stalled in her crumenall" (*September,* 11. 118–19), from *crumena,* a leather pouch for money. In the *January* eclogue "ysicles depend" (1. 42) rather than hang as in Shakespeare's song in *Love's Labour's Lost,* and there is a reference in the *November* eclogue to the "vitall threds" (1. 149). And, as at least one Elizabethan critic was quick to note, Spenser made great play with the word augment, for William Webbe in his *Discourse of English Poetrie* (1586) pointed to Spenser's "singular rare devise of a dittie framed upon these sixe wordes Woe, sounds, cryes, part, sleep, augment, which are most prettily turned and wounde uppe mutually together, expressing wonderfully, the dolefulnesse of the song," referring to the *August* eclogue where augment appears six times (11. 156, 157, 164, 171, 185, 189).[17] Spenser uses the verb to deck, one he grew increasingly fond of, four times, once to describe Queen Elizabeth "decked . . . in royall aray" (*April,* 1. 145), and the other three times to describe a shepherdess, a dame, and a grave.[18] He refers to the sky as the welkin twice (*March,* 11. 12, 155), uses honor for a tree's foliage (*February,* 1. 114), has gaudy garlands (*June,* 1. 45, and *November,* 1. 108); his meadows are mantled (*November,* 1. 128), and his boughs are crowned with blooms

(*December*, 1. 103). Other words which were to attain greater currency are crew, glittering, madding, pensive (anxious), and troop. Rubel states quite categorically that it "was Spenser . . . Who ultimately determined the diction of the pastoral to the very close of the period," i.e., the English Renaissance,[19] and while Rubel's poetic diction is only in small part the poetic diction studied here, his conclusion may be extended to the diction in *The Shepherd's Calendar.*

Of other prominent writers in the pastoral mode and with particular emphasis on the use of poetic diction in pastoral drama, George Peele, in his *Arraignment of Paris* (1584), has massy gold, the sylvan chase (three times), bowers decked with parti-colored flowers, a heavenly crew of goddesses, gaudy soil, and the painted paths of pleasant Ida, all to be used with greater and greater frequency by later writers. Three years after Peele's play Abraham Fraunce published *The Lamentations of Amyntas,* translated from Thomas Watson's Latin. His fondness for watery, especially with fountains to describe tears (four times), is also shown by his coupling it with fountains (literal ones), countenance, and Kingdom (twice).[20] He has "wythy twiggs" (5. 90), two uses of mantled in the figurative sense (4. 43 and 7. 45), and a few more uses that already were or were to become part of poetic diction.[21] The anonymous *The Maid's Metamorphosis* (1600), attributed to John Lyly, is largely comic and largely written in prose; what poetic diction it has is little, though some of it is distinctive. For example, one finds "this grassie bed, / With sommers gaudie dyaper bespred" (2. 1. 55–56), Echo's "airie tong" (2. 1. 71), a "grovie" ground (3. 1. 26), "verdant" fields (5. 1. 104), flowers described as "Floras painted pride" (5. 1. 105), and streams are, of course, "chrystall" (5. 1. 106). Of these, however, the anonymous author could have derived his "airie tong" of Echo either from Spenser's "airy echo" (*Gnat*, 1. 232) or from *Romeo and Juliet* act 2, scene 2. (Echo's "airy tongue"), his "verdant fields" from *The Faerie Queene* (1. 1. 17.9) or elsewhere, and his description of flowers as "Flora's painted pride" from the famous description of Spenser's Bower of Bliss, which contains the description of flowers as "all the ornaments of *Floraes* pride" (2. 12. 50.5). Samuel Daniel had virtually nothing to add to all this in his *Queene's Arcadia* (1605), nor in his later pastoral tragicomedy *Hymen's Triumph* (1623), except possibly to have his little spring not only "christall" but "purling" (2. 4. 832; the play is continuously lined). Possibly the most famous English pastoral is John Fletcher's *Faithful Shepherdess* (acted about 1608), but poetic diction is very sparse therein also, with gaudy, evidently a favorite, used to describe a shepherd's hook (act 1, scene 1), flowers (act 1, scene 3), and the abstraction, youth (act 1, scene 3). There are sylvan powers (act 3, scene 1, the sole use of that adjective in the play), verdant grass (act 2, scene 2), two uses of the coronation figure ("crown thy chaste hopes" in act 1, scene 2 and "crown my appetite" in act 2, scene 3), and a use of enamelled, descriptive, not of nature, but of human veins (act 2, scene 3).

Later pastoral dramas such as Ben Jonson's *Sad Shepherd* (left unfinished at his death in 1637), Thomas Randolph's *Amyntas* (1638), and James Shirley's *The Arcadia* (adapted from Sidney in 1640) are of no significance in the history of poetic diction, though the first two repeat some of the increasingly more frequently encountered words and phrases of that diction. "Genial bed," for example, occurs in Randolph's play (2. 1. 64). Abraham Cowley gave an impetus to the use of sylvan as adjective in *Love's Riddle, A Pastoral Comedy* (1638), there joining it to deities, goddesse, habit, weeds, friends,[22] and he also has such expressions as "springs flowry birth" (act 1, scene 1, p. 73), "fleecy tribute" (act 2, scene 1, p. 89), and "spring crown'd with the glories of the earth" (act 2, scene 1, p. 90). No one pastoral play, therefore, can be said to have exerted much influence on the course of poetic diction, and it must be remembered that the last four plays discussed are almost exactly contemporary with *Comus,* published in 1637, and *Lycidas,* published in 1638. One more pastoral play of this period should, however, be mentioned. Fanshawe's translation of Guarini's *Il Pastor Fido* was published in 1647; the amount and kind of poetic diction in the play may suggest the "advances" made in that direction. Fanshawe can still write of the sky as the welkin (1. 845, continuously lined), the sea is the briny main (4105), a way is craggy (4997), foliage is verdant honour (4533), the head of a boar is horrid (i.e., bristly, 3338), groves are described in terms of gloomy and silent horrors (73 and 1653), imbrue is coupled with blood (3047–48), a stone is massy (3197), meads are painted (230), grass is pearled (1692), night's "canopie" is sable (887), and spirits and blood are vital (2512 and 2513).[23] The evidence leads to the conclusion that pastoral poetry and drama, for the most part, borrowed poetic diction from other genres rather than contributed notably to it. Perhaps some significance can be attached to the nonappearance in Arthos's study of most of the pastoral poems and dramas examined in this brief survey, for only Googe's eclogues are quoted in Arthos's work, only a few times and then in illustration of beam, climate, frame, globe, sphere, train—only the last of which can be considered part of poetic diction. Googe is quoted for two periphrases only: "Neptunes rayne" for the sea and "golden globe" for the sun. None of this can be considered to have made any lasting impression on anybody.

As a footnote to the discussion of the influence of Spenser, Shakespeare, and Milton on English poetry, Havens wrote that "since Spenser was less read than the other two poets and seemed more antiquated and remote, his diction was used more consciously than theirs, by fewer writers, and in more definite imitations of his manner. Shakespeare's language seems to have attracted a still smaller degree of attention and, until the beginning of the nineteenth century, to have had less influence than one would expect. Yet no one can speak with anything like certainty in these matters until extensive researchs have been made into the entire subject of poetic diction, a neglected field in which the many recent concordances are of invaluable service."[24] Some fifty years after this statement there is still no adequate study of Spenser's diction in its entirety, although some aspects of that diction have been closely examined. Henry Cecil Wyld's three lectures are devoted largely to Spenser and are partly an expansion of an earlier essay;[25] the limitations of Wyld's work are discussed on pages 56-9. And there is, of course, Groom's study, already discussed, which treats primarily of "the diction of poetry, not with 'poetic diction' " and hence is of relatively little value for present purposes.[26]

John Arthos writes that

> the vast majority of the terms which belong to eighteenth-century diction belong also to the diction of Lucretius and Virgil. Phrases like *humid King-doms* and *painted birds* are almost indubitably to be traced to those writers. Accordingly, the first important fact gained from studying the extensive and ancient use of many elements of stock diction is that most of them are to be found in classic Roman poetry—commonly among the Augustan writers, and rather fully among earlier Roman poets.[27]

Certain English writers of the sixteenth and seventeenth centuries, influenced by Lucretius and Virgil, were themselves important in the transmission of this body of poetic diction. For Arthos, chief among these English writers is Joshua Sylvester, for he states quite categorically that "the great source of English poetic diction in the description of nature is Sylvester's translation of DuBartas",[28] i.e., *Bartas His Devine Weekes and Works*, 1605, parts of which appeared in 1592, 1595, and 1598. Tillotson had written in 1938 that English poetic diction of the eighteenth century began with Sylvester, but that it was probably his imitator George Sandys "who did most to fix the vocabulary of 'progressive' English poetry for more than a century."[29] One must deduce from his absence in Tillotson's discussion that Spenser played no role in the formation of poetic diction. This is the more curious in that Sandys's "group of favourite and semi-favourite words: *anxious* (often with *cares*), *pensive, ratify, promiscuous(ly), sad, trembling, glittering, nodding, sylvan, refulgent, pale, alternate, sing* (of hail and arrows), *yielding, involve,* " include six of which one might also claim as Spenser's favorites or semi-favorites: glittering (or glistering), pale, pensive, sad, trembling, and yielding. Tillotson wrote that "among these [the listed words] an important word is *sad*".[30] Sad appears in the canon of Spenser's poetry more than three hundred times. There are thirty-two uses of glittering (or glistering), twenty-three of pale, twenty-one of pensive, sixty-one of trembling, and thirteen of yielding, but none of anxious, alternate, involve, nodding, ratify, promiscuous(ly), refulgent, sylvan, or sings (with hail of arrows). Since Tillotson does not indicate what frequency of use makes a word a favorite with an author and since he does not give examples of the later use of words such as ratify, alternate, and nodding—to name but three whose frequency in English poetry is not particularly striking—one can only register a general disagreement. But when he proceeds to demonstrate that "Milton's minor poems and, to a less extent, his major poems, show the debt to Sylvester and Sandys perfectly combined among all those other debts to earlier English poetry" and selects sad, pensive, and trembling as examples of this combined influence, one can only point to the number of times these words were used by a poet whose popularity far overshadowed that of either Sylvester or Sandys. Sandys's translation of Ovid, as will be demonstrated,[31] had little influence upon subsequent translators of that poet, further evidence that his was a minor role in the history of English poetic diction.

Arthos wisely qualifies his sweeping statement about the primacy of Sylvester's translation of DuBartas as an influence upon poetic diction by writing that "though the diction of eighteenth-century English poetry owed immeasurably to Sylvester, many of the individual poets may have been quite ignorant of his work. They may have modelled themselves upon Lucretius and Virgil, and have been unaware that their English vocabulary came from Sylvester at second or third hand."[32] But Edmund Spenser, Sylvester's contemporary, of whose poetry few individual poets were ignorant, was without a rival "in the strength of his continuous influence, direct and indirect, on the diction of English poetry" according to Groom. It should be repeated that Groom uses "poetic diction" (his quotation marks) where he means "to imply a charge of convention or of mechanical repetition," and it is in the light of this distinction that he can write that "in Spenser too are the clear beginnings of what came to be known as the 'poetic diction' of the eighteenth century: 'the *watry* Gods' (F.Q. IV. xi. 10), 'the *nation* of . . . birds' (II. xii. 36), 'his *finny* drove' (III. viii. 29)."[33] Actually,

Spenser is a more important originator and, especially, transmitter of poetic diction than either Arthos or Groom recognizes. Indeed, because of his stature as a poet and his reputation, as well as his influence, it is safe to say that he not only influenced the course of English poetry by those aspects of his poetry that can properly be called Spenserian, but that he was almost equally influential in the formation and transmission of poetic diction. Such a distinction, that between what is considered peculiarly Spenserian—for example, adding the y- prefix to a word—and that which was shared by a number of poets and poetasters, has not been enough insisted on. Failure to make this distinction, both with Spenser and with Milton, has inevitably led to much confusion in the attempt to chart the rise and progress of English poetic diction. And if, as has been maintained, "most Elizabethans turned chiefly to Ovid, [but] Spenser was more vitally affected by the finer art of Virgil,"[34] one comes again to the Roman poet the translation of whose works into English in 1697 marked the virtual codification of a great body of that same English poetic diction.

One indication of the extent of Spenser's influence can be had from John Dryden's scattered remarks about him. Late in life, in his dedication to his translation of Virgil, published in 1697, Dryden wrote quite unambiguously, "I must acknowledge that Virgil in Latin, and Spenser in English, have been my masters" and "Spenser and Milton are, in English, what Virgil and Horace are in Latin; and I have endeavoured to form my style by imitating their masters." And in his last critical work, the preface to *Fables, Ancient and Modern,* Dryden linked Spenser and Milton again, calling the later poet "the poetical son" of the earlier, and claiming that Milton had "acknowledged" to him that "Spenser was his original." Earlier, in *A Discourse Concerning the Original and Progress of Satire,* he had written of Milton that "his antiquated words were his choice, not his necessity; for therein he imitated Spenser, as Spenser did Chaucer." His admiration for Spenser is also expressed in a passage on "the turn"—i.e., "a stylistic grace or characteristic idiom"—in which he writes that after not finding this particular kind of poetic beauty in either Cowley, "the darling" of his youth, or Milton, "at last I had recourse to his [Milton's] master Spenser, the author of that immortal poem called the *Fairy Queen;* and there I met with that which I had been looking for so long in vain. Spenser had studied Virgil[35] to as much advantage as Milton had done Homer; and amongst the rest of his excellencies had copied that." And as far as pastoral poetry was concerned, Dryden was emphatic that "the *Shepherd's Calendar* of Spenser is not to be matched in any modern language."[36] If one adds to Dryden's opinion Pope's avowal in a letter to John Hughes of October 7,

1715, "Spenser has been ever a favourite poet to me: he is like a mistress, whose faults we see, but love her with 'em all"; his remarks to Joseph Spence that "the great landmarks" in "the general course of our poetry" are "Chaucer, Spenser, Milton, and Dryden" and that Drayton, Fairfax, and Milton "in his famous *Allegro* and *Penseroso* and some others" were imitators of Spenser; as well as a number of other laudatory comments recorded by Spence, one has further impressive firsthand evidence of Spenser's popularity with and influence upon two succeeding poets who themselves influenced the course of English poetry.[37]

The claim made by Arthos for Sylvester's pre-eminence as a source for the diction of eighteenth-century poetry merits some further consideration. Thomas Seccombe writes that "after 1660 Sylvester ceased to be read, and was referred to, like his original in French, as a pedantic and fantastic old poet, disfigured by bad taste and ludicrous imagery."[38] Earlier, one editor of Spenser's works stated bluntly "the fact is, that Sylvester often plunders Spenser, but often also accommodates the theft to his purpose with little taste or judgement,"[39] Dryden confesses, in his dedication of *The Spanish Friar,*

> I remember, when I was a boy, I thought inimitable Spenser a mean poet in comparison of Sylvester's *Dubartas;* and was rapt into an ectasy when I read these lines:
>
>> Now, when the Winter's keener breath began
>> To crystallize the Baltic Ocean;
>> To glaze the lakes, to bridle up the floods,
>> And periwig with snow the bald-pate woods.
>
> I am much deceived if this be not abominable fustian, that is, thoughts and words ill sorted, and without the least relation to each other.

George Gordon, remarking on the Elizabethans' penchant for hunting "words and verbal patterns," notes that "the virtuoso of the business was Sylvester, and his work its rag-bag. Yet ought one to sneer at a poet whom Milton studied, and who coined, perhaps, such words as *deathless, star-spangled,* and *princeling?*"[40] Perhaps it is significant that editions of Sylvester's translation stopped with that of 1641 and that there were none in the eighteenth century. Spenser, on the other hand, fared extremely well in the eighteenth century, commanding editorial and critical attention for which Sylvester had to wait almost to the beginning of the twentieth century. Spenser knew DuBartas and praised him in the envoy of his *Ruins of Rome,* published in 1591, by which time there had been a number of translations of parts of the French writer's work, one of them being Sylvester's first translation. Perhaps it is also significant that Spenser, in the envoy, speaks of DuBartas's "heavenly Muse," which is taken to be a reference to the French poet's *Uranie,* or *Heavenly Muse* in 1584 (with a second edition in 1585) and translated into Latin in 1589 by Robert Ashley. Spenser might, in 1591, have known only the one poem by DuBartas in translation. *If* there is influence upon Spenser's poetry it is almost surely from the original French[41] and not from Sylvester's translation, a fact which is borne out by comparison of the first appearances in Spenser or Sylvester of the words in Arthos's Appendix A, "Certain Words Significant in Eighteenth-Century Poetry, with Illustrations from Earlier Poetry and Scientific Literature." For what little significance may attach to it, the fact is that of those words held in common by Spenser and Sylvester there are seventy-six first appearances in Spenser to twenty-one in Sylvester. Since the question of influence does not include later English poets' knowledge of the French of DuBartas but rather the diction of his translator, there is no need to ascertain, if that were possible, how much, if any, of his poetic diction Spenser owed to DuBartas himself.[42]

Wyld distinguishes four different categories of a poet's vocabulary; two are germane to this study: "Words, some of them in familiar daily use, employed in new ways by the poet, and endowed in a particular context with a special emotional value," and, "Words not used in ordinary prose, nor in familiar speech, but peculiar to poetry, many of which are felt to have some special 'poetical' value and associations."[43] Wyld sensibly adds that it is best to regard his categories "as to a great extent fluid and variable, and as often passing one into the other."[44] According to him "it is not too much to say that the poetic diction of the eighteenth century, the diction of Pope and his school, is all to be found in Spenser, either actually, or as a germ which was later expanded, worked up, and emphasized." The special language of poetry, for Wyld, is made up of "archaisms, Latin words, and conventional 'poetical' words, derived from different modern languages, words from English provincial dialects, current colloquialisms, and new formations from already existing materials."[45] Wyld's analysis of what he terms "conventional poetical words of various origins" comes to the heart of the matter. Among these poetical words are a certain number "often held to belong to a conventional, artificial diction, in fact to 'poetic diction' in the narrower meaning of the term." Some of these words, we are told, are associated with "the style of the later eighteenth-century imitators of Pope, derived from the master himself." Still others are favored by poetasters who "seize upon them, apparently in the belief that to use a certain range of words is in itself to make poetry, in spite of vacuity of thought, and insincerity of feeling." And with the further remark that "nearly all" of the words he is going to mention in this section "have been used at one time or another by great poets from Spenser onwards, and some of them go back, with the sense they still bear, to Middle English poets,"[46] Wyld is ready to quote examples.

The brevity of Wyld's ensuing discussion can be put down to the fact that he was delivering a series of three lectures, and one cannot try the patience of an audience too far. Whatever the reason, while he accumulates a number of interesting examples, largely from the poets before 1800, much poetic diction is neglected. Additionally, some of his conclusions are based on a woefully small number of examples, inspiring little confidence in statements about the role of the words in question in the history of poetic diction. And there is also reason to suspect his judgment on the merit of some of the lines he quotes. One example of this last shortcoming is his comment on the word verdant. "Verdant," he writes, "becomes with many later poets a mere conventional epithet, often awaking no particular emotion; but the word has specific value in Spenser's

And streams of purple blood now dye the verdant fields.

Faerie Queene, I. ii. 17."

He continues, "And how splendid is Milton's use:

the parting sun
Beyond the earth's green Cape and verdant Isles
Hesperean sets.

Paradise Lost, VIII. 630–2."[47]

Spenser's line has no particular merit; indeed, the very contrast of verdant, one poetical word, with purple, a poetical word used almost inevitably with blood or wounds (at least twelve more times in Spenser, some ten in Shakespeare) seems to rob the line of any possible freshness.[48] As far as Milton's lines go, a note on them in a recent edition of his poetry reads, "Here the *green cape* is Cape Verde and the *verdant isles* the Cape Verde Islands," and the same note suggests a source for his use of "Hesperean" also. Returning to Spenser and verdant, it is interesting to note that of the other four uses of the word in his poetry three are unstrikingly in description of grass and one is the name of a character. And I cannot, for another example, from a different poet, even half-heartedly concur that two quoted passages from Milton which contain the word welkin somehow escape the charge of belonging to a "pseudo-poetic diction."[49]

As example of the untrustworthiness of some of Wyld's conclusions, there are the statements he makes about the "widespread use" of the adjective sable for black. He quotes Spenser once (night's sable mantle) and Milton three times (sable cloud, sable shroud, and sable stole). Dryden's use is exemplified by sable night from his translation of the *Aeneid.* "For Pope," Wyld states, "the word is a convenient and more imposing synonym for 'dark' or 'black,' " and he gives as examples: sable weeds, sable fumes, sable waste, and sable ship, Jove's sable brows, sable loves, and Africa's sable sons. (I have remarked above on sable waste in the line "Like verdant isles [did he take it straight out of Milton?] the sable waste adorn" from *Windsor-Forest.*) First of all, in two of these uses—i.e., with shroud and weeds—Milton and Pope are using sable as what the *OED* defines as "a symbol of mourning." Other uses of sable, although not exemplified in the passages quoted by Wyld, have reference to it as a heraldic color, something equally true of azure. But the statement about the "widespread use" of sable for black needs correction. Spenser uses sable only five times, twice to describe night's mantle, if not already a cliché soon to become one, and three times as a symbol of mourning, but he uses black fifty-seven times. Shakespeare, curiously absent from Wyld's study, uses sable as an adjective three times in the plays and four times in the poems, but black appears between two and three hundred times in the plays and twenty-seven times in the poems. Wyld exhausted Milton's use of sable in his three quotations; he might have added sable-stoled and sable-vested, the latter to describe a personified Night, a practice, that of describing Night or her garments as sable, that is seen in the quotations from Spenser. Milton, incidentally, uses black twenty-three times. Dryden uses black forty-six times in his *Virgil* as opposed to fourteen times for sable, five of which latter uses are with night. For Pope's translation of the *Iliad,* from which Wyld quotes, the frequencies are sixty-four times for black and forty-four for sable. There are five sable ships, two vessels, and one bark, as well as four shields, two brows (Jove's), and two clouds—all of which had become pretty standardized by this time. Indeed, one has only to remember Swift's line in *A Description of a City Shower* (1710), "A sable cloud athwart the welkin flings," to realize how sick one writer had become of sable clouds, Milton's as well as anybody else's.

Curiously enough, in Wyld's discussion of "Latinism in Spenser," his examples, both in terms of their small number and in terms of the infrequency with which the Latin words in those examples appear in the canon, rather than enforcing his argument about the major importance of Spenser in the formation of poetic diction in this area tend to disprove it. He quotes examples of daedal, eternize, ruinate, delectable, verdant, fume (as verb), and humid. Humid and ruinate appear six times each, verdant and fume (as verb) five times each, eternize four times, daedal twice, and delectable once. What is more, Wyld then proceeds to quote examples of "dozens of other Latin words which have long been sanctified by the usage of poets, words already dignified by their classical associations, and given a permanent and exalted place in English poetry by their use in some splendid passage."[50] The quotations range in time from Milton to Swinburne and exemplify the words lucid, circumfuse, interfuse, sanctitude, dome, irriguous, depending, emulate, refulgent, pellucid, irremeable, diurnal, lave, and exhalation—fourteen words in all. Of these fourteen, only three (lucid, depending, emulate) appear in Spenser's work, with depending appearing only twice and lucid and emulate only once each. Wyld's examples would seem to show that Spenser's use of Latinisms had little effect on the history of poetic diction. Nor were these Latinisms Spenser's in the sense that he was the first to use them, for the *OED* credits him only with the introduction of daedal and verdant (in the sense of green with vegetation). One might wish to have Shakespeare share in the dissemination of ruinate, for he uses it four times. Similarly, he uses fume as a verb twice, while delectable appears twice in his work as opposed to the single appearance in Spenser. Again, this is not an attempt to claim precedence for one poet as opposed to another in the matter of the introduction or popularization of certain words, but rather further proof of the existence of a fund of words being introduced or favored by a group of poets at a particular time. As one scholar has put it, "to say definitely that Shakespeare or any other author invented a word or phrase is to say, very often, what we cannot know."[51]

Wyld's earlier essay named a number of words used by Spenser as forming "part of that 'poetic diction' of the eighteenth century which Wordsworth attacked."[52] Among these are the adjectives griesly, sunshiny, glittering, glistering, flaggy, horie, pompous, moystie, humid, and the verbs to deck and to embrew. Among the metaphorical expressions or periphrases in Spenser, he lists watrie wildernesse, leavy cages, this vitall aire, finny drove, milkie mothers, sable mantle (night's), grassie flore and gives examples of similar expressions in Milton, Dryden, and Pope. It is immediately noticeable that a number of the examples listed depend on the device of forming an adjective by adding the -y suffix to a noun, one of the mainstays of poetic diction. Now this is not, of course, peculiar to Spenser, as has already been demonstrated, but his recourse to this device has attracted some notice. H. C. Hart, editing the first part of Shakespeare's *Henry VI* in 1909, remarked that "adjectives from nouns formed with the suffix -y are very conspicuous in Spenser. Many of them are his own undoubted introductions. He has grassy, calmy, watery, hoary, misty, frothy, sappy, dewy, starry, foamy, rosy, filmy, shiny, airy, fleecy, plumy, snowy, scaly, frory, pearly, gloomy, briny, leany, heady, vetchy, bushy, weedy, cloudy, horsy, whelky, fenny, slimy, snaky, ashy, muddy, balmy, cooly, in his early work. A very great list with numbers of interesting words. It must not be assumed that several of these, now very common, were so in his time, or ever in use at all. Golding is not noteworthy in this respect."[53] However, it has since been remarked that Spenser did not coin hoary, frothy, dewy, foamy, rosy, fleecy, plumy, snowy, pearly, fenny, balmy, ashy, all being quoted in earlier authors or works in the *OED*. Despite this, Groom writes, "it is possible that the currency of such words in verse was largely due to the popularity of Spenser's poetry."[54] Rubel comments that "to a modern reader these at times become enervating to the style, but they are quite in the tradition from Chaucer through Skelton and Wyatt and Surrey and . . . they become increasingly common in the polite verse of such poets as Turbervile and Warner."[55]

Gloomy, not in Hart's list, is claimed by George Gordon as one of the words "either coined or introduced" into the language by Shakespeare[56] a curious error in that it first appears in *1 Henry VI* and *Titus Andronicus*, both of 1592, but had been used by Spenser in *Mother Hubbard's Tale* ("gloomy glades," 1. 951) and in *Daphnaida* ("gloomie evening," 1. 22)— both poems published in 1591. Gordon adds that "it is amusing to see" how "Spenser and Marlowe almost dispute by their nimbleness as connoisseurs the Shakespearian paternity of *gloomy.*"[57] But the exact paternity of the word is less important than that three major literary figures were willing to adopt it at about the same time.

In the matter of Latinisms, at least of those that occur with sufficient frequency in later poets to qualify for inclusion in poetic diction, Spenser occupies a curious position. One scholar, writing in 1926, stated that "Spenser's vocabulary may be characterized as essentially English and essentially simple. . . . His Latinisms are few and well established." She singled out "trinall triplicities" as his only "inkhorne terms," but listed as Latinisms abiects (to cast down or out), caerule, conceipt, deceipt, crumenall (Latin *crumena,* pouch for money), edify, re-aedify, porcpisces, protense *(Faerie Queen,* 3. 3. 4.7) and adward (*F.Q.* 4. 10. 17.5 and 4. 12. 30.4), claiming only the last two as peculiar to him.[58] One could add intricate from "Their clasping armes, in wanton wreathings intricate" (*F.Q.* 2. 12. 53.9); macer-ate, whose first use the *OED* gives to Spenser (*Virgil's Gnat* 94); and jovial, to mean "under the influence of the planet Jupiter," which was, again according to the *OED*, first used in this sense in *The Faerie Queene* (2. 12.

51.1). Wyld's claims for Spenser's influence in this direction are, therefore, exaggerated, although one should add that his initial statement is an admirable one, for he writes that

> Spenser is too great an artist ever to pile up Latin words after the manner of Hawes; you may read many pages of *The Faerie Queene* without being disturbed by the startling extravagances of indiscriminate Latin borrowings. By the side of numerous Latin words which had passed into the fabric of our language and were known and used by everybody, alike in poetry and in common speech, Spenser makes a judicious use of certain rarer and more striking words from this source. But he generally so uses them that they are in harmony with the general atmosphere of the passages. He may be said to have given them a life in poetry. One of the few Latin words used by Spenser which might with advantage have been replaced by a more ordinary word is *singult:* "deep sighs and singults few" (*Faerie Queene*, V. vi. 13).[59]

Earlier in his study Wyld had singled out Spenser's use of improvided (unseen), expire (to breathe out), pretended (stretched out), and edifyde (built) as examples of unusual Latinisms.[60] There are, of course, others, i.e., exprest, which in *The Faerie Queene* 2. 10. 43 means expelled or ejected and in 2. 11. 42 means crushed out, but, on the whole, Spenser is not remarkable in this respect. With what is evidently the first use of daedal, in "the daedale earth" (*F.Q.* 4. 10. 45.1) taken bodily from Lucretius's *daedala tellus,* he may have started a minor ripple in the sea of poetic diction, for Phineas Fletcher takes the word over and uses it three times in *The Locusts* (1627) and once in *The Purple Island* (1633);[61] Drummond of Hawthornden has both "the daedale hare" and "deadal nets" in his poetry (see *OED*). Thomas Warton, an admirer of Spenser's work, uses it twice in *The Pleasures of Melancholy* (11. 107, 248) and his brother Joseph has "daedal fancies" in his Ode III; Wordsworth has "the daedal earth" in the "sequel" to *The Beggars,* which Shelley echoes in his *Hymn of Pan* (1. 26). Keats has "daedale heart" in *Endymion* 4. 459.

Spenser is no Milton in the matter of Latinisms. Indeed, his most famous contemporary has a greater range and frequency of use of them in his plays and poems than he, despite the fact that Shakespeare had to put so many of these words into the mouths of his characters. Spenser, to take a few examples of Latin words used by Shakespeare, never has adverse, cordial (as adjective), fluent, grateful (to mean pleasing), meridian, obsequious (he has obsequy once), officious, peculiar, pendent, popular, sinister, and unctuous. He uses congregate only once and then as an adjective, and decent, distinguished, provoke (as in to provoke war), and successively also once only. He rarely uses care in its Latinate sense, has two uses of revert as verb (none as adjective), and only two examples of liberal, both times to mean generous. All in all, then, on the basis of this incomplete and somewhat random analysis of some Latinisms in both poets, Shakespeare would appear to have exerted the greater influence on later poets in this direction. An additional check of a greater number of Latinisms that were or became quite popular further reveals that Spenser's diction is even less Latinate than Shakespeare's. The following are some words never used by Spenser in their Latinate meaning: adverse, ambient, attract, confest (manifest), conscious (guilty), devote(d) (doomed), error, invert, intercept, impend, incumbent, involve, lambent, latent, oblivious, obnoxious, obscene, obtuse, obvious, opponent, perplex, pristine, prodigal, promiscuous, protend, protrude, redundant, refulgent, relume, revolve, social, specious, supine, various, varied, vocal—and the list could be extended.

Since Spenser's influence upon later English poets, and possibly upon those contemporary with him, is said to have been pervasive, although one would wish to know how strong that influence was at particular times, it is likely that some Latin usages were first encountered in his work and imitated by later poets, even though those usages may have appeared before Spenser and even though they had been current for many years before the imitator took them up. With the Wartons and Collins, avowed disciples of Spenser, there can be little doubt, and one can be relatively sure that Joseph and Thomas Warton found daedal in *The Faerie Queene* rather than in Phineas Fletcher or in Drummond of Hawthornden, to adduce one admittedly weak example, for daedal had not endeared itself to many poets. And so flames aspire, air is liquid, a funeral is decent, delicious always means pleasing, icicles depend, a war is doubtful, sights are fantastic, courage is generous, a bed is genial, a helmet is horrid with gold, to infest is to attack, prevent can mean anticipate, and vital is used to describe breath, air, blood, and powers in Spenser's poetry and in the poetry of many poets after him. It is true, as Arthos has shown, that "liquid air," to take but one obvious example, had been used by, among others, Lucretius, Virgil, and DuBartas before Spenser, but whatever its pre-Spenserian history there is always the strong probability that later poets remembered it and other uses of liquid from Spenser's poetry.

What holds true for the probable influence of some of Spenser's Latinisms should also hold true for certain other words and phrases much used by later poets. Thus, the seemingly unremarkable words cleave and cut, both in Arthos's list of significant words, are used to describe the progress of gods and goddesses, angels, birds, ships, fish, and swimmers through air and water. As one would expect, there are classical precedents for the use of these words in this fashion but Spenser has angels "cleave / The flitting skyes"; he has a dove who "with her pineons cleaves the liquid firmament," a juxtaposition, of cleave and liquid, which achieved overmuch popularity; and he has Mercury cleaving "the liquid clowdes, and lucid firmament."[62] Similarly, one finds "winged ships" which were seen "In liquid waves to cut their fomie way" (note not only "liquid-cut" but also "fomie," all items of poetic diction); there is a ship which "cut [s] away upon the yielding wave" (yielding, too, is poetic diction);[63] and Sir Guyon's guardian angel is described in a passage that merits quotation because of the cluster of poetic diction in it:

> His *snowy* front curled with golden heares,
> Like *Phoebus* face adorned with *sunny* rayes,
> Divinely shone, and two sharpe winged sheares,
> *Decked* with diverse plumes, like *painted* Iayes,
> Were fixed at his back to *cut* his *ayerie* wayes.
> [2. 8. 5.5–9; my italics].

In another passage, a dragon is described as "cutting way / With his broad sayles" (1. 9. 18.6–7; the same stanza contains "yielding aire"); and, finally, in *An Hymne of Heavenly Love* there are angels "with nimble wings to cut the skies" (1. 66).

Despite the intervention of several generations of poets between Spenser and his professed admirers, Dryden and Pope, it is of some interest and significance that in the former's *Virgil* and in the latter's *Homer* the verbs to cut and to cleave appear in contexts much similar to those quoted from Spenser's poetry. In the *Aeneid*, Cyllenius "cleaves with all his wings the yielding skies" (1. 413) and a "long team of snowy swans" "clap their wings, and cleave the liquid sky" (7. 965–66).[64] Dryden is even fonder of the verb to cut, with fourteen uses descriptive of progress through air or water, among them "cut their liquid way" twice (5. 274 and 667), "cut the liquid sky" (7. 97), "cut the liquid glass" (8. 128), and "cuts his wat'ry way" (5. 1). Pope, in his version of the *Iliad,* has "cleave the liquid plain" (2. 821), "cut the liquid road" (1. 409), "cuts the liquid sky" (5. 927), "cuts the aerial way" (18. 710), and "cut the yielding tide" (2. 640); and in his part of the translation of the *Odyssey* he has "cleave the yielding deep" (9. 200), "cleave the hoary deep" (9. 116), "cut the cleaving sky" (5. 189), "cut the liquid way" (3. 215) "cut the wat'ry way" (7. 47; note Dryden's "cuts his wat'ry way" above), "cuts the liquid skies" (13. 105), "cuts the aerial road" (15. 573), and close to Spenser's ships which were seen in "Liquid waves to cut their foamy way" (*The Ruins of Time*, 1. 149), "he cut the foamy way" (1. 355).[65] Arthos quotes Waller's *His Majesty Escaped* for "cleave the yielding deep," which may or may not have influenced Pope's identical words in the *Odyssey* (9. 210); Sandys's *Ovid's Metamorphoses* for "cuts the ayrie Maine"; and Evelyn's *Lucretius* for "they cut the liquid way," all earlier than Dryden's and Pope's work.[66] And there are, of course, other conjunctions of cut or cleave with liquid, yielding, foamy before Dryden, but they are also there in Spenser, from whom, directly or indirectly, Dryden may have got them. Pope could have got them directly from Spenser or through Dryden, for Dryden's *Virgil* was much in his thoughts as he translated Homer.

Perhaps, too, Spenser's use of distain with blood (twice) and with gore (once) is largely responsible for later poets' comparative reluctance to use stain with those words or their synonyms.[67] There are six uses of distain in Spenser's poetry as opposed to thirty-four of stain, but it was the rarer word that attracted his admirers. Gower and Marlowe, among others, had used distain, although not with blood, but it was not long after 1590 that it became almost imperative, especially in poetry at all remotely epic, to link distain and blood.[68] Spenser, to go to another possible example, combines airy with a number of nouns (Echo, coast, plumes, flight,[69] wayes, spirit, dove, spright, towers, wide) and frequently describes the sky as azure, an adjective he also couples with wings, field, and streams. He is fond of glistering (or glittering), often to describe weapons, and of scaly (with creasts, gold, back [of a snake], breast, tayle, neck, Phocas, trouts), and he is somewhat lavish of shady, that requisite feature of the *locus amoenus*. He, with others who share some of the above preferences, overdoes silver in the description of water, and he may have started a minor trend with his "silver streaming Thamesis" (*The Ruins of Time*, 1. 2), for Pope, for one, has "silver Thames" three times and "silver Thame" once, and Wordsworth has "silver Thames" in *Artegal* and in the *Ode 1850*. The latter also describes the rivers Isis and Meuse as silver. Even with words that Spenser uses relatively few times and in certain contexts it may have been his example, rather than that of others, that prompted later poets to essay the same usages. As a final instance, then, consider Spenser's use of doubtful to mean "uncertain as to the event" in a context of war and battle. In *The Faerie Queene* one finds "End of the doubtfull battaille" (1. 5. 11.7), "the doubtfull battel" (1. 6. 46.4), "this doubtfull warre" (1. 8. 26.3), "very doubtfull was the warres event" (5. 2. 17.1), and "battailles doubtfull proofs" (5. 4. 6.2).

64

Again having recourse solely to Dryden's *Virgil* and Pope's *Homer,* one comes upon the following: in the *Aeneid,* "doubtful war" (1. 5, 9. 48, and 10. 1090), and in the fourth *Georgic,* "doubtful combat" (128). Pope's translation of the *Iliad* reveals a decided preference for the phrase "the doubtful day" [of battle], for it occurs six times (2. 477; 6. 8, 96, and 481; 7. 246; and 13. 945), but "doubtful war" also occurs three times (10. 22; 12. 414 and 428). Pope also has "a doubtful field" and a "doubtful plain" of battle (3. 12; 5. 192). Only once, however, in the *Odyssey,* that far less battle-torn epic, does Pope have a "doubtful day," and here it is descriptive of the coming of night (15. 317), a phrase and a meaning that number among their ancestors Spenser's "doubtfull night" (*F.Q.* 6. 3. 41.4).

Arthos's Appendix B lists many two-word phrases made up of a noun and an adjective—"fine element" for air, is the first English example—under a number of what Arthos considered "the most popular subjects of periphrasis."[70] The citations are not exhaustive, although if any of them do approach exhaustiveness it is those from DuBartas and Sylvester, his translator, for Arthos did a detailed study of Sylvester and "the diction of neo-classic poetry" for a Master's thesis at Harvard (1937), which is the source of his book. Hence, there is no use trying to ascertain strict priority and strict frequency of appearance of periphrases used by both Spenser and Sylvester in Arthos's Appendix B. Arthos does, however, place Spenser first, of English writers, in his periphrases for air, animal, body, dew, fish, flowers, goats, man, sky, stars, water. One must observe, of course, that there is only one periphrase for sky cited from Spenser as against thirty-five for Sylvester; the same proportion is roughly true for the citations from both poets under stars. The only other periphrases cited from Spenser's work appear under death, sea, sheep, and tears. Sylvester, it may be added, is given priority in his periphrases for corn, hive, honey, ice, insects, leaves, serpents, ships, snow, volcano, winds, and wine. By the very nature of his subject and because of their presence in the French of DuBartas, one would expect to find more periphrases for the phenomena of nature in Sylvester than in Spenser. There is, therefore, the possibility that Sylvester's greater use of periphrases in this area acted as a stimulus to some later poets, a statement phrased so tentatively because there is no good evidence as to the extent to which Sylvester was read for his manner as opposed to his matter. That his translation went through a number of editions up to 1641 is a matter of fact. We know, too, that Milton read the translation, leaned upon it for his paraphrases of Psalms 114 and 136 (he was fifteen when he wrote them), and in *Paradise Lost* adopted some of Sylvester's mannerisms but not his phraseology. But the influence of Spenser on Milton, especially in his early poetry, either directly or through such admirers of the older poet as the brothers Fletcher (Phineas and Giles) and Edward Fairfax, the translator of Tasso, was of profoundly greater depth and significance. All things considered, finally, there are cogent reasons to believe that despite the greater frequency of poetic diction descriptive of natural phenomena in Sylvester's translation of DuBartas and despite the influence of the hexae-meral content of DuBartas, English poets contemporary with Sylvester and Spenser, as well as later ones, were almost surely more greatly aware of and attracted by Spenser's use of poetic diction than Sylvester's.[71]

NOTES AND REFERENCES

1. "The Poetic Diction of the English Classicists," in [*Kittredge*] *Anniversary Papers* (Cambridge, Mass.: Harvard University Press, 1913), p. 432.

2. See p. 28.

3. V. L. Rubel, *Poetic Diction in the English Renaissance* (New York: Modern Language Assn. of America, 1941), p. 49 and n. 18.

4. Editor, *Tottel's Miscellany*, rev. ed. (Cambridge, Mass.: Harvard University Press, 1965), vol. 1, p. 107; see pp. 107–24 for Rollins's brief survey of that influence.

5. This is true of Sir Philip Sidney. He has "callmy thoughtes," "flamy breath," "vaultye skye," and "dimmy clowdes"; see Rubel, *Poetic Diction*, p. 155.

6. The influence of Gavin Douglas's translation of the *Aeneid* on Surrey's versions of Books 2 and 4 has been studied by Florence H. Ridley in *PMLA* 76 (1961):25–33 and by Emrys Jones in his edition of Surrey's *Poems* (Oxford: Clarendon Press, 1964), pp. 134–40. Douglas anticipated Surrey only in "massy gold" of the listed examples from Surrey.

7. I take these from the edition by Dirk van der Haar (Amsterdam: H. J. Paris, 1933), p. 39; the asterisks indicate a first use, according to *OED*.

8. J. W. Hebel and H. H. Hudson, eds. (New York: F. S. Crofts, 1947), p. 924.

9. Rubel, *Poetic Diction*, p. 169; specific examples of the debt to Surrey's *Aeneid* are given on pp. 169–70.

10. Surrey has "hugie great temples," *Aeneid* 4. 257.

11. Rubel, *Poetic Diction*, pp. 169–70 suggests that "Sackville's frequent use of 'griesly' may have come through his reading of Surrey."

12. I have used the numbering of stanzas in Marguerite Hearsey's edition of the *Induction*, which has 79 stanzas, and the *Complaint*, which has 111, numbered consecutively (New Haven: Yale University Press, 1936).

13. See Arthos, *Language of Natural Description*, p. 360, for Sylvester's periphrases.

14. Lodge also has stormy, grassy, hilly, ruddy, and bushy; his most unusual adjective is "branchie," used of saplings, st. 52.

15. Rubel, *Poetic Diction*, p. 143.

16. There are some "pendant cliffes" in the fourth eclogue, 1. 824.

17. Webbe is quoted in *Elizabethan Critical Essays*, ed. G. G. Smith (Oxford: Clarendon Press, 1904), vol. 2, p. 76.

18. *August*, 1. 65; *September*, 1. 115; and *November*, 1. 108.

19. Rubel, *Poetic Diction*, p. 160.

20. Respectively, *Lamentation* 1. 79, 6. 86, 7. 93, 9. 64; 10. 11, 1. 8, and 1. 11 and 5. 42.

21. A use of "deckt" (4. 43), "vital" heat (5. 68), and "christall" and "silver" descriptive of water (7. 91 for both).

22. 1. 1., p. 80; 3. 1., pp. 96 and 102; and 5. 1, pp. 139 and 143.

23. For a full list of the poetic diction in the play, add azure, beauteous, crew, crown (2), crystal, deck, dire, impetuous, influence, meridian, ponderous, promiscuous, purling, and purpled.

24. R. D. Havens, *The Influence of Milton*, p. 66, n. 1.

25. Wyld, *Some Aspects of the Diction of English Poetry* (Oxford: Basil Blackwell, 1933); the earlier essay being "Spenser's Diction and Style in Relation to those of Later English Poetry," in *A Grammatical Miscellany Offered to Otto Jesperson on his Seventieth Birthday* (Copenhagen: Levin and Monksgaard; London: G. Allen and Unwin, 1930), pp. 147–65.

26. Groom, *Diction of Poetry*.

27. Arthos, *Language of Natural Description*, pp. 14–15.

28. Ibid., p. 75.

29. Tillotson, *On the Poetry of Pope*, 2nd ed., p. 66.

30. Ibid., pp. 66 and 67.

31. See pp. 132-5.

32. Arthos, *Language of Natural Description*, p. 79 n.

33. Groom, *Diction of Poetry*, pp. 3 and 17.

34. *The Poetical Works of Edmund Spenser*, ed. J. C. Smith and E. de Selincourt (Oxford: 1912), p. ix.

35. Compare *Poetical Works of Edmund Spenser*, p. 106.

36. Respectively, Watson, 2. 237, 242, 270, 271, 84, 150, 220; the definition of a "turn," is Watson's (2. 304).

37. Spence, *Observations, Anecdotes*, pp. 178, 187, and passim.

38. Seccombe, *Dictionary of National Biography* (New York: Oxford University Press).

39. Henry J. Todd, 1805, vol. 4, p. 2 n.

40. "Shakespeare's English," in *Society for Pure English*, Tract No. 29 (1928), p. 273 and n.

41. Gabriel Harvey wrote that "M. Spenser conceives the like pleasure in the fourth day of the first Weeke of Bartas. Which he esteemes as the proper profession of Urania." Harvey's *Marginalia*, ed. G. C. Moore Smith (Stratford-upon-Avon: Shakespeare Head Press) p. 161. Harvey was fond of DuBartas and he praised Sylvester twice (pp. 231 and 233).

42. A. M. Upham, *The French Influence in English Literature from the Accession of Elizabeth to the Restoration* (New York: Octagon Books, 1908, reprinted in 1965), pp. 167–70, tries to show that Spenser was indebted to DuBartas, but I find his argument without merit.

43. Wyld, *Some Aspects*, p. 7.

44. Ibid.

45. Ibid., p. 18.

46. Ibid., p. 39.

47. Ibid., p. 34.

48. Compare John Ogilby's translation of the *Iliad* (1669): "A purple Flood then dy'd the verdant Plain" (17. 383) and "And purpled with his Blood the verdant Plain" (21. 444).

49. Wyld, *Some Aspects*, p. 23.

50. Ibid., p. 35.

51. George Gordon, *Shakespearian Comedy and Other Studies* (New York: Oxford University Press, 1944), p. 141; three pages further on he says that Shakespeare introduced "balmy slumber" in *Othello*, 1604.

52. Wyld, "Spenser's Diction and Style" (see note 25), p. 153.

53. Hart, ed., *1 Henry VI* (London: Methuen and Co., 1909; 2nd rev. ed., 1930), p. xlii. I have noted clammy, craggy, fenny, hoary, massy, pitchy, ruddy, sedgy, and watery in Golding (p. 47); fenny figures in East Anglian place names—i.e., Fenny Drayton as opposed to Dry Drayton. Of these, Spenser has all but clammy and sedgy.

54. Groom, *Diction of Poetry*, p. 10. Spenser also has chalky, crazy, downy, dreary, flinty, rushy, rusty, shady, steely.

55. Rubel, *Poetic Diction*, p. 241.

56. Gordon, *Shakespearian Comedy*, p. 142.

57. Ibid., p. 150.

58. Emma Field Pope, "Renaissance Criticism and the Diction of *The Fairie Queen*," *PMLA* 41 (1926):605, 612. W. L. Renwick had anticipated the matter of the relative scarcity and unobtrusiveness of Latinisms in Spenser in his "Critical Origins of Spenser's Diction," *MLR* 17 (1922):12.

59. Wyld, *Some Aspects*, p. 33.

60. See respectively, *The Faerie Queen* 1. 12. 34; 1. 11. 45; 6. 11. 19; and 1. 1. 34.

61. Canto 2, st. 32; 3. 35; and 4. 31 and 12. 44.

62. *The Faerie Queen* 2. 8. 2. 3; 3. 4. 49.9; *Mother Hubbard's Tale*, 1. 1258.

63. *The Ruins of Time*, 1. 149 and *The Faerie Queen* 2. 6. 5.6.

64. Cleave the sky or skies appears at 4. 328, 5. 279, and 7. 569 and ships "cleave the briny floods" at 3. 18.

65. Shakespeare has only "the strong-ribbed bark through liquid mountains cut" (*Troilus and Cressida* 1. 3. 40).

66. Harington has "fishes cut the liquid stream with fin," *Orlando Furioso*, Bk. 34. st. 49.

67. The Earl of Surrey described the dead Hector in Aeneas's dream as "distained with bloody dust," *Aeneid* 2. 346.

68. Thus used in its five appearances in Dryden's *Aeneid* and in seven of its eight appearances in Pope's *Iliad*. There is only one occurrence in the *Odyssey*, Broome's use at 23. 119.

69. "Airy flight" demonstrates no great imaginative powers in its users, hence its appearance in *Paradise Lost* 2. 407 and *Samson Agonistes*, 1. 974, as well as five times in Dryden's *Aeneid* (5. 969; 6. 280, 343; 7. 98 and 396) is probably of little significance, though worth noting.

70. Arthos, *Language of Natural Description*, p. 356.

71. The following words, not to be found in Spenser, occur in Sylvester, and his work may have done something to promote their popularity: adverse, aerial, ambient, ball (earth), bearded (not of humans), callow, enamel, enlighten (to illuminate), fluent (not of speech), scud, sequestered, smoke (of moisture), steepy, waft.

Chapter 3.

Shakespeare

Samuel Johnson wrote in the preface to his *Dictionary* (1755) that he had taken "the language of poetry and fiction from Spenser and Sidney; and the diction of common life from Shakespeare"; yet Shakespeare has cadent tears, operant powers, multitudinous seas incarnadine; and in one short passage in one play the words conflux, tortive, protractive, and persistive are either original with him or first used by him in the sense in which they are used in the passage.[1] Johnson turned again to the subject of Shakespeare's language soon after the publication of his *Dictionary,* for in the 1756 proposals for an edition of Shakespeare's plays he stated that Shakespeare "wrote at a time when our poetical language was yet unformed," although he added that the Elizabethan age was one "above all others [in which] experiments were made on language, which distorted its combinations, and disturbed its uniformity." Shakespeare's role in the formation and transmission of poetic diction is, therefore, a curious one, if only for the additional reason that he is usually the only dramatist to be considered in this connection at all. And this is not, of course, because he also wrote nondramatic poetry. One supposes the reason for his inclusion in Groom's *The Diction of Poetry from Spenser to Bridges* resides almost solely in the fact that he is Shakespeare and cannot, hence, be safely omitted from any examination of the diction of poetry or of poetic diction, two distinctly different terms and phenomena for Groom, of course. Poetic diction, characterized by

Groom as conventional or traditional, is found to occur in "the less characteristic and inferior parts of Shakespeare's work," but is also declared available to and used by him "for interesting and even exciting dramatic effects" because of its familiarity to his audiences.[2] While this is partly true, and while it is also true that some of Shakespeare's personages are made to indulge in poetic diction as one mode of characterization, there remains much more to be said about the heavier concentrations of poetic diction in a few plays, the dramatic propriety of certain uses of that diction, and the true nature of Shakespeare's place in its history. As Groom's is the most recent work to touch on this matter, some of the following discussion concentrates on his statements and suggestions.

Initially, it must be said that Groom is somewhat of a bardolater, proof of which resides, among other places, in the statement that "no one has shown a finer sense of the fit use of accepted equivalents, e.g., the various words for 'sea': *surge, deep, main, flood*" than Shakespeare.[3] This statement requires examination. Main never occurs with a descriptive adjective in the plays and is modified by wat'ry and by broad in its only appearances in the poems (*Sonnets* 64 and 80), neither adjective placing any strain on the poet's imagination. Surge is absent from the poems but appears seven times in the plays, twice meaning wave, not sea. We are left with "liquid surge" (*Timon* 4. 4. 442), which employs a stock adjective; "turbulent surge" (again from *Timon* 5. 1. 221, and following fast upon "the beached verge of the salt flood" in that scene, 1. 219); "murmuring surge" from *King Lear* (4. 6. 20); "rude imperious surge" (*2 Henry IV* 3. 1. 20), an echo of the "imperious flood" (another of Groom's "accepted equivalents") of an earlier scene in the same play (1. 1. 13) which precedes the well-known "enchafed flood" by four lines. Note, however, the similarity of "wind-shaked surge" to the "always-wind-obeying deep" of *The Comedy of Errors* (1. 1. 63), further evidence of Shakespeare's willingness to repeat himself. Nor is the analysis of deep, for sea, in Shakespeare as impressive as Groom's statement leads one to believe. Only once does it appear in the poems, there described as soundless (*Sonnet* 80, the same sonnet that has the "broad main" in it). I have already mentioned the "always-wind-obeying deep" of *Errors,* an epithet I cannot bring myself to admire. "Salt deep" of *The Tempest* (1. 2. 253), like its companions, "salt flood" of the conceit in *Romeo and Juliet* (3. 5. 135), and in *Timon* (5. 1. 219),[4] is stock, and there remains only the "confined deep" of *Lear* (4. 1. 75). For three of the four "accepted equivalents" for sea the record for freshness is not exactly overwhelming. For flood, the same conclusion is warranted. Two salt floods have already been disposed of. There is an "imperious flood" in *2 Henry IV* (1. 1. 62), which looks forward to the "rude imperious surge" of the same play (3. 1. 20); a "wild and wand'ring flood" in Troilus's lover's rant (1. 1. 105), part of an elaborate conceit; and the "high-wrought flood" of *Othello* (2. 1. 2), followed by "the enchafed flood" (2. 1. 17). These last two rightly merit some respect, a respect it is not perverse to withhold from the "boundless flood" in *The Rape of Lucrece* (1. 653), the only time the word is modified in the poems. Shakespeare's "finer sense of the fit use of accepted equivalents" does not, then, emerge from the analysis of the various words he uses for sea.

Some aspects of Shakespeare's diction, or his "English," have been studied more than others. For example, the matter of -y suffix adjectives is examined, albeit briefly, by Hart in his edition of *1 Henry VI*[5] where, after listing thirty-seven examples of these adjectives in Spenser's poetry, he writes that

> Shakespeare has many of the above. He has also slumbery, vasty, and paly in his later works. Mothy and pithy belong to *Taming of a Shrew*. But I only find him once indulging in a bout of such terms, and that is in a very appropriate place, *Midsummer-Night's Dream*, wherein he is especially reminiscent of Spenser. He has there, only: wormy, sphery, starry, rushy, barky, batty, brisky, unheedy. He sets a friendly seal of approval on Spenser's trick.[6]

The trick is hardly Spenser's, as has been seen, although he may have had more recourse to it than other poets writing before, or contemporaneously with, him. Another scholar, George Gordon, writes that "there was tumbled into the language by one poet or another, from Sackville and Golding to Spenser and Shakespeare, a whole race of new adjectives on the old model" and selects, from Shakespeare, "finny, fleecy, bosky, briny, horsy, snaky, gloomy, dusky, shiny, as a small but impressive handful from the mob of newcomers in -y." He, too, taking his cue from Hart, finds Spenser "the chief executant in this way" and conjectures that "*Finny, briny, horsy,* and *shiny* seem all to be his." "*Bosky,*" he states, "is first found in Peele, *snaky* in Turbervile, and *gloomy* in Shakespeare."[7]

Still influenced by Hart's pioneering work, Gordon gives as one example of what he terms Elizabethan writers' tendency "to group their verbal fancies, and to give them out in clusters, two or more at a time," the number of -y adjectives in *A Midsummer-Night's Dream,* a run which he feels has "a special meaning and appropriateness there." His explanation merits full quotation:

> *Rushy, unheedy, sphery, brisky, barky,* and, in some twenty-eight lines between Oberon and Puck (III. ii. 356–84), the further complement of *starry, tasty, batty, wormy,* are drops in that delicate rain of nicely calculated rusticity with which Shakespeare has sprinkled the language of this play. Four of the nine, *sphery, brisky, batty, barky,*[8] he made for the purpose. There is a simplicity about this suffix which pleased the pastoral Spenser, but, like all simplicities, it was easily overdone. Ben Jonson thought Marston clownish with his *clumsy, barmy, puffy,* "outlandish terms." Shakespeare is more tactful, and his fun is gentler. But *brisky* is a joke; *starry* is mated with the archaic and ludicrous "welkin"; and even *sphery,* though Milton found it here and placed it in the firmament of *Comus,* can hardly by its maker have been intended seriously. It is Hermia's "eyne" that are sphery, as it is the "welkin" that is starry, and the adjectives incur some part of the rusticity of their nouns.[9] So in *Antony and Cleopatra,* when he invented *plumpy* for the triumvirs' drunken song, archaic "eyne" keeps up the note:
> Plumpy Bacchus, with pink eyne
>
> [II. vii. 120]

Part of this criticism is excellent; part needs closer analysis. First, the remark that *"starry, testy, batty, wormy,* are drops in that delicate rain of nicely calculated rusticity"* is, at the very least, misleading. Rusticity, one assumes, implies rustic speakers, but these adjectives, as well as the other poetic diction in the play, are placed in the mouths of Oberon, Titania, and Puck and in those of Lysander and Helen—no rustics these. What is more, when Shakespeare went in for rustic language he wrote, as one example, things like this:

> When icicles hang by the wall,
>   And Dick the shepherd blows his nail,
> And Tom bears logs into the hall,
>   And milk comes frozen home in pail,
> When blood is nipp'd, and ways be foul,
>   Then nightly sings the staring owl,
>   Tu-who!
> Tu-whit to-who, a merry note,
> While greasy Joan doth keel the pot.
> When all aloud the wind doth blow,
>   And coughing drowns the parson's saw,

> And birds sit brooding in the snow,
>   And Marian's nose looks red and raw,
>   When roasted crabs hiss in the bowl,
>   [Refrain of 4 11.]

A later poet called icicles, very poetically, "pendent chrystal"[10] and Spenser has "ysicles depend," not hang, in *The Shepherd's Calendar* (*January*, 1. 42). But icicles also hang in *Twelfth Night* (act 3, scene 2) and in *Henry V* (act 3, scene 5). Possibly, to return to *A Midsummer-Night's Dream*, it may be best to think of the pastoral genre, which has little relationship to actual rustic life, as the begetter of some of these adjectives and of the other poetic diction in this play, for it comes closer to pastoral drama and poetry than any other of Shakespeare's plays.

Before returning to Gordon's remarks it is necessary to digress to redirect attention to the Masque in the fourth act of *The Tempest*, "redirect" because Groom writes of "the almost ultra-Spenserianism" of its diction. "Nowhere else in Shakespeare," he goes on, "is the style so entirely built up on epithets: *turfy* mountains, *spongy* April, *pole-clipt* vineyard, *short-grass'd* green, *windring* brooks, and the like—scarcely a significant noun in the first forty lines of the Masque but has its 'rare,' if not always felicitous epithet."[11] This is all very well, possibly, for Groom's belief that the diction of English poetry has its fountainhead in Spenser, but it only touches on the matter of poetic diction in citing turfy and spongy. For not only does one get the rainbow described as the "wat'ry arch," but there are also "dusky Dis" and "bosky acres." Other poetic diction resides in "thy sea-marge," a use of the coronation figure ("thy blue bow dost crown / My bosky acres"), a goddess cutting the clouds, and the description of the "bosky acres" and "unshrubb'd down" as a "rich scarf" to the "proud earth." Curiously enough, critics are divided in their opinion of the Masque, some thinking it so bad that they have argued that it is not Shakespeare's.

None of the poetic diction in *The Tempest* is given to the comic characters. It is Prospero who uses the verb to deck, who calls the ocean "the salt deep" and the sky "the azur'd vault," and who bids Miranda "the fringed curtains of thine eyes advance / And say, what those seest yond'." And here digression is mandatory, for a later poet, in *Peri Bathous, or The Art of Sinking in Poetry* (1727), uses these words as one example of the "buskin" style, querying, "Will not every true Lover of the *Profound* be delighted to behold the most vulgar and low Actions of Life exalted in this Manner?" (Chapter XII), for all Prospero is saying, according to Alexander Pope, is

"See who is there." Almost a century later Coleridge, in the course of a lecture on Shakespeare, defended him against "the very severe, censure of Pope and Arbuthnot."

> Putting this passage as a paraphrase of "Look what is coming," it certainly did appear ridiculous, and seemed to fall under the rule Coleridge had laid down, that whatever without injury could be translated into a foreign language in simple terms ought to be so in the original or it is not good. . . . But Coleridge was content to try this passage by its introduction: How does Prospero introduce it? He has just told Miranda a story which deeply affects her, and afterwards for his own purposes lulled her to sleep, and Shakespeare [makes her] wholly inattentive to the present when she awakes, and dwelling only on the past. The Actress who truly understands the character should have her eyelids sunk down, and living as it were in her dreams. Prospero then sees Ferdinand, and wishes to point him out to his daughter, not only with great but also scenic solemnity, himself always present to her, and to the spectators as a magician. Something was to appear on a sudden, which was no more expected than we should look for the hero of a Play to be on the stage when the Curtain is drawn up: it is under such circumstances that Prospero says,
>
> > The fringed curtains of thine eye advance,
> > And say, what thou seest yond.
>
> This solemnity of phraseology was, in Coleridge's opinion, completely in character with Prospero, who was assuming the Magician, whose very art seems to consider all the objects of nature in a mysterious point of view, and who wishes to produce a strong impression on Miranda at the first view of Ferdinand.[12]

All this is very ingenious, but probably needs the corrective of Dr. Johnson's remark about emendations, which can be extended to critical interpretations: "I have always suspected that the reading is right, which requires many words to prove it wrong; and the emendation wrong, that cannot without so much labour appear to be right" (Preface to Shakespeare, *ad finem*).

To return, however. It is Alonso who speaks of the "oozy bed" where his son lies; Ariel describes swords as massy; and Miranda says that "the sea, mounting to the welkin's cheek, / Dashes the fire out," And with Miranda's serious use of welkin in what is almost surely Shakespeare's last play one comes back to Gordon's contention that in *A Midsummer-Night's Dream* the adjective "*starry* is mated with the archaic and ludicrous 'welkin'." Now

Shakespeare makes comic capital of welkin in *The Merry Wives of Windsor, Love's Labour's Lost, The Taming of the Shrew, Twelfth Night,* and *2 Henry IV,* using as speakers Nym, Armado, and Holofernes, the Lord who addresses Sly in the Induction to *The Taming of the Shrew,* Sir Toby Belch and the Clown, and Ancient Pistol. Incidentally, it is the Clown in *Twelfth Night* who uses welkin in preference to element because the latter is "overworn" (3. 1. 65–66). Serious uses of welkin are found in *King John* (2), *Richard III,* and three times in the space of sixteen lines in *Titus Andronicus* (3. 1. 212, 224, 227), one of Shakespeare's earliest plays. It will not do, therefore, to dismiss welkin as "archaic and ludicrous" when Oberon speaks of the "starry welkin,"[13] although there is some reason to accept the statement that "sphery eyne" "can hardly by its maker have been intended seriously." Gordon quotes a line from *Antony and Cleopatra* as additional evidence that eyne was archaic and hence, combined with sphery, not to be taken seriously in *A Midsummer-Night's Dream.* He might have added that eyne occurs four times in that play, with additional appearances in *Love's Labour's Lost, As You Like It, The Taming of the Shrew,* and *Pericles,* almost all the uses occurring in comic contexts. One might add that Shakespeare glances in fun at another bit of poetic diction when he has Thisby stab herself after crying out "Come, trusty sword; / Come, blade, my breast imbrue" (5. 1. 350–51), for it is Ancient Pistol who is given one of the only other two uses of the word: "What! shall we have incision? Shall we imbrue" (*2 Henry IV* 2. 4. 210). And in *Titus Andronicus,* that early play in which there is a cluster of welkins, a character cries out that "Lord Bassianus lies embrewed here" (2. 3. 222). But the appearance of imbrue in such diverse later poets and works as Samuel Johnson, Milton, Ogilby's translations, Arthur Murphy, the 1717 translation of Ovid's *Metamorphoses,* Richard Glover *(Leonidas),* Nicholas Rowe *(Pharsalia),* Thomas Gray, Michael Drayton, Chapman, Dryden, Pope, and John Hoole *(Jerusalem Delivered)* is proof positive that Shakespeare did not laugh it out of existence. Imbrue was a handy word for the tragedian and the writer or translator of epics, but its handiness made it fair game.

To focus solely on the -y adjectives in *A Midsummer-Night's Dream* is to overlook other words and usages which combine to make what is probably the greatest concentration of poetic diction in any single play of Shakespeare's. And, indeed, some uses of the -y adjective are not even mentioned by Groom or Gordon as, possibly, too common even for comment. But Shakespeare falls back upon wat'ry three times in this play, first in a passage heavy with poetic diction, "To-morrow night, when Phoebe doth behold / Her silver visage in the wat'ry glass, / Decking with liquid pearl the bladed grass" (1. 1. 209–11). Twice wat'ry is pressed into service to describe the moon, once simply as wat'ry, once to describe the moon's eye (2. 1. 162 and 3. 1. 203). "Watery moon" is also found in *Richard III* (2. 2. 69), "watery eyne" in *Love's Labour's Lost* (5. 2. 206, the King is the speaker), and "wat'ry eyes" in *Titus Andronicus* (3. 1. 269) and in *A Lover's Complaint* (1. 281). It might also be noted that wat'ry appears twice in *The Merchant of Venice,* twice in *Pericles,* and makes a single appearance in eleven other plays. There are three uses in *The Rape of Lucrece,* none remarkable. Gordon's suggestion that Shakespeare and other Elizabethans tended to group their verbal fancies is further borne out, then, by the three uses of wat'ry in *A Midsummer-Night's Dream.*

Robin Goodfellow, or Puck, describes how Titania withholds "a lovely boy, stolen from an Indian king" from Oberon and "crowns him with flowers" (the old coronation figure). Hence, the King and Queen of fairies "never meet in grove or green, / By fountain clear or spangled starlight sheen" (2. 1. 26–27). Again digression is necessary, for Groom, by implication, lauds Shakespeare's use of sheen and points to Milton's echo in *Comus,* "spangled sheen" (1. 1003), overlooking the fact that it occurs only once more in the Shakespeare canon, and then in the opening lines of *The Murder of Gonzago,* the play within a play in *Hamlet.* There the word, part of a passage which Groom characterizes as made up of "conventional allusions," helps to "distinguish the artificial play from the real one".[14] The lines read

> Full thirty times hath Phoebus' cart gone round
> Neptune's salt wash and Tellus' orbed ground
> And thirty dozen moons with borrow'd sheen
> About the world have times twelve thirties been
> [3. 2. 145–48]

Whether in *A Midsummer-Night's Dream* or in the player King's speech in *Hamlet,* sheen is a word that Shakespeare uses self-consciously, making a noun of an adjective. Only later did sheen become popular, possibly because of Milton's four uses of it. Milton had earlier made a new adjective of the noun in his poem *On the Death of a Fair Infant Dying of of a Cough,* written when he was seventeen, for there he wrote of "the wall / Of sheeny heaven" (11. 47–48). And, of course, he was imitated in this, as in almost everything else he wrote; for in the next century, Fenton wrote of "the sheeny form of Epicaste" in a translation of the eleventh *Odyssey,* which he labeled "in Milton's style."

Clustered in act 2, scene 1, are other examples of poetic diction in *A Midsummer-Night's Dream:* "the farthest steep of India," the "beached margent of the sea," the conceit of young corn rotting before it "attain'd a beard," "hoary-headed" frosts that fall in "the fresh lap" of the crimson rose, and a flower, formerly milk-white, now "purple with love's wound." The same scene contains a "rushy brook," the "wat'ry moon," and the snake's "enamell'd skin"; the speakers are Titania and Oberon. Shakespeare evidently thought well enough of beached to use it later in *Timon of Athens,* where it describes the "verge of the salt flood" (5. 1. 219). Fortunately, he did not see fit to employ beachy more than once, for "the beachy girdle of the ocean / Too wide for Neptune's hips," in *2 Henry IV* (3. 1. 50–51), is almost too much for the risible muscles. Perhaps, however, there is partial explanation for what appears such a lapse. With the passage of time, girdle has come to mean an undergarment associated with the desire to seem trimmer; in the Elizabethan age it was "a belt worn round the waist to secure or confine the garments; also employed as a means of carrying light articles, esp. a weapon or purse" *(OED).* The fault here, then, is in the reader's eye. However, the speaker, King Henry IV, has been ill for a fortnight—he enters in his nightgown—and his soliloquy, his first speech in the play, reflects a disturbed mind. One recent editor of the play comments that "once or twice the King, so much in command of his language in Part 1, is nearly its victim in Part 2," citing "his melancholy contemplation of futurity" in this soliloquy as one of the two times.[15] The principal offender is, of course, beachy employed in an unfortunate image, for in the two other examples given in exemplification of the word in the *OED,* Sandys's "beachy Sands" and Watts's "beachy shore," there is no element of the ludicrous.

Shakespeare, in *A Midsummer-Night's Dream,* was one of the first English poets to use beard or bearded of corn; his only other such use was in an image in *2 Henry VI* (3. 1. 175–76). Sylvester, taking his cue from DuBartas, has "bearded eares," Milton has a "bearded grove," Dryden has "bearded product of the golden year" and "bearded harvest," Rowe has "bearded ear" (Lucan's *Pharsalia,* 1722 ed., 6. 184), Lovelace has "oaten beard" in *The Grasshopper* (1. 2), Pope has "bearded grain," and Richard Jago has "bearded store".[16] Groom makes too much of the metaphorical use of lap in "Nature-description" in *Richard II* and *A Midsummer-Night's Dream,* "twice in the former play, 'the fresh green lap of fair King Richard's land' and 'Violets . . . That strew the green lap of the new-come spring.' These were phrases too beautiful to escape the notice of a selective poet like Milton who, in *Lycidas,* repeats the 'fresh lap' of Shakespeare, expanding

77

it into 'Earth's freshest softest lap' in *Paradise Lost.* "[17] But Milton is himself both a transmitter and propagator of poetic diction in his use of lap, both in Groom's examples and in "the flowery lap" of *Paradise Lost* (4. 254) and of the *Vacation Exercise* (1. 84), as well as the "green lap" of "flowery May" (*Song on May Morning,* 1. 3). What is worthier of remark is Shakespeare's use of another item of poetic diction, the verb to enamel, used largely by earlier or contemporary poets to describe inanimate natural phenomena (the ground, for example) but used by him to describe the cast skin of a serpent, "And there the snake throws her enamell'd skin, / Weed wide enought to wrap a fairy in," in a context, not only the tiny world of fairies but also as part of the so-admired passage beginning "I know a bank where the wild thyme blows." Incidentally, Shakespeare uses enamell'd in only one other place, the "enamell'd stones" of an extended conceit spoken by Julia in *The Two Gentlemen of Verona* (2. 7. 28).

Twice, both times in speeches by Titania, Shakespeare writes of a "flow'ry bed" (3. 1. 132 and 4. 1. 1); the adjective occurs only twice again in the canon, once in a figure, the "flow'ry tenderness" of *Measure for Measure* (3. 1. 83), and once as a periphrasis, "flow'ry way," for the "primrose path" that leads to hell. The latter is spoken by the Clown in *All's Well That Ends Well* (4. 5. 57). Given the extreme popularity of that adjective, Spenser, for example, linking it with grass (twice), banks (twice), garlands (thrice), marge, and dales, Shakespeare showed marked restraint, albeit his indulgence in it twice in the *Dream* adds little to his originality as poet. Even Chaucer has flowery green, year, and mead. Twice, too, Shakespeare uses airy, an "airy spirit" and, in Theseus's speech on the poet's eye "in a fine frenzy rolling," the "airy nothing" to which the poet's pen gives "a local habitation and a name" (3. 1. 164 and 5. 1. 16); he used the adjective three times in *Romeo and Juliet,* memorably in endowing Echo with an "airy tongue,"[18] mechanically in describing heaven as an "airy region" (2. 2. 21). And there is, in the poems, "the airy scale of praise" (*A Lover's Complaint,* 1. 226). Another word, one which he used sparingly in his descriptions of nature, gains much from its inclusion in another delightful speech of Titania's, her injunction to Peaseblossom, Cobweb, Moth, and Mustardseed to "be kind and courteous to this gentleman," i.e., Bottom. I refer to the "painted butterflies" whose plucked wings were to "fan the moonbeams from his sleeping eyes" (3. 1. 175–76). Only once again did Shakespeare use painted in the description of one of nature's creatures and that was in *The Taming of the Shrew* when Petruchio speaks of the "painted skin" of the adder (4. 3. 180). Chaucer uses the term only once in nature description: "May peynted with his softe showres / This gardyn ful of leves and floures"

(*Franklin's Tale,* 1. 907). Spenser was fond of painted to describe natural objects, linking it with lap, plumes, (twice), blossoms, jays, wings, and flowers (twice), and although Milton was chary of it, the poets of the Restoration and eighteenth century worked it almost to death.[19] The "barky fingers" of Titania's simile, "the female ivy so / Enrings the barky fingers of the elm" (4. 1. 46–47), part of an old and much-used figure, is a nonce word, and one does not regret its nonreappearance. There remains Shakespeare's use of the epic verb to cut, used, usually in epics, of deities, noble birds, and ships, in Puck's "night's swift dragons cut the clouds full fast" (3. 2. 379), paralleled only in *Troilus and Cressida,* "The strong-ribb'd bark through liquid mountains cut" (1. 3. 40)—note that other bit of poetic diction in "liquid mountains." Finally, there are the "wormy beds" to which "damned spirits" must return before dawn (Puck's speech above) and one of Shakespeare's four uses of dew as a verb. "Wormy beds," as Polonius says of "mobled queen," is good, and Milton thought it worth repeating in his youthful poem *On the Death of a Fair Infant Dying of a Cough* (1. 31); the verb to dew, not original with Shakespeare, is not equally felicitous in all its appearances, almost surely finding its most natural habitat in the line in the *Dream,* "To dew her orbs upon the green" (2. 1. 9).[20]

To return to Shakespeare's -y adjectives, the point can be made that, for the most part, taking poems and plays together, Shakespeare rarely overworks any that are relatively new or that he has himself coined—although the *OED* is no sure guide to precedence in this matter. For example, no matter whether Spenser or Shakespeare coined or introduced the word gloomy,[21] it is a fact that there are eleven more appearances in *The Faerie Queen,* while Shakespeare used the word only twice in his plays and once in his poems. Consider also the following, by no means a complete list of these adjectives that are used once only in the accepted canon: barky, batty, bosky, brassy, brawny, brisky, browny, busky, cloddy, corky, craggy, crudy, crusty, dreary, finny, foamy, grassy, leafy, oozy, palmy, pearly, plumpy, ruddy, rushy, scaly, seamy, sedgy, shelly, shelvy, shiny, snaky, snowy, sooty, sphery, starry, swarthy, turfy, unheedy,[22] weedy, wormy. Used twice are the following: ashy, bristly, chalky, dungy, leavy, shadowy, slimy, steely, steepy, wiry. Some of these had proved popular with poets writing before or contemporaneously with Shakespeare and were to continue as part of accepted poetic diction into the nineteenth century; Shakespeare contented himself with infrequent recourse to them. Sometimes, however, he seems to have been taken with a -y adjective, not necessarily one of those mentioned, and consequently one gets the "vasty fields of France," a "vasty Tartar," and the "vasty jaws" of war, all in *Henry V.* Often, too, it must be said, these adjectives are predictably linked with certain nouns: cliffs are chalky, mountains are craggy, hearts are flinty,[23] morn is dewy, spring is gaudy, weapons are massy, sleep is downy, lips and cheeks are rosy. But Shakespeare would not be Shakespeare if he did not also have such passages as this from *Richard III:*

> DUCHESS OF YORK. Why should calamity be full of words?
> QUEEN ELIZABETH. Windy attorneys to their client woes,
>   Airy succeeders of intestate joys,
>   Poor breathing orators of miseries,
>   Let them have scope!
>
> [IV. iv. 126–30]

Such uses of windy and airy are rare.

Another aspect of English poetic diction, that which was later to attain even more widespread popularity with the publication of *Paradise Lost,* is the use of words in their original Latin meanings. Shakespeare's plays are not usually considered remarkably Latinate in their diction, but it was inevitable that he would make some use of some of the many words of Latin origin in their special meanings. Thus, to cite some obvious examples, Shakespeare uses depend to mean to hang, determine to mean to fix the limits of, and generous to mean of noble birth. A quick and incomplete check reveals his use of adverse (opposite, against), aspire (of flames, hills, fire), care (from *cura*), curious and curiously (in the sense of careful, attentive, diligent), congregated (with college and sands), cordial (*cordis,* of the heart), decent (*decet,* proper, seemly, fitting), distinguish (to separate), fluent (flowing as in "fluent as the sea" in *Henry V* 3. 7. 36), grateful (*gratus,* pleasing), liberal,[24] obsequious (obedient, compliant, yielding). Here, it is fitting to quote notes by Johnson, Steevens, and Malone on King Claudius's "obsequious sorrow" in the first act of *Hamlet.* Johnson notes that *"obsequious is here from obsequies or funeral ceremonies,"* and Steevens adds another passage, "To shed *obsequious* tears upon his trunk" *(Titus Andronicus),* while Malone finds the same use in Shakespeare's thirty-first sonnet, "How many a holy and *obsequious* tear, / Hath dear religious love stoll'n from mine eye." Shakespeare also has meridian (of or at midday, southern), officious (obliging, courteous, attentive), peculiar (belonging to one's private property, one's own, special), pendent,[25] popular (always to mean of the people), prevent (to come before, to anticipate), provoke (to call forth, excite, arouse—as in *Antony and Cleopatra,* "provoke not battle" (3. 8. 3), reverted,[26] sinister,[27] spoil (*spolium,* the skin or hide stripped from an animal), successive (to come after or into the place of), unctuous (*unctus,* greasy—as in *Timon of Athens,* "morsels unctious," 4. 3. 195), and vital (*vitalis,* of life). A number of these are used only once; others, only twice. Doubtless one could add to this admittedly sketchy list, yet the only point to be made, that Shakespeare also had his part in the formation and transmission of this aspect of poetic diction, would not be thereby altered. Thus, his "peculiar care," *Cymbeline* (5. 5. 83), deriving ultimately from Virgil's first *Eclogue,* "nec spes liberatis erat nec cura peculi" (1. 32), turns up again in Davenant's *Gondibert* (1672, Bk. 2, Canto 2, st. 60), twice in Blackmore's *Prince Arthur* (1714, Bk. 1, p. 20 and Bk. 7, p. 240) twice in his *Eliza* (1705) as "God's peculiar care" (Bk. 7, p. 201 and Bk. 10, p. 273), once in his *The Nature of Man* (1720 ed., Bk. 2, p. 39) and once in his *Alfred* (1723), as "Heav'n's peculiar care" (Bk. 1, p. 15); in Ozell's translation of Tassoni's *La Secchia Rapita* (1713), as "the Gods, by whose peculiar care" (Canto 2, p. 44); and, mock-epically, in Matthew Concanen's *A Match at Football* (1724) as Flora's "peculiar care" (Canto 1, p. 32) and in William Hawkins's *The Thimble* (1744), as "Heav'n's peculiar care" (Canto 3, p. 20); in Rowe's translation of *Lucan* (1719, 10. 258); four times in Dryden's *Virgil* (1697, *Aeneid* 7. 617; 9. 136; 11. 470; and *Georgics* 2. 6); once in Dryden's *Baucis and Philemon,* in Swift's *On Poetry: A Rhapsody,* and some six to eight times in Pope's poetry—depending on how one regards certain of Norman Ault's attributions—and by at least three minor poets of the early eighteenth century (Mrs. Singer, Thomas Tickell, and Samuel Croxall). One cannot say that any of these later writers were consciously echoing Shakespeare nor can one say that they were not recalling Virgil, but the former of these possibilities of course exists.

Certain words and usages that were to become increasingly convenient parts of poetic diction in the latter part of the seventeenth century and throughout the eighteenth already had an existence in Shakespeare's plays and poems. For some, he may have been indebted to Spenser, although their being contemporaries and the presence of some of these same words and usages in others writing at the same time makes for very nice questions of precedence. Probably some of this diction was in the air at this time, common property. Some can be traced back to Golding's translation of Ovid's *Metamorphoses* (1567), for he has his craggy shore, his christall stream and pool, his fenny grounds, his hoary beard and hair, his massy gold, his pitchie darkness, his ruddy cheeks and ruddy blood, and his "Southerne winds . . . with watry wings." The verb to embrew occurs at least twice, and he is fond of headlong, a word much used, especially in translations of epics. Harington's translation of Ariosto's *Orlando Furioso*

(1591) also did something to formulate and transmit poetic diction; and there were, of course, others, poets, dramatists, and translators, all of whom contributed their part. Shakespeare's conventional use of much of this diction should not, hence, be unexpected. In his work, waves and billows curl, the earth is a ball, there is much use of crew (and as the last word of a line), his use of the coronation figure is conventional ("crowns him with flowers," *Midsummer-Night's Dream* 2. 1. 27), and he has few surprises in store after such adjectives as glassy, silver, and liquid, although there is the description in Sonnet 5 of perfume or rosewater as "summer's distillation left / A liquid prisoner pent in walls of glass." Once in a while one sees, or thinks he sees, Shakespeare borrowing a word and an image from an earlier poet, for in Sonnet 63 the lines "when his youthful morn / Hath travell'd on to age's steepy night" echo Golding's "Through drooping ages steepy path he ronneth out his race" (*Metamorphoses* 15. 249). Occasionally, as with sway, a poetical counter for rule, as in "sceptered sway" (*Merchant of Venice* 4. 1. 193; Portia's speech on "the quality of mercy"), "kingly sway" (*Richard II* 4. 1. 206), and "sovereign sway" (*Macbeth* 1. 5. 71) there is a surprise, for in Sonnet 66 strength is by "limping sway disabled." Another surprise comes in Sonnet 143 which is one prolonged conceit beginning "Lo, as a careful housewife runs to catch / One of her feathered creatures broke away," a use of feathered in a homely context which takes the curse of poetic diction off a word which Spenser had used to describe Cupid, and Shakespeare to describe both Cupid and Mercury—and which poets and poetasters for generations to come were to use repeatedly and mechanically.

Shakespeare's "feathered creatures" of Sonnet 143 and his "limping sway" of Sonnet 66 are two of his more unusual variations on poetic diction, but he could be as conventional as the next nondramatic poet elsewhere in his poetry. Some of the poetic diction of the nondramatic poetry is repeated or anticipated in the plays; so that while hills aspire in the plays, mountains do the same in the poems, and night is pitchy in both. Bosoms or their possessors are flinty, wounds and blood are purple, eyes or tears are crystal, events are dire, and water and tears are silver. Such words as steepy, vaulty, spongy, airy, balmy, gaudy, and watery are common to both, although, as would be expected, their use varies widely with the contexts in which they are employed. Thus, the "vaulty heaven" of Romeo's aubade (3. 5. 22) is consonant with the mood of scene and play, and the "vaulty prison" of night in *The Rape of Lucrece* (l. 119) serves to help set the tragic tone. Spring is gaudy, and so is the sun, in the poems (*Venus and Adonis*, l. 1088 and

Sonnet 1); in the plays it is largely descriptive of the works of men (four of five times). So, too, with sable, used only in *Hamlet* (as noun and adjective) and in *Pericles,* and then of arms and banners; more in the tradition of poetic diction, it is Night, "mother of Dread and Fear" who is sable (*The Rape of Lucrece,* l. 117; note the proximity to the "vaulty prison" of l. 119). Shakespeare, if the poem is his, uses spongy in its primary meaning of "having a soft elastic or porous texture resembling that of a sponge. . . . Of flesh, animal tissue, etc. sometimes with special reference to morbid conditions" *(OED)* in "the spongy lungs" of *A Lover's Complaint* (326) in a context rife with the artificial conventions of love poetry. In the plays, however, he uses the word to mean "resembling a sponge in absorptive qualities; absorbent. Chiefly fig.", as in the "spongy officers" of *Macbeth* (1. 7. 71), quoted by the *OED,* and as in "spongy April" and "spongy South" (*Tempest* 4. 1. 65 and *Cymbeline* 4. 2. 349). "Spongy officers" is an admirable example of Shakespeare's imaginativeness in language; "spongy April" and "spongy South" are such phrases as other poets and playwrights of his time could, and did, employ. Sylvester had anticipated him in "spongie lungs" and also had the moist "braines spongie bone," the "spongie globe," and "spongie fannes."[28] Spongy was to reappear in Chapman's *Odyssey,* Fletcher's *Purple Island,* and in Ogilby's translations. Dryden picked it up early in his career, as witness "the cloth of spongy softness made" in *Annus Mirabilis* (826), and found a pastoral setting for it in his elegy *On the Death of Amyntus* (15) and in his translation of Virgil's first *Georgic* (438)—in both these poems it is clouds that are spongy. Possibly he remembered Milton's sole use in the "spongy air" of *Comus* (154); Pope eschewed the word.[29]

Whatever the extent of poetic diction in Shakespeare's nondramatic poetry—and he is capable also of such phrases as "pearly sweat" and the "snail's shelly cave"—its influence was probably slight, at the very least until 1710, for it was not until then that the poems were reprinted with an edition of the plays. In that year the poems, and some critical remarks on the plays by Charles Gildon, were published as a seventh volume to Nicholas Rowe's edition of Shakespeare (1709). The poems were again reprinted in the 1714 edition of Rowe's *Shakespeare* and in 1725 as a supplement to Pope's edition of Shakespeare; by the latter date there could no longer be much chance of influence. Whatever influence Shakespeare may have had on the course of poetic diction came almost surely from the plays, for they never ceased to be read.

NOTES AND REFERENCES

1. See *Troilus and Cressida* (1. 3. 7–21); I take these examples from F. P. Wilson, *Shakespearian and Other Studies,* ed. Helen Gardner (Oxford: Clarendon Press, 1969). Act, scene, and line references are to the *Complete Works,* ed. G. L. Kittredge (Boston: Ginn and Company, 1936).

2. Groom, *Diction of Poetry,* p. 30.

3. Ibid., p. 35.

4. "Salt" flood or flood appear three times in Surrey's poems: in "O happy dames. . . ," 1. 29; in "Syns fortunes wrath. . . ," 1. 19; and in Eccles., Chap. 1, 1. 34.

5. Hart (ed.), *1 Henry VI.*

6. Ibid., p. xlii.

7. Gordon, *Shakespearian Comedy,* p. 149 and n. 8.

8. Nicholas Breton borrowed barky for the line "The trees their barky silence break" (*The Passionate Shepherd,* 1604, 1. 17); Shakespeare had written of "the barky fingers of the elm," 4. 1. 47.

9. Milton used "eyn" once in his poetry, in the line "The rays of Bethlehem blind his [Osiris's] dusky eyn" (*On the Morning of Christ's Nativity,* 1. 223); there is no comic intent here.

10. James Ralph, *Night,* 1728, Bk. 4, p. 59.

11. Groom, *Diction of Poetry,* p. 47.

12. *Coleridge on Shakespeare, The Text of the Lectures of 1811–12,* ed. R. A. Foakes (Charlottesville: University of Virginia Press, 1971), pp. 114–15.

13. Both George Herbert and Thomas Vaughn use welkin without humorous intent.

14. Groom, *Diction of Poetry,* p. 32.

15. *2 Henry IV,* ed. A. R. Humphreys, Arden ed. (London: Methuen and Co., 1966), p. lxv n. 1.

16. Arthos, *Language of Natural Description,* pp. 363–64.

17. Groom, *Diction of Poetry,* p. 39.

18. *Romeo and Juliet* (2. 2. 163). Spenser had described Echo as "ayrie in *Virgil's Gnat* (1. 232), and Lyly or whoever wrote *The Maid's Metamorphosis* (1600) took Echo's "airie Tong" (2. 1. 71) either from *Romeo and Juliet* or elsewhere. Milton took "aery tongue" for a line in *Comus* (208).

19. Reynolds, *Treatment of Nature,* pp. 20 and 41.

20. "Bladed grass" (1. 1. 211) is echoed in *Macbeth* "bladed corn" (4. 1. 55) and in Dryden's *The Hind and the Panther* (1. 255), "Nor bladed grass, nor bearded corn succeeds," and makes an appearance in Wordsworth's *The Excursion* (1. 740).

21. See p. 60.

22. From *Midsummer-Night's Dream* (c. 1595); Spenser uses it in *The Faerie Queen,* 2. 10. 6.5 (1596).

23. A "heart as hard as flint" is one of the proverbs in Morris Tilley's *Dictionary of the Proverbs in England in the 16th and 17th Centuries* (Ann Arbor: University of Michigan Press, 1950) with one example more than twenty years before Shakespeare.

24. "Such as a freeman ought to be," Schmidt's *Lexicon,* see *2 Henry VI,* 4. 7. 67–68, "Sweet is the country, because full of riches; / The people liberal, valiant, active, wealthy."

25. To hang suspended; Shakespeare anticipated Milton's "pendent world" of *Paradise Lost,* 2. 1052, in *Measure for Measure,* 3. 1. 126.

26. Turn back, return, with a notable use in *The Comedy of Errors,* part of the catalogue of the charms of the kitchen wench: "Where France? / In her forehead; arm'd and reverted, making war against her heir," 3. 2. 125–27.

27. Shakespeare used this word and "dexter," for left and right, to distinguish the cheeks on the face in *Troilus and Cressida,* "my mother's blood / Runs on the dexter cheek, and this sinister / Bounds in my father's," 4. 5. 127–29.

28. Translation of DuBartas, ed. F. C. Faber (Gainesville: University of Florida Press, 1965), Second Day of the first Week, p. 47; Sixth Day of the first Week, p. 210; Handicraftes, p. 382; and Sixth Day of the first Week, p. 215.

29. Gay has the "spongy fleeces" of "floating clouds" in *Rural Sports.*

Chapter 4.

Milton

The confusion that has arisen in modern times between poetic diction and Miltonic diction need not be traced any farther back than the publication in 1900 of Walter Raleigh's *Milton*. In the chapter on Milton's style and influence, Raleigh not only confuses these two terms but adds to his error by identifying Milton's poetic diction with the poetic diction Wordsworth attacked. He writes that Milton "may fairly be called the inventor and, by irony of fate, the promulgator of that 'poetic diction' which, in the time of its deformity and decay, Wordsworth sought to destroy."[1] Matters are made worse when Raleigh adds that "there was little or no poetic diction, of the kind condemned by Wordsworth, before the time of Milton. In the Elizabethan age all diction was free to poetry, and was freely used. Drawing on his accumulated stores of literary reminiscence, and using them for his own special purpose, Milton invented 'poetic diction,' and bore a main part in the founding of the English school of poetry which is classed 'Classical.' "[2] Raleigh defends Pope against Coleridge's accusation that the source of "our pseudo-poetic diction" was Pope's *Homer* by stating that Pope "was from boyhood a sedulous student of Milton, and a frequent borrower" and that "in the translation of Homer, above all, reminiscences of Milton abound."[3] Finally, he adds Thomson and Gray to Pope as examples of poets who were much influenced by Milton's diction.

Tracing Wordsworth's theory of poetic diction, Marjorie L. Barstow, more properly distinguishes between the popular misconceptions of Milton's diction—"we must turn aside for a moment to do honour to the splendid and lonely figure of Milton"—and that decried by Wordsworth. Indeed, she concludes that Milton, "who certainly was responsible for some of the *dulcia vitia* in the poetry of the eighteenth century, proves upon examination to hold an ideal not altogether different from that of Wordsworth."[4] Havens put the matter of Pope's indebtedness to Milton's diction in the translations of Homer into truer perspective when, after quoting Pope's remark in the postscript to the *Odyssey* that "in order to dignify and solemnize these plainer parts . . . some use has been made . . . of the style of Milton," he states that "from these remarks the reader might expect to find considerable Miltonic diction in the translation, but he would be doomed to disappointment."[5] Havens acknowledges, as do all critics of Milton's diction, the presence of what he terms "the strongly Latinic, learned, and grandiloquent vocabulary" of *Paradise Lost,* a feature which, at least in the "Latinic" part of that statement, is found in poetic diction.[6] But it is also necessary to point out, as Helen Darbishire has, that Milton's Latin words "were part of an inherited poetic vocabulary" with roots in Lucretius, Virgil, and Horace, and, one might add, in their English translators.[7] Deane had expressed the difference between the two kinds of diction as "the lofty Miltonic kind in which Latinism of construction and wealth of vocabulary predominated, and the Dryden-Pope type in which set-phrases and *gradus* epithets were variously confined."[8]

Before proceeding to a closer analysis of the differences between poetic diction and Miltonic diction, it may be well to call attention to the repetition, two years after Havens's painstaking study of Milton's poetry and his temperate remarks on Milton's part in the formation of English poetic diction, of Walter Raleigh's turn-of-the-century statements about Milton's role as founder of this diction and of his influence upon Pope, especially in his *Homer.* Thomas Quayle's study is based on the premise that most poetic diction was "mainly to be found in the descriptive poetry of the period," a descriptive poetry which contained "a common stock of dead and colourless epithets,"[9] statements which, while true enough, exclude the poetic diction prevalent in other genres, notably in epics and in English translations of epics. Quayle, unlike other modern students of eighteenth-century poetic diction, sees Latinisms as "another type of eighteenth-century poetic diction," a type as widespread as that encountered in descriptive poetry. But there is so much that is wrong in Quayle's work that one quotation on the descent of poetic diction should suffice.

Pope was a frequent borrower from Milton, and, in his "Homer" especially, very many reminiscences are to be found, often used in an artificial, and sometimes in an absurd, manner. Moreover, Pope's free and cheapened use of many of Milton's descriptive epithets did much to reduce them to the rank of merely conventional terms, and in this respect the attack of Wordsworth and Coleridge was not without justice. But on the whole the proper conclusion would seem to be that what is usually labelled as "the *Pope* style" could with more justice and aptness be described as "the pseudo-Miltonic style."[10]

Later, Quayle is even more specific, asserting that "if it is necessary to establish a fountainhead" for this "conventional poetical language," *Paradise Lost* "will be found to contain most of the words and phrases which the eighteenth century versifiers worked to death."[11] Perhaps this last statement may serve as a convenient point of departure, or possible whipping boy, for detailed analysis of this question.

A logical approach to the Milton-Pope theory of the origin and transmission of poetic diction would begin by asking what part Dryden had in this process. Quayle, who acknowledges a debt to the earlier work by Myra Reynolds,[12] glances in the direction of Dryden and sees "many of the characteristics of this 'spurious poetic language' " in his poetry but still finds that Milton "originated" most of it.[13] Miss Reynolds gives a number of examples of poetic diction from the work of Dryden and, for the most part, poets of the eighteenth century, with here and there an example from Dryden's contemporaries, including Milton,[14] but neither she nor any other student of the question has made a systematic effort to trace any great body of this poetic diction back to its origins in earlier English poetry. The one exception is Arthos's work, and that covers only the poetry of natural description. While a not inconsiderable part of poetic diction can be shown to have its source in the Latin poets, and while any English poet may have gone directly to them, the frequency with which some of these identical words and phrases occur over at least two centuries makes the theory of strong English influence more probable. Then, too, the practice of making adjectives of nouns by adding a -y suffix is not one which can be traced to Latin origins. What is more, given a point of departure such as the fact that Latin *liquidus* not only means fluid, flowing, liquid, but also bright, clear, any poet or poetaster could progress from Virgil's *liquidi fontes* to some combination of liquid and a fitting noun—or a far-fetched one, for that matter, as witness Blackmore's "clouds of liquid dust" which "obscure the sky" in *Prince Arthur* (Bk. 10, p. 323 in the 1714 revised ed.).

Milton's position in the transmission of poetic diction is similar to Spenser's in that they both contribute to and pass on a body of common poetic diction at the same time that they employ a vocabulary and create a diction of their own. With Milton, employing blank verse as he does in his major poems, certain very convenient monosyllables that served as rhyme words for other poets and became part of poetic diction are used but rarely.[15] Thus, Milton in the entire canon of his poetry uses breed only as a verb; Dryden uses the modified noun eight times in the rhyme position in his *Virgil,* and Pope uses it similarly seven times in his *Iliad.* Race appears with a modifier three times in Milton (I discount "human race"); it appears fifty-seven times with modifier and in the rhyme position in Dryden's *Virgil,* with seventy-three such occurrences in Pope's *Iliad.* The same general disparity in use between all Milton's poetry and Dryden's *Virgil* and Pope's *Iliad* obtains for such words as brood, crew (although Milton modifies this word fifteen times) kind, train (here the disparity is very great), tribe (not once modified in Milton) and some others. As a result one gets such combinations or periphrases as heav'nly breed, woolly breed, promis'd breed, the mastiff's gen'rous breed, and celestial breed in Pope, but none, of course, in Milton. And where Milton has solely human kind, serpent-kind, and brutal kind Dryden, among many others, has the degenerate kind, the salvage kind, the laborious kind, the sinking kind (*Georgics* 4. 363, to describe bees "oppress'd by Foes, or Famine pin'd"), the generous kind, and the salacious kind, and Pope has the beauteous kind, that tempestuous kind, the boastful kind, a noxious kind, and Priam's faithless kind, among others. One moves from such usages to Thomson's the bleating kind (sheep) and the mixed household-kind (*Spring,* 1. 772, 1746 ed., used to distinguish domestic fowl from rooks).

"Milton," writes Quayle in another undocumented and irresponsible statement, "indeed seems to have been one of the great inventors of adjectives ending in *y,* though in this respect he had been anticipated by Browne and others, and especially by Chapman."[16] The bare truth of the matter is that Milton invented no adjectives ending in y, except possibly sheeny, which appears in one of his earliest and worst poems, that *On The Death of a Fair Infant Dying of a Cough,* where it describes heaven, and cany in "cany wagons" (*Paradise Lost* 3. 439). He is far surpassed in such inventions by Spenser, Shakespeare and a host of less influential poets. While it may seem paradoxical, the term poetic diction encompasses both words and phrases that occur with such great frequency as to become stale as well as certain rare and even nonce words either invented or taken bodily from the Latin and used only once or twice in the entire corpus of a poet's work. Thus, Milton's "sheeny heaven" is as much poetic diction as his repetition of earlier poets' "hoary frost." In this respect, and for these adjectives, he is mostly a transmitter rather than an originator of poetic diction. Not only was Milton no inventor of these adjectives, he was also most conservative in his use of them. Those he uses with greatest frequency are airy (19), starry (17), flowery (14), shady (13), and watery (12), all very conventional and affording no surprises in the contexts in which they appear. Of the approximately seventy-five such adjectives in the canon of his poetry, thirty-four make single appearances, while another twelve appear only twice.[17] For the most part, Milton is as conventional in his use of these and his other -y adjectives as he is with those he favors. And he is not given to any great daring in his borrowings from earlier English poets. The following are among his more unusual -y adjectives: arrowy showers, bosky bourn, coaly Tyne, corny reed, gulfy Dun, [a swan's] oary feet, smutty grain, sphery chime, and wormy bed. Of these Shakespeare could have been the source for bosky, sphery, and wormy. But Milton is as predictable as other, and lesser poets, in airy flight, bushy shrub, craggy cliff, dewy sleep, dusky clouds, finny drove, fleecy flock (of clouds), flowery vales, hoary frost, horny beaks, massy gold, mossy trunk, pearly shells, ruddy flame, shady grove, snowy Alp, spicy shore, starry Sphere (or train), tawny lion, and watery desert.

A negative way in which to put Milton's influence in the matter of -y adjectives into perspective is to list some of those already coined or used by his predecessors, other than Spenser and Shakespeare, which he eschews. Golding has clammy and fenny; the Earl of Surrey has hugy (from Chaucer) and steepy; Harington has drossy and flinty; R. Carew, who translated five Cantos of Tasso's *Godfrey of Bulloigne* in 1594, has blacky, largy, shrilly, and straungy (i.e., strangy); Sylvester has branchy, bristly, chaffy, poysonie, and wiry; Drayton has bracky, tusky, and vasty (the last of which he shared with or took from Shakespeare); Gorges has brusky, flaggy, frothy, globy, lithy, and moisty; Sandys has beachy, fishy, flamy, foamy, herby, leavy, plashy, sappy, spiny, and unknotty; and Vicars, to make an end to a list that could be much expanded, has beamy, calmy, flaly, fumy, goldy, hooky, shieldy, shippy, swarmy, waxy, wheely, and wingy. Vicars's translation of the *Aeneid* was published in 1632, by which time Milton had been writing poetry for some eight years. It should be pointed out that *Comus,* published in 1634, contains the single appearances in the Milton canon of bosky, corny, feathery, finny, hilly, leafy, musky, shrubby, smoky, sphery, and spungy; one of the two appearances of bushy, glassy, rosy, sooty, and tawny; as well as occurrences of airy, balmy, dusky, fleecy, flowery, gloomy, grassy, hoary, mossy, scaly, shady, snowy, and starry. *Comus,* then, with some of the other early poems, accounts for much of Milton's use of one aspect of poetic diction. Finally, it might also be noted, that Ernest de Selincourt puts Milton down as probable source for six of a list of forty-five -y adjectives in the poetry of John Keats.[18] The six are bloomy (Drayton has bloomy bier), gummy, oozy (already well established by Milton's time), sphery (which de Selincourt also notes as probably influenced by Shakespeare), spongy (but see p. 83), and wormy (which, in "wormy bed," Milton had taken verbatim from Shakespeare). Thus reduced, Milton's role in the transmission of -y adjectives does not loom very large as far as Keats is concerned.

Milton's Latinity and its part in the history of English poetic diction is more difficult of assessment. At the outset it may be said that the Miltonic style, including the use of Latin-derived words with their root meanings, has been perhaps exaggeratedly described, both as to extent and originality. Walter Raleigh, for one, gives as examples of Milton's Latinity: intend (consider), arrive (to come to the shore of), obnoxious (liable to), punctual (point-like, minute), sagacious (keen of scent), explode (to shout down, to drive off the stage), retorted (requited), and infest (attack, harass, destroy). A first point to make is that these words, with these meanings, occur very infrequently: of twenty-one uses of intend only one means to consider; in sixteen appearances of arrive only two are used as above; obnoxious appears three times and explode twice; and punctual, sagacious, retorted, and infest occur only once. Other words that have been associated with the Miltonic style also appear but once, and too much has been made of their contribution to that style. Among these are circumfluous, fulgent (and refulgent), effluence, chequered, dubious, irriguous, luxuriant, mural, nocent, procinct, profluent, respire, obscene, suppliant (as adjective), and unctuous. Secondly, the *OED* is authority for the previous appearance of each of the words in Raleigh's list as used by Milton, with arrive appearing in Gower and in the Bible, among other places. Milton's "Thus was the applause they meant, / Turned to exploding hiss" (*Paradise Lost* 10. 545–56) had been anticipated in Burton's *Anatomy of Melancholy,* "Virtue and Wisdom . . . were hissed out, and exploded" and in Cowley, "Why they did not hiss, and explode him off the stage." His use of sagacious had the lexicographical sanction of Blount's *Glossographia* (1656), where it is defined as "quick of scent, taste, or sight." And he had precedents for his use of intend, obnoxious, punctual, and retorted.[19] That Milton was mistakenly credited with certain Latinisms which he either did not use or used only once or twice is evident, among other places, in the satiric remark attributed to a friend of Pope's that "without abundance of words such as these [dulcet, gelid, umbrageous, redolent] a poem will never be esteemed truly Miltonic"[20] for the truth is that Milton did not use either gelid or redolent, and that he used umbrageous once and dulcet twice.

The problem is an old one. In a systematic "Examination of Milton's Style," Francis Peck lists no less than forty-nine characteristics of that style.[21] Among these, listed eighth and ninth, are "He naturalizes many Greek words" followed by "and almost innumerable Latin ones." But Peck gives no examples nor figures. David Masson, however, is specific in his essay on "Milton's English," writing that the words Milton used only once in his poetry "will be found on examination greatly more numerous than might have been supposed beforehand."[22] He then lists 118 words beginning with the first letter of the alphabet which occur only once in the corpus of Milton's poetry. Of 375 words beginning with un- he counted "no fewer than 241 occurring only once—the reason being that so many of those words are negative adjectives." He concluded that he would not be surprised if between 2,000 and 3,000 of the estimated 8,000 words in Milton's poetic vocabulary were found to be used only once.[23] Most of the words in his first list, those beginning with a- are of Latin derivation.

Perhaps it would be well now to list some of the Latin words used in their root meanings in a few of Milton's predecessors. Chapman, in his translation of Homer's epics, has adverse, ambient, circumfluous, confluence, decent, deject, devoted, err, frequent, generous, horrid, implide (see Milton's much-condemned "fizzled hair implicit" in *Paradise Lost* 7. 323), instruct, involve, meridian, officious, procinct ("in all procinct of warre," *Iliad* 12. 89, with which compare Milton's "war in procinct," *Paradise Lost* 6. 19), refluent, refulgent, respire, servile, unctuous, vital. Sandys's translation of Ovid's *Metamorphoses* contains, among others, aetherial, care, circumfluent, confess, conscious, ductile, effuse, exalt, extrude, fluent, fulgent, generous, grateful, horrid, invest, involve, luxurious, obsequious, obvious, peculiar, perplex, promiscuous, protend, rebate, refulgent, retort, revert, servile, spoils, supine, vernal, vital. Vicars's translation of Virgil's *Aeneid,* already cited in connection with the use of -y adjectives, has adverse, animate, armipotent, aspire, auspicious, confluence, conglomerate, congregate, conscious, curious, ejaculate, fluent, frequent, generous, ignipotent, infest, ingeminate, obsequious, obtestates, obvious, officious, perplexed, refulgent, retorted, sublunary, supine, vital. Of the above lists, Milton does not use circumfluent, confess (to be manifest), confluence, conglomerate, deject (to throw), ductile, ejaculate, exalt (of objects), extrude, fluent, ingeminate, instruct,[24] obtestate, protend, rebate, refluent, revert, spoils (hide or fur of animals), supine. Nor does he use aspire of material objects (fire, smoke,

92

mountains, towers, trees); only once does he use conscious to mean guiltily conscious or simply guilty (*Paradise Lost* 9. 1050); only twice, unless one is perennially on the lookout for puns, does he avail himself of obvious to mean in the way of. Groom in his discussion of "the large Latin element" in Milton's diction, an element which he terms "the most conspicuous general feature" of that diction, quite properly notes that "many of the words derived from Latin in *Paradise Lost* [I would include the whole poetic canon] are simply part of the literary diction of the sixteenth and seventeenth centuries." Groom lists a number of these and uses the *OED* to show previous appearances in other writers and to characterize some words as obsolete, rare, or archaic.[25] It is not, however, the extent and frequency of use of Latinity that distinguishes the Miltonic style so much as the memorableness of the context in which these Latinisms appear added to such other recognizable and agreed-upon features of that style as inversion, omission of words, archaisms, parenthesis and apposition, "collocations of more or less exotic proper names," and "unusual and compound epithets."[26] And yet it is chastening to know, as was long ago pointed out, that the line "Immutable, immortal, infinite" (*Paradise Lost* 3. 373) comes unchanged from Sylvester's *DuBartas*

With the above in mind, the distinction between Miltonic diction and poetic diction should be more easily demonstrated. Tillotson compares the landscapes of Broome and Fenton, published in the *Miscellany* of 1712, to show "with what uniform completeness external nature could be commanded" and concludes that "the motto of both these passages is *Everything of the Best*. Broome and Fenton are self-elected Tweedledum and Tweedledee. They are two poets playing for safety."[27] Now, Broome and Fenton were the two poets pressed into service by Pope to assist him in translating the *Odyssey*. Broome translated eight books (2, 6, 8, 11, 12, 16, 18, 23) and Fenton translated four (1, 4, 19, 20). What is more, Fenton had already translated the eleventh book of the *Odyssey*, "In Milton's Style," prompting Dr. Johnson to write that "it is observable" that Fenton did not take that book to translate, "neither did Pope claim it, but committed it to Broome."[28] And Broome, taking his cue from Fenton, but not until after the *Odyssey* was completed, translated *Part of the Tenth Book of the Iliads of Homer: In the Style of Milton* for his *Poems on Several Occasions* (1727). His version of part of the eleventh *Iliad*, "In the Style of Milton," also appeared in this collection. One has, therefore, what seem to be ideal conditions for a possible discrimination between the Miltonic style—or imitations thereof, which are even better, since imitations must exaggerate stylistic features in order to be recognizable as imitations—and epic diction as practiced by two poetasters steeped in poetic diction, but, in their collaboration in the *Odyssey,* subject to Pope's revisions.

Fenton's translation of the eleventh book of the *Odyssey* is, unlike Broome's much later version of part of the tenth *Iliad,* uninfluenced by his collaboration with Pope. For this reason, it may be termed a purer imitation of Milton's style, since Broome labored under the disadvantage of having fairly recently translated eight books of the *Odyssey* under Pope's supervision. And while Broome had Pope's version of the tenth *Iliad* to help him, if need arose, Fenton had no such crutch. One would expect Fenton's version to be much more an imitation of Milton's style than Broome's, and one's expectations would be fulfilled.

Broome's dependence upon Pope can be seen in his version of part of *Iliad* 10 in such a passage as "A mortal! born to die! but such his deeds / As future Grecians shall repeat with tears / To children yet unborn"[29] which owes much to Pope's "Yet such his Acts, as *Greeks* unborn shall tell" (1. 61). Broome's "But if thy wakeful cares (for o'er thy head / Wakeful the hours glide on) have aught matur'd / Useful, the thought unfold" plainly derives, even to the parenthesis, from Pope's couplet, "If ought of use thy waking Thoughts suggests / (Since Cares, like mine, deprive thy Soul of Rest)" (ll. 106–7).[30] This same dependence on Pope can also be seen in Broome's version of part of *Iliad* 11; one example will suffice: Broome's "As toiling reapers in some spacious field / Rang'd in two bands, move adverse, rank on rank" (p. 176) closely parallels Pope's "As sweating Reapers in some wealthy Field, / Ranged in two Bands, their crooked Weapons wield" (ll. 89–90). As far as poetic diction is concerned, Broome owes little to Pope, and indeed his versions of parts of *Iliads* 10 and 11 are relatively free of that diction.[31]

Elements in Broome's versions which warrant his claim to be writing in Milton's style are the occasional inversion (which of course is epic rather than solely Miltonic), the use of one part of speech for another, parenthetic expressions, Latinisms, adjectives made from proper names, and words from Milton's poems. Broome is not up to the long, complicated sentence that is an essential feature of Milton's verse in *Paradise Lost.* All these elements, plus a very infrequent archaism, are also to be found in Fenton's imitation. Epic inversion and parenthetic expressions, and there are but a few of each in Broome's versions, may be dismissed as not distinctive enough to make a real difference between Milton's style and epic diction in general. A feeble attempt at Miltonics is seen in "Panting the spy they seize" (p. 122), where one has to compare Pope's "The panting Warriors seize him" (1. 447) in order to learn that it is the warriors who are panting, not the spy—who has also been running. In *Iliad* 10 Broome has two adverbial uses of nocturnal (pp. 105, 123); a verb is formed from an adjective in "the dark veil of night / Sabled the pole" (p. 114); obscure is used as an adverb in "why wanderest thou obscure" (p. 106);[32] and terrific also functions adverbially in "He spoke terrific" (p. 126). With this use of terrific and an earlier one, "a leopard's spotted spoils / Terrific clad his limbs" (p. 103), there is the additional link with Milton's sole use of the word in the description of the serpent's "eyes and hairy name terrific" (*Paradise Lost* 7. 497). In *Iliad* 11 Broome uses orient as a noun rather than as the adjective it is in its thirteen appearances in the canon of Milton's poetry, but there are no other examples of the transposition of parts of speech.[33]

Among the Latinisms in Broome's versions are frequent, a lion's spoils, a power omnipotent, intricate and various (ways), florid with purple wool, elate with joy, armipotent, sagacious, precipitant in *Iliad* 10, with pernicious beams, dubious, penurious meal, grateful, the foe incessant, care, generous in *Iliad* 11, for most of which he finds precedent in Milton. It may be worth noting, however, that there are only single appearances of penurious and sagacious in the Milton canon. Broome's adjectives from proper names are few: in *Iliad* 10 he calls Nestor the "Pylian sage" twice (Pope has "sage Nestor" *and* "the *Pylian* sage") and "Oëlean Ajax" once; in *Iliad* 11 he has "Saturnian Jove," "noble Orthean song" (Pope had "loud *Orthian Song*" in the same passage) and "Olympian bowers" (Pope had "th' *Olympian* Hill" in the same passage). And in one passage Broome has "Pelasgian train," the "Thrymbroean plain," and the "Maeonian bands"—Pope has four such adjectives in the parallel passage.

Miltonic words are those Milton used frequently, or those which, although used only once or twice by him, were sufficiently unusual to remain associated with him. Perhaps terrific would qualify for the latter category; beamed, in *Iliad* 10, for the former. Others, not mentioned either as Latinisms or as transposed parts of speech, are dun in "the dun shades of night" (compare *Comus,* 1. 127, "these dun shades") and "th' ensanguin'd field" (verbatim from *Paradise Lost* 11. 654, and also used by Fenton). In *Iliad* 11 there is orient (thirteen times in the canon), flamed (another favorite), battailous array (see *Paradise Lost* 6. 81, "in battailous aspect," the sole occurrence), blazed, and the steep of Heaven. All in all, considering that there are about 550 lines in the two versions, the Miltonic elements are not impressive. The blank verse is there, of course, instead of the usual heroic couplets, but the jagged rhythm of Milton's long sentences is not present.

Very briefly, the epic diction which coincides in part with what some

95

might consider Miltonic diction in Broome's two versions consists of spoils, hoary, generous, glittering (of weapons and apparel), ponderous (of weapons, stones), athwart, war (battle, encounter), tawny lion, band, train, crown, sable, social feast, elate with joy, horrid in arms, plumy crest, ambient gloom, care, the vital air, refulgent car, adverse Greece, aerial in *Iliad* 10. In the shorter of the two versions, that of part of *Iliad* 11, he has trench profound, noise rends the sky (common in epics but absent in Milton), beamy, aerial, blood distain (but no distain in Milton), refulgent, more than mortal (another epic formula not found in Milton), ranks tumble on ranks (a collocation of words that goes back to Homer), th' immortal train, the steep of Heaven, promiscuous Greek and Roman, war (battle, encounter), grateful, generous savage (the lion), fell headlong. It is not unremarkable that most of the lines in these two versions end in monosyllables, among them bands (eight times) and train (three times), a throwback to the heroic couplets that Broome had been turning out for some time.

Fenton first tried his hand at Miltonic blank verse in his *Part of the Fourteenth Chapter of Isaiah Paraphrased,* published in the bookseller Bernard Lintot's *Miscellaneous Poems and Translations* (1712). Earl Harlan, Fenton's modern biographer, calls the poem "really good blank verse, of an intentionally Miltonic tone."[34] The biblical paraphrase contains sixty-one lines and may be considered a preliminary exercise, for five years later Fenton's *Poems on Several Occasions* included his *Eleventh Book of Homer's Odyssey: Translated from the Greek: In Milton's Style,* a much more ambitious piece of some 760 lines. He, much more than Broome, who may even have followed him instead of Milton in ensanguined field and battailous array, and who almost certainly followed him in nocturnal used as an adverb, and sabled used as a verb in their identical sabled the pole, was able to capture the Miltonic tone. How he did this can partly be seen in the speech of Ulysses's mother to her son when he visits the underworld.

> My Son! how reach'd you these *Tartarean* Bounds,
> Corporeal? Many a River interfus'd,
> And Gulfs unvoyageable, from Access
> Debar each living Wight; besides th' Expanse
> Of Ocean wide to Sail. Are you from Troy
> With your associate Peers but now return'd,
> Erroneous from your Wife and Kingdom still? [p. 96]

The passage has the inevitable inversion of noun and adjective, the adjective formed from a proper name in Tartarean (compare Milton's Tartarean sulphur, *Paradise Lost* 2. 69), the archaism in living Wight (taken bodily from *Paradise Lost* 2. 613), the Latinisms in corporeal (itself an example of one part speech used for another, another Miltonic feature) and erroneous (compare *Paradise Lost* 7. 20, "erroneous there to wander"), and a complicated sentence structure. "Associate Peers" echoes, or is meant to recall, Satan's "associate powers" (*Paradise Lost* 10. 395). What is more, except for the use of Latinisms, and erroneous is quite Miltonic, with the *OED* giving but one prior use and that in a prose chronicle, there is no poetic diction in the passage, it is pure Milton.

Poetic diction and Miltonic diction overlap in the use of Latinisms. Fenton, to quote the first of these to appear, has "devoted Victims" (p. 88), and one is told by William Frost in the Twickenham *Homer* (7. 132) that " 'devoted' in the sense of 'doomed' is a peculiarly Miltonic Latinism." Two examples from *Paradise Lost* are quoted, two from the four in the canon. Here it is necessary to pause and correct a misconception that results in the description of a word as a "peculiarly Miltonic Latinism" when it had already appeared in the sense used by Milton in Fairfax's *Tasso,* Fanshawe's *Lusiads,* Chapman's *Odyssey,* Vicars's *Aeneid,* Gorges's *Pharsalia,* May's *Pharsalia,* and Ross's *Silius Italicus.* Devoted is part of poetic diction; it is decidedly not peculiar to Milton. This is a distinction that must be insisted upon and holds for words, all in Fenton, such as vital, promiscuous, grateful, dome, decent, obvious, circumfluous, peculiar, fallacious, effuse, luxurious, adverse, opponent (adj.), lenient, oblivious, frequent, luxuriant, and incumbent. Having made this point, one must also call attention to Fenton's Miltonic echoes in his use of certain Latinisms, some of them in the above list. His circumfluous seas (p. 106) looks back to Milton's circumfluous waters (*Paradise Lost* 7. 270); his journeying obvious (p. 95) to Milton's obvious hill (*Paradise Lost* 6. 69); his penurious hand (p. 108) to Milton's penurious niggard (*Comus,* l. 726); his erroneous wanderers (p. 108), to Milton's erroneous there to wander (*Paradise Lost* 7. 20); his illustrate his descent (p. 118), to Milton's illustrate his high worth (*Paradise Regained* 1. 370, to mean make clear, display to advantage); his vernant with asphodel (p. 120), to Milton's with vernant flowers (*Paradise Lost* 10. 679); his lenient of wrath (p. 121), to Milton's lenient of grief (*Samson Agonistes,* l. 659); his oblivious doom (p. 121) to Milton's oblivious pool (*Paradise Lost* 1. 266); and his frequent and full (p. 122), to Milton's identical words (*Paradise Lost* 1. 797).

Fenton's Miltonic tone was also made possible by the employment of archaic words, but he almost surely went directly back to Spenser for disparted, disarrayed, ensample, and portance, the third of these words a

97

particular favorite of Spenser's. None of these four is used by Milton, but Milton does have parle, puissant, hoar (adj.),[35] marish (for marsh), unweeting, battailous, and prowest,[36] all used by Fenton. None of the above can be considered poetic diction; that it to say, the words are peculiar to a school of poetry but do not form part of the large reservoir of words, phrases, and images that is called poetic diction. The same holds true for the transposition of parts of speech: sabled the pole, nocturnal (adv.), my earthy (noun), the dry (for land), scepter'd (verb), homag'd, tempesting, to peal (of the ear). All these are in Fenton; some are in Milton, even verbatim.[37] Fenton's visual orb for eye (p. 93) derives from Milton's use of visual with ray, nerve, beam; his ensanguin'd field (p. 90) derives from Milton's "th' ensanguin'd field" (*Paradise Lost* 11. 654); and his sanguine pool (p. 90) from *Lycidas* 106, "that sanguine flower." Other examples occur, but the point has been made; in what has been quoted, Fenton is employing Milton's diction. However, in the following, he is in the tradition of poetic diction, in some part of which Milton may coincide, but in which, to put it perhaps too boldly, Milton is not the Milton of the traditional view. Fenton has dewy shade, foamy strand, goary pool, Maia's wingy son, foamy flood, fleecy fold, hoary sire, bloomy son, sheeny form,[38] airy circles, slopy (flood and side), rosy youth, wavy locks, flow'ry mead, and massy portal. The statement is equally true of deep (for ocean), sable fleece, sylvan lodge, the lady-train, Nature's savage train (wild animals), and aerial arrow. In "a vessel not your own" Fenton falls back on an epic formula absent from Milton's work.

Fenton and Broome can conveniently be forgotten now. Since much poetic diction appears in or results from—or stigmatizes—the language of much poetry of natural description, the famous description of the Garden of Eden in Book 4 of *Paradise Lost,* squarely in the tradition of the *locus amoenus,* offers itself as a logical place to examine more closely the matter of Miltonic, as opposed to poetic, diction. The sole concern will be with the words used, not the syntactical structure in which they appear. Before all else, it is worth noting that Milton sets his stamp on the passage, consisting of lines 210 to 285, by a short introductory passage (11. 210–14) containing the names Eden, Auran, Selevcia, and Telessar (and "Grecian kings") and by a concluding passage (11. 269–85) even richer than the first in proper names and adjectives made from proper names: Enna, Proserpine, Dis, Ceres, Daphne, Orontes, Castalian spring, Eden, Nyseian isle, Triton, old Cham, Ammon, Lybian Jove, Amalthea, Bacchus, Rhea, Abbasin kings, Mount Amara, Ethiop, Nilus, and Assyrian garden. Between these passages is the description of the garden. F. R. Leavis, referring to lines 233–51, wrote of "the laboured, pedantic artifice of the diction"[39] without reference to the tradition of the *locus amoenus* and the almost mandatory aspects of the ideal landscape. Poetic diction in the description resides in: the shaggy hill, the nether flood, the crisped brooks, mazy error, pendent shades, curious knots, palmy hillock, flowery lap, irriguous valley, umbrageous grots, the mantling vine, creeps luxuriant, "a lake, / That to the fringed bank with myrtle crowned, / Her crystal mirror holds," vernal airs, gloomy Dis, florid son, and trembling leaves.[40] There are forebears for some of the above: rivers' heads are "crisped" by Zephyr's stroke in Ben Jonson's *The Vision of Delight;*[41] "gloomy Dis" may be a reminiscence of "dusky Dis" in *A Midsummer Night's Dream;* and there was already "a green mantling vine" in *Comus* (1. 293). Comparison with Spenser's bower of bliss in *The Faerie Queene* (2. 12. 50–76) reveals "a faire grassy ground / Mantled with greene" (st. 50), "trembling groves" (st. 58), "Christall waves" (st. 64), and other similarities which do not necessarily fall into the category of poetic diction. Milton's "fruit burnished with golden rind" (1. 249) almost surely owes something to Spenser's grapes "of burnisht gold" (st. 55), although the presence in Spenser of a stanza full of proper names (52) is probably coincidental. Both have other traditional elements of the *locus amoenus* without, however, any verbal echoes. Perhaps it is worth remarking that Milton's Latinity is not intrusive in these seventy-five lines of description, that he does not pile it on as he does often enough to make this another recognizable feature of his style, one that is best seen, if one admires that sort of thing, in Book 7, the creation of the world.[42]

Since Milton is Milton, it is worth repeating, critics have found excellence where, with lesser poets, they have found fault. Havens writes that "many phrases that sound absurd when transferred to the writings of his imitators are harmonious and beautiful in their original settings. The expression 'vernal bloom,' for example, is not good, but who has objected to it in Milton's great lament over his blindness?"[43] Possibly no one has objected precisely because it is the lament of a man over his blindness, and to suggest that something like "spring flower" is better than "vernal bloom" borders on lack of feeling. Most twentieth-century readers of poetry almost surely prefer the "summer's rose" of the same line (*Paradise Lost* 3. 43) to that "vernal bloom." In similar manner, Tillotson states that "when a poet like Milton takes up a fashion, he does so because he wants to. He spoke of a moonlit 'finny drove' [*Comus*, 1. 115] because he wanted the reader to be aware of an exquisite propulsion of fins."[44] It is known that Milton probably took the phrase from Spenser's "Proteus abroad did rove, / Along the fomy waves driving his finny drove" (*F.Q.* 3. 8. 29.8–9), and to the unprejudiced eye both passages are guilty of reliance upon poetic diction. Both are imbedded in contexts rich in poetic diction, Milton's *Comus* being especially remarkable for the frequency with which he has recourse to it. Samuel Johnson's statement that "Milton's style was not modified by his subject: what is shown with greater extent in *Paradise Lost* may be found in *Comus*"[45] is, then, only partly true with respect to poetic diction. And then, too, there is the occasional poem which, except for its topical matter, would defy identification as Milton's; his Sonnet 11, "A Book was writ of late call'd *Tetrachordon*," might easily be mistaken as Browning's.

One should not be left with the impression that Miltonic diction and poetic diction are two separate entities and can therefore be nicely discriminated. One should realize, however, that the differences between the two are at the very least as great as the similarities. And it should be equally borne in mind that Milton's part in the formation and transmission of poetic diction is an important one, more especially in its transmission than in its formation. An example may help. Proudfoot makes very much, indeed far too much, of Dryden's "habitual periphrases," of which "the most fearsome of all is his use of the word 'war.' " He quotes fifteen examples, confessing rather unnecessarily to uncertainty as to the meaning of the word in some of the passages he quotes.[46] Nothing is said of the possibility that Dryden had himself inherited the periphrase and was using it (possibly abusing it) in the full knowledge that he had powerful precedent for it. The word, in some periphrastic sense, is used three times in *Paradise Lost,* the first two occurrences coming in Book 6, as might be expected. In the first, "his chariot; where it stood retired / From off the files of war" (338–39), war means battle, as it does in many of Dryden's uses of the word. In the second, "bring forth all my war. / My bow and thunder" (712–13), war, according to Alastair Fowler, is "a synecdoche for 'weapons of war.' Whether or not M.[ilton] invented the figure, it was soon after a popular one; cp. Dryden (*Aen.* viii 572: 'His broken Axel trees, and blunted War'); Addison, *Cato* i 4 ('th' embattled Elephant / loaden with war'); etc."[47] In the third, an account of the passage of the Red Sea, "On their embattled ranks the waves return, / And overwhelm their war" (12. 213–14), war is glossed by Fowler as "soldiers in fighting array (perhaps poetic diction; first example in this sense in *OED*)" (p. 1038). The *OED* also gives, as a fourth definition, "Actual fighting, battle; a battle, engagement. *Obs.* (chiefly poet.)" and quotes examples from c. 1320 through Dryden's *Aeneid* (two examples) and up to and beyond Sir Walter Scott. Definition 4b reads "A hostile attack, invasion, assult. *Obs.* " and there are examples ranging from Chaucer's *Knight's Tale* through Knolles's *History of the Turks* (1603). One suspects that Milton may not have invented the special meanings, "weapons of war" and "battle array," but use them he did and thereby gave them a currency they would not otherwise have had. The extremes to which the periphrastic use of war could be pushed may be gauged by Broome's lines in the eleventh book of the *Odyssey*: "*Greece* gave her latent warriors to my care," says Ulysses, " 'Twas mine on *Troy* to pour th' imprison'd war" (641–42) where the "latent warriors" and "th' imprison'd war" both describe the Greek warriors hidden in the wooden horse. Here, then, one can say with considerable assurance that Milton had a part in the formation and transmission of one bit of poetic diction. Multiplication of similar examples would allow a more accurate assessment of his total contribution, but at no time should the one, his contribution to poetic diction, be confused with the other, those features which make up Miltonic diction.

Addendum on "War"

War for battle is to be found in John Vicars's *The XII Aeneids of Virgil* (1632), Book 10, p. 308, "all maintain the warre." Shakespeare had used the word to mean single combat, or so it is glossed in Schmidt's *Lexicon* for its appearance in *A Midsummer Night's Dream* (3. 2. 408) "Telling the bushes thou look'st for wars." Ross joined it with the verb to provoke to mean to challenge to battle in his translation of *Silius Italicus* (1661, Book 3, p. 69) and it is so used by Dryden in the *Aeneid* (5. 569; 7. 616; 10. 123 and 793) and Pope in the *Iliad* (3. 4; 4. 355; 16. 914; 17. 136). Davenant writes of the fishes' "hungry war" in *Gondibert* (2. 5. 48); "the servile War" appears in Sherburne's *The Sphere of Marcus Manilius Made an English Poem* (1675); and Addison has the bees' "humming war" in his translation of the fourth *Georgic* (1694)—in all three examples war means battle. Proudfoot would find cause to censure Dryden's translations from Ovid, for there in the twelfth book of the *Metamorphoses* one comes upon "the rowling War" (1. 76, thunder), "a sanguine War" (1. 139, where the word appears to mean the object of a battle), and "in closer War" (1. 508, where the purpose is to discriminate between hand-to-hand fighting and battle done from a distance with missive weapons). In the story of Ceyx and Alcyone, Dryden has "the wat'ry War" (1. 100) as a periphrase for "the storm at sea." Earlier, however, than Dryden's translation of the *Aeneid* (1697) and of the passages quoted from his translations of Ovid (1700) Blackmore in his *Prince Arthur* (1695) had described a navy as "the sailing war" (Bk. 4, p. 126) and Prince Arthur as "himself a fearful war" (Bk. 10, p. 281, presumably to mean that the prince was an army in himself). In his revision of *Prince Arthur* in 1714, Blackmore introduced a "floating war" (Bk. 4, p. 136—i.e., a naval battle) and "th' advancing war" (Bk. 5, p. 146

101

—i.e., the line of battle). Young Alexander Pope, translating the episode of Sarpedon from the twelfth and sixteenth books of the *Iliad* availed himself of the word, and thus shepherds "gaul" a lion "with an Iron War" (1. 18, unglossed in the Twickenham *Pope* but meaning weapons of iron, a phrase he probably took bodily from Dryden's *Georgics* (1. 232), where it is explained in the next line as the "Rakes and Harrows" used in clearing a field). Pope, in the Sarpedon episode, writes of "th' approaching War" (1. 60, which is glossed as "Soldiers in fighting array *(OED),*" with a reference to "1. 134, below" which turns out to be "A mighty Breach appears, the Walls lye bare, / And like a Deluge rushes in the War." The "doubtful War" of line 70 is merely a battle whose outcome is in doubt. Rowe's translation of Lucan's *Pharsalia* contains, besides some ambiguous uses of the word, "a winged War" (3. 682—i.e., a shower of arrows), "the closing War" (3. 843 —i.e., two ships grappling), and "a distant War" (10. 853—i.e., fisherman throwing darts at a sea serpent). In Richard Glover's *Leonidas* (1737) man-to-man combat is described as "in single war" (3. 651) and in Christopher Pitt's translation of the *Aeneid* (1753) "their whole collected war" (9. 1081) means their combined might. In an epic simile Thomson describes the preliminaries to a combat between two bulls as "the bellowing war" (*Spring, 1746 ed.*, 1. 803) and echoes Dryden and Pope in "iron war," i.e., that waged with iron weapons (*Spring,* 1. 842). Hunting is "the sylvan war" in *The Castle of Indolence* (1. 37). Later in the century William Julius Mickle wrote of "the flying war," i.e., the hurling of "flints, clods, and javelins" in his translation of the *Lusiad* (1778 ed., 1. 33–34). One notices that the word occurs most frequently in epics and translations of epics, and once in an epic simile; hence it can be thought a part of epic diction.

NOTES AND REFERENCES

1. Raleigh, *Milton* (London: Edward Arnold, 1900), p. 246.
2. Ibid., p. 251.
3. Ibid.
4. Barstow, *Wordsworth's Theory of Poetic Diction* (New Haven: Yale University Press, 1917), pp. 17, 18.
5. Havens, *The Influence of Milton,* pp. 115–16.
6. Ibid., p. 66.

7. Darbishire, "Milton's Poetic Language," in *Essays and Studies by Members of the English Association,* 1957, p. 44.

8. Deane, *Aspects of Eighteenth Century Nature Poetry,* p. 35.

9. Quayle, *Poetic Diction, A Study of Eighteenth Century Verse* (London: Methuen and Co., 1924), pp. 25, 26.

10. Ibid., p. 36

11. Ibid., p. 184

12. Ibid., p. 28 n.

13. Ibid., pp. 32, 33–4.

14. Reynolds, *Treatment of Nature,* pp. 39–48.

15. See Tillotson, *APD,* pp. 36 and 74 for some of these.

16. Quayle, *Poetic Diction,* p. 35.

17. "Approximately," because some -y adjectives were already so very common by this time that they need not be taken into account.

18. De Selincourt (ed.), *The Poems of John Keats,* 6th ed. (London: Methuen and Co., 1935), pp. 624–26.

19. See also Lalia Phipps Boone, "The Language of Book VI, *Paradise Lost,*" in *SAMLA Studies in Milton,* ed. J. Max Patrick (Gainesville: University of Florida, 1953), p. 118: "A closer examination of the ultimately Latin words will, I believe, show that the Latinity of Milton's language has been overestimated."

20. Quoted in Havens's *Influence of Milton,* p. 65.

21. Peck, *New Memoirs of the Life and Poetical Works of John Milton,* 1740.

22. Masson, introduction to his edition of the *Poetical Works,* (London: Macmillan, 1874). 3 vols., 1–xii.

23. Ibid., pp. xii–xiii.

24. *OED,* "Furnished or equipped with something." See Chapman's *Odyssey* (4. 755), "ship instruct with oars."

25. Groom, *Diction of Poetry,* pp. 81–83.

26. James H. Hanford and James G. Taaffe, *A Milton Handbook,* 5th ed. (New York: Appleton-Century-Crofts, 1970), pp. 244–46.

27. Tillotson, *APD,* p. 19.

28. Johnson, *Lives,* vol. 2, pp. 259–60.

29. *Poems on Several Occasions* (1727), pp. 104–5.

30. There is no need to catalogue other parallels; this has already been done in the Twickenham *Homer* (10. 586).

31. But Broome's "a lion's spoils" coincides with Pope's "a Lion's yellow Spoils" in *Iliad* 10 and his "the immortal train" with Pope's "th' immortal Train" in *Iliad* 11, for example.

32. See *Samson Agonistes,* 1. 296, "they walk obscure."

33. Broome also falls back upon "terrific" again in "the dread sire of men and gods descends / Terrific from his Heavens," p. 181.

34. Harlan, *Elijah Fenton, 1683–1730* (Philadelphia: University of Pennsylvania Press, 1937), p. 71.

35. *L'Allegro,* 1. 55, "on some hoar hill," with which compare Fenton, p. 105, "on Olympus hoar."

36. *Paradise Regained,* 1. 342, "many prowest knights," with which compare Fenton, p. 118, "many a prowess'd knight."

103

37. *Paradise Lost* 7. 412 "tempesting the ocean" is repeated by Fenton, p. 112; Milton has "nor was his ear less pealed," with which compare Fenton's "tho' she peal / Your Ear," p. 114.

38. These last two are from Milton's "bloomy spray," Sonnet 1, and "On the Death of a Fair Infant Dying of a Cough," 1. 48, "sheeny Heaven."

39. Leavis, *Revaluation, Tradition and Development in English Poetry* (New York: G. W. Stewart, 1947), p. 49.

40. On "trembling," see Tillotson, *APD,* p. 49.

41. *OED* gives as the second definition, "Having a surface curled into minute waves, folds, or puckers" and quotes Dekker, "crisped Spring," and the Douay Bible, "a crisped lily."

42. Some scholarly attention has focused on *Paradise Lost* 4. 239, "With mazy mirror under pendent shades"; see my article in *MLR* 67 (1972),:745–51.

43. Havens, *The Influence of Milton,* p. 139.

44. Tillotson, *APD,* pp. 20–21.

45. Johnson, *Lives,* vol. 1, p. 190.

46. L. Proudfoot, *Dryden's Aeneid, and Its Seventeenth Century Predecessors* (Manchester: Manchester University Press, 1960), pp. 225–27.

47. *The Poems of John Milton* (London, 1968), p. 761. Milton's is the first use according to *OED.*

Chapter 5.

Dryden

By the time of Dryden's appearance on the poetic scene the store of poetic diction had been markedly building up for at least a century and had been added to and given fresh sanction by Milton. Dryden's chief role in the history of poetic diction was to be that of inheritor and hander-on. There has, however, been some misunderstanding about his position. Long ago Miss Reynolds suggested that Dryden was too fond of watery, giving a number of examples of his use of that adjective, noting that many "occur in translations by Dryden but in none of the instances quoted is there any justification in the Latin phrase for the adjective 'watery'."[1] Although the quoted remark is true, it does not take into account Virgil's five uses of *aquosus,* sufficient warrant for the combination of watery with any word Dryden or others chose. Miss Reynolds also remarked that -y adjectives were "favorites with Dryden"[2] and, giving a few scattered examples of Latinisms from his poetry, went on to other poets, not seeking to make him the originator of poetic diction. Havens found Dryden "singularly free from any objectionable diction," adding in a note that this could be seen by comparing Dryden's translation of the fourth *Georgic* with "the earlier one made by Addison."[3] Quayle gave a few examples of Dryden's periphrases, but he was after bigger game—Milton.[4]

Mark Van Doren was only partly right when he stated that in Dryden's use of briny waters, sylvan scenes, and cristal streams, all from an eleven-line passage in his *Aeneid*, "are the beginnings of the stereotyped Nature which graced the verse of England for at least two generations. No one can be held more strictly accountable for its vogue than Dryden, whose *Virgil* was read by every poet and served as a storehouse, like Pope's *Homer,* of cultivated phrases." He was right in stating that Dryden's *Virgil* did most for the vogue, especially since it served Pope, whose *Homer* in its turn was read by every poet; he was wrong, of course, in finding the origins of this diction in Dryden. Van Doren goes on to add:

> Nor did the young poets in the time of Queen Anne need to go further than Dryden for models of periphrasis. The circumlocution, that pale ghost of the Roman epithet . . . was everywhere in the later Dryden. In the *Aeneis* an arrow is a feathered death; in the *Georgics,* honey is liquid gold, tenacious wax, ambrosial dew, gathered glue; and always the fish are finny.[5]

George G. Loane remarked of "feathered death" in Dryden's *Palamon and Arcite* (3. 222) that it was "a phrase worked to death in D.'s translations," evidently as much struck by it as was Van Doren.[6] And yet besides the cited occurrences in the *Aeneid* and *Palamon and Arcite,* there was only one other use in the canon—in 1693 in the translation of the first book of Ovid's *Metamorphoses* (1. 617). Three uses hardly constitute a working to death of the phrase, and while I have not come upon the phrase before Dryden's use in 1693, feathered had been used to describe weapons by a small number of poets before that time.[7] To return to Van Doren and Dryden's periphrases for honey. His "liquid gold" comes in *Georgics* 4. 50, a translation of Virgil's *mella . . . liquefacta* (35–36); Virgil later in the same *Georgic* calls honey *liquido nectare* (164), and thus Dryden had two precedents in his source for half his periphrase. Arthos quotes Góngora's *liquido oro,* Drayton's "liquid gold," and Milton's "liquid sweet" as periphrases for honey, as well as Sylvester's "delicious Deaw" and Milton's "mellifluous Dewes."[8] Dryden, it can be seen from these examples, is not so much an originator as a follower. As far as Van Doren's jocular reference to the inevitable finniness of Dryden's fish is concerned, it simply is not true.[9]

Most recently the editors of the first volume of the California *Dryden* felt it necessary to defend Dryden against the anticipated charge that he initiated poetic diction. Their comment comes in a note to "the feather'd train" of *Annus Mirabilis* (l. 440):

> Lest this be noted as a harbinger of what is thought of as the plague of neoclassical diction, let it be observed that the device of elegant periphrasis

was an inheritance from the golden age of English poetry, brought to perfection by the middle of the seventeenth century. A glance at Joshua Poole's *The English Parnassus* (1657), under such a heading as Bird, or Fish, will reveal how fully developed was the technique of translating the simple term into a polite circumlocution, and how great was the stock of examples ready at hand. In view of this development, it is surprising that Dryden indulged so seldom in the periphrastic diversion at this time.[10]

Again, as with Van Doren's remarks, part of this is true, part debatable, the latter being the extent to which Dryden indulged in periphrases. If "at this time" means 1666, the date of *Annus Mirabilis*, then there is not much point in the note, since Dryden had published little poetry up to 1666, none of it poetry in translation.

While there is some poetic diction in Dryden's early poetry, it is unusually little for an apprentice poet, possibly because Dryden, unlike Pope after him, did not attempt any verse translations early in his career and was not, as a result, influenced in his original poetry by his work as translator. Possibly, too, the occasional nature of much of Dryden's early poetry and his work as a playwright account for the relative paucity of poetic diction in the poetry up to the publication of *Sylvae, or the Second Part of Poetical Miscellanies* (1685). He writes in the preface of *Sylvae*, "For this last half Year I have been troubled with the disease (as I may call it) of Translation"; the results are versions of parts of the first five books of Lucretius's *De Rerum Natura*, of three of Theocritus's *Idyllia*, and of four of Horace's poems. It is in this collection, and not in the earlier translations, those of a few of Ovid's *Epistles*, published in 1680, nor in his translation of Ovid's nineteenth *Elegy* or Theocritus's third *Idyllium*, both published in 1684, that the amount of poetic diction begins to obtrude itself upon the reader. There is, it is true, some observable poetic diction in *Annus Mirabilis*, but it is virtually lost sight of because of the sheer length of that poem.[11] But eight years after *Sylvae*, with the publication of *Examen Poeticum, Being the Third Part of Miscellany Poems* (1693), containing the translations of the entire first book of Ovid's *Metamorphoses*, of the "Fable of Iphis and Ianthe" from the ninth book, of the "Fable of Acis, Polyphemus, and Galatea" from the thirteenth book, and of "The Last Parting of Hector and Andromache" from Homer's sixth *Iliad*, that Dryden really leans rather heavily upon poetic diction. And it is, of course, with the translation of Virgil in 1697 and with *Palamon and Arcite*, the translation of the first *Iliad*, and the further translations from Ovid's *Metamorphoses* in *Fables Ancient and Modern* of 1700 that Dryden virtually codifies poetic diction. Only one, or possibly two, more poets were to complete the codification: Pope with his translations of Homer and, for the language of poetry of natural description, Thomson with *The Seasons.*

One must realize that the bulk of Dryden's poetry, apart from the plays, resides in *Sylvae, Examen Poeticum,* the *Virgil,* and *Fables Ancient and Modern,* and hence it should not be surprising to find that a number of words in the vocabulary of poetic diction make their first appearances in the *Virgil* and then reappear in the *Fables Ancient and Modern.* Sometimes; too, the first use of an item of poetic diction will be in one of the two earlier collections, but for the most part it is in the *Virgil* that Dryden tries some words for the first time. The following are but a few words of poetic diction used for the first time in the *Virgil:* beamy, craggy, glassy, incumbent, devoted (doomed), luxuriant, smoky.[12] Another large group of words, of which I list only those beginning with one of the first three letters of the alphabet, occur remarkably more often in the poetry of 1697 and thereafter than in the poetry up to the *Virgil:* abode, adverse, aetherial, ambient, animate, augment, band, beauteous, brood, care, conscious, crew, crystal, cut. There is no need to beat the track of the concordance for further examples of the above or for examples of words first used in the poems and, more particularly, in the translations in *Sylvae* and *Examen Poeticum;*[13] it is obvious that Dryden's translations were the begetters, or the transmitters, of poetic diction.

Dryden's major translations, in order of extent, are of Virgil, Ovid, Lucretius, and Theocritus. His dependence upon the versions of seventeenth-century translators of the *Aeneid,* or at least upon versions of the fourth book of that epic, is the subject of Proudfoot's study,[14] while Helene Maxwell Hooker studied the matter of his English predecessors in the translation of the Georgics.[15] Both scholars show how much Dryden was indebted to his predecessors in the matter of phrases and single and double rhyme words; neither is concerned with the possible debt in the matter of poetic diction.[16] Robert Stapylton translated the fourth book of the *Aeneid* in 1634, and James Harrington translated Books 3–6 in 1659. However, the earliest of Dryden's seventeenth-century predecessors was an anonymous poem titled *Didos Death* (1622); Sidney Godolphin and Edmund Waller collaborated in *The Passion of Dido for Aeneas* (1658); Sir Robert Howard included his translation of the fourth book in his *Poems* (1660); and Sir John Denham wrote *The Destruction of Troy* (1656) and *The Passion of Dido for Aeneas* (1668). Fanshawe translated the fourth book in Spenserian stanzas in 1652, and for that reason, i.e., the stanzaic form, is only mentioned in

Proudfoot's work. Three translations of the entire *Aeneid* were known to and used by Dryden: John Vicars's, published in 1632, John Ogilby's, published in 1649 and revised in 1654, and Richard Maitland's (Earl of Lauderdale's) posthumously published around 1708 or 1709. Dryden saw Lauderdale's manuscript and acknowledged in print that it clarified Virgil's "sense" for him when he was in doubt. According to Proudfoot, Dryden,

> referred to eight English translations [all but Vicars's and the anonymous *Didos Death*] in Book IV alone. And the total for the whole *Aeneid* might be even more impressive. In addition . . . there are vestiges in his work of the early version of Ogilby (received by way of Lauderdale) and of *Didos Death*. Moreover, there is a possibility that he used a ninth translator, Vicars.[17]

All in all, Dryden is said to have taken about one rhyme word in four from his predecessors, to have been significantly influenced by the earlier versions in one line in five, and to have taken over "either verbatim or nearly so" forty lines from eight translators, from the twenty-one he took from Lauderdale to the single lines borrowed from Denham, Howard, Harrington, and Ogilby.[18] Although I do not consider Proudfoot's conclusions completely acceptable, there is no doubt that Dryden was considerably indebted to his predecessors in translating the *Aeneid*.

In the matter of diction and decorum, Dryden is guilty in Proudfoot's eyes of using a large number of abstract words in the poem; among these are sway, reign, empire, imperial, sovereign, and beauteous.[19] "Much worse" than these "are some of Dryden's habitual paraphrases," of which "the most fearsome of all is his use of the word 'war'."[20] Other periphrases to which attention is called are "wing'd inhabitants of air" for birds, "woolly care" for sheep, and "sacred honours" for hair. Since Proudfoot is the chief and most recent accuser, it is obviously necessary to examine his charges at some length. Although his study was published in 1960, he makes no mention of the previous work on poetic diction by Tillotson nor of Arthos's indispensable book on the language of natural description. Recourse to Tillotson's conclusions, summed up in *Augustan Poetic Diction*, published in 1964 but available in earlier works, would have revealed that Dryden was merely following precedent in his use of beauteous[21] and care, as in "woolly care."[22] Sway, needs no explaining, given the subject of the *Aeneid* and, if need be, the practice of Milton (fourteen times in the canon), plus its convenience as a monosyllabic rhyme word, a consideration that holds equally true for reign. Reign is, furthermore, one of Arthos's "signifi-

109

cant words," as are empire and inhabitants;[23] all were used a sufficient number of times before Dryden as to make them quite traditional.

Proudfoot writes, of another aspect of poetic diction:

> Thus, of adjectives in "-y," apart from the familiar ones, he shows the following: "beamy" (in one place for "antlered," in another for "scintillating"), "sickly" (for "sick"), "plumy," "visionary" (for "seen in a vision"), "forky," "nightly" (for "by night"), "briny," "foamy," "ridgy," "steepy," "pitchy," "massy," "fenny," "palmy" (for "where palms grow"), "piny," "fishy," "wreathy," "sulphury," "hugy," "shelfy," "shoaly," "horny" (for "made of horn"), "fumy" and "moony." Of these several, for example "tusky," "forky," "steepy" and "fishy," are very frequently repeated: the reader hardly ever meets a boar but it is tusky, or encounters lightening that fails to be forky. The frequency of these two conjunctions may well mean that Dryden was trying to establish the classical characterizing epithet in English verse. If so, he failed.[24]

First of all, Arthos has an appendix of "epithets with suffix -y" that includes examples, largely from scientific and topographical works published before 1697, of briny, pitchy, horny, sulphury, woolly of the above list. In the second place, beamy,[25] piny, pitchy, briny, foamy, massy, steepy, fishy, horny, shoaly, fumy had all been used by Dryden's predecessors in translations of the *Aeneid*. John Vicars alone, for example, used beamy, piny, pitchy, foamy, massy, steepy (three times), fishy, horny, fumy. Milton, whose use of these epithets is relatively rare, has horny, pitchy, fishy, fumy, palmy, and massy (eleven times). Hugy has a long history, going back to Chaucer (see p. 43) and was used no less than seven times in Gorges's translation of Lucan's *Pharsalia*. Shakespeare has fenny, fishy, foamy, massy, pitchy, steepy of Proudfoot's list. As for the other epithets, the *OED* gives Dryden's *Virgil* pride of place for forky and ridgy only. Dryden could have derived moony from Sidney's *Arcadia* or, more probably, from Sylvester's *DuBartas;* tusky from Drayton's *Second Nymphall* (1. 31);[26] shoaly from Drayton's *Poly-Olbion;* nightly from Milton. In the special meaning of visionary, as "Seen only in a vision; unreal, nonexistent, phantom, spectral," Dryden's *Aeneid* is first, as is his use of wreathy to mean "decked with a wreath or wreathling."

Proudfoot can see little to commend in Dryden's Latinisms. He brands "sacred honours," of the lines "The Thund'rer said, / And shook the sacred honours of his head" (*Aeneid* 10. 171–72), and "woolly cares" and "wing'd inhabitants of air," of two other passages, "Dryden's own deliberate enhancement of diction, intended to set his poem apart from the common style of lesser themes," after having declared that these three phrases are "hardly ever transcripts of Virgil."[27] Proudfoot is guilty of the fault he shares with the editors of the Twickenham *Homer* of looking for parallel uses only in the identical passages, i.e., "woolly cares" must be a "transcript of Virgil" for the words of the English phrase translated at that specific juncture in the *Aeneid.* Overlooked is the presence of the lines in the third *Georgic, superat pars altera curae, / lanigeros agitare . . .* (286–87), which Dryden, *at that juncture,* translated as "woolly sheep" (1. 452), but which he recalled for the "woolly care" of the line in the third book of the *Aeneid.* So, too, with "shook the sacred honours of his hair" which is not a transcript of the passage in Virgil being translated but *is* a translation of Virgil's *decussit honorem* in the second *Georgic* (1. 404), there used of leaves, not of hair, it is true. Spenser, long ago, in his February *Eclogue* had given Dryden and others a precedent, in English, with the lines, "His [a tree's] toppe was bald, and wasted with wormes, / His honor decayed, his branches sere" (ll. 113–14). Pope has "tow'ring Oaks" rear their "growing Honours" in *Windsor-Forest* (1. 221), an expression that John Scott of Armwell termed "an affected kind of catachresis."[28] The *OED*'s definitions and examples are confused for this special meaning of honours. Fanshawe described foliage as "verdant honour" in his translation of *Il Pastor Fido* (5. 2. 4533 in the continuously lined edition). Broome used honours both of foliage and of hair in Pope's *Odyssey* (11. 235 and 18. 182). Proudfoot also objects to "brown horror" in "a wood, / Which thick with shades and a brown horror stood" (*Aeneid* 7. 40–41) on the grounds that in Latin horror can be used for a shag of almost anything but not in English. Here, so far as being the first so to use the term, and except for a literal translation in the Wyclif Bible of 1382 according to the *OED,* Dryden is guilty. Objection to "erected eyes" as Dryden's getting on his high horse may, like the other objections already discussed, be true, but as with the other examples Dryden did not introduce the Latinism or indeed the phrase. There are "erected eyes" in Drayton's *Eclogue* 10. 26 and examples of the word in its primary sense of uplifted in Sidney's *Apology For Poetry* and in Clarendon and Southerne—all before Dryden. Milton describes Mammon as "the least erected spirit that ever fell" (*Paradise Lost* 1. 679), glossed as uplifted by Alastair Fowler, and writes of the "most erected spirits" in *Paradise Regained* (3. 27) which is strangely glossed by John Carey as "elevated, exalted: an obsolescent sense: *PL* i. 679 is the last instance of it recorded in *OED.*" Whatever the confusion in the Longmans *Milton,* it is clear that Dryden had sufficient precedent for his use of erected.[29] Another objection, that of gore being described

111

as purple may be dismissed with the observation that poets had been describing blood and gore and wounds as purple for generations.[30] Dryden used the adjective as automatically, virtually, as one would sign his name. Dryden was unquestionably the great transmitter of poetic diction, a poetic diction to which he made original contributions, but the extent and kind of those contributions are grossly exaggerated in Proudfoot's account, an account that makes Dryden appear the only begetter of that diction.

Dryden's first major effort as a translator of poetry is the 762 lines devoted to parts of the first five books of Lucretius's *De Rerum Natura,* which appeared in *Sylvae, or the Second Part of Poetical Miscellanies,* published in 1685. The same collection contained Dryden's versions of the eighteenth, twenty-third, and twenty-seventh *Idyllia* of Theocritus. In the preface to *Sylvae,* Dryden, "having with much ado got clear of Virgil," turned "to consider the genius of Lucretius, whom I have translate more happily in those parts of him which I undertook."

> If he was not of the best age of Roman poetry, he was at least of that which preceded it; and he himself refined it to that degree of perfection, both in the language and the thoughts, that he left an easy task to Virgil; who, as he succeeded him in time, so he copies his excellencies; for the method of the Georgics is plainly derived from him. Lucretius had chosen a subject naturally crabbed; he therefore adorned it with poetical descriptions, and precepts of morality, in the beginning and ending of his books; which you see Virgil has imitated with great success, in those four books which, in my opinion, are more perfect in their kind than even his divine Æneids. The turn of his verse he has likewise followed in those places which Lucretius has most laboured, and some of his very lines he has transplanted into his own works, without much variation.[31]

But Lucretius "was so much an atheist that he forgot sometimes to be a poet."[32] One has, then, Lucretius choosing a subject "naturally crabbed" and therefore adorning it with "poetical descriptions," at the same time that he is so wrapped up in what he is saying that he forgets how he is saying it.

Thomas Creech of Wadham and later of All Souls, Oxford, had translated the *De Rerum Natura* in 1682 and *The Idylliums of Theocritus* in 1684; in the latter year he also translated *The Odes, Satyrs, and Epistles of Horace,* dedicating that work to Dryden. The editors of the California *Dryden* observe that "Dryden's translations of Lucretius, Theocritus, and Horace all show resemblances to Creech's versions and perhaps more general inspiration to Dryden's friendship with the young classicist."[33] About Creech as translator of Lucretius, there is no ambiguity in Dryden's praise. Dryden speaks of what he owes to "the ingenious and learned translator of Lucretius," although their translations are "very different," Creech not allowing himself to be too voluminous, as he had the whole of the work to translate, whereas he, took "more liberty, because it best suited with my design, which was to make him as pleasing as I could."[34] Virtually every contemporary reference one encounters attests to the popularity of Creech's translation.

In the course of his handsome tribute to Creech's translation of Lucretius, Dryden, referring to his own versions of parts of that poet, writes, "If I have been anywhere obscure in following our common author, or if Lucretius himself is to be condemned, I refer myself to his [Creech's] excellent annotations, which I have often read, and always with some new pleasure."[35] A few of Dryden's "occasional debts to Creech" in his translation of "The Latter Part of the Third Book" are pointed out by James Kinsley; the few borrowings do not, however, fall into the category of poetic diction.[36] Where Creech and Dryden coincide in expressions such as "flow'ry plain[s]" or "supinely lies" in the beginning of Book 1 the debt, if such it can be called, is to a common reservoir of poetic diction on the part of both rather than of the later translator to the earlier. The greatest concentration of poetic diction in Dryden's versions is in Book 1; Creech's recourse to poetic diction is fairly frequent and offers no surprises, unless one excepts a use of turgent (Bk. 4, 1. 1054) and a fondness for yielding,[37] one of Arthos's "significant words" and Tillotson's "recurrent favourites".[38] By 1682, then, the date of publication of Creech's *Lucretius*, there was already such a considerable body of poetic diction that it seems pointless further to pursue the matter of indebtedness in works published so close in time, for Creech's translation preceded Dryden's *Sylvae* which contains his translations from Lucretius, by a mere three years. And since Dryden publicly acknowledged his obligations to Creech's notes on Lucretius, it seems less than likely that he would have followed Creech's text to any great extent without some similar acknowledgment.

Few English poets before Dryden took it upon themselves to translate any number of Theocritus's *Idyllia*. An anonymous poet translated six of them under the delightful title *Six Idillia, That Is, Six Small, or Pretty, Poems, or Aeglogues, Chosen out of the Right Famous Sicilian Poet Theocritus* in 1588. He selected the eighth, eleventh, sixteenth, eighteenth, twentieth, and thirtieth, in three of which, the sixteenth, twentieth, and thirtieth, he was followed by Sir Edward Sherburne, the next English poet to translate

113

Theocritus.[39] Sherburne's *Poems and Translations* was published in 1651, well after the date of Sylvester's translation of DuBartas (1605) and the two editions of Sandys's translation of Ovid's *Metamorphoses* (1626 and 1632), considered by some scholars to be the two most important documents in the establishment of poetic diction. Dryden's translations of the third, eighteenth, twenty-third, and twenty-seventh idyllia in 1684 and 1685 are so close in time to Creech's translation that James Kinsley notes briefly that "there are correspondences of line and phrase between Dryden's versions of Theocritus here [*Miscellany Poems,* 1684] and in *Sylvae* [1685], and Creech's complete translation (1684). It is impossible to distinguish debtor and creditor."[40] Dryden thought highly of Theocritus as a poet. Like others, he praised what he termed "the inimitable tenderness of his passions, and the natural expression of them in words so becoming of a pastoral." He adds that "a simplicity shines through all he writes: he shows his art and learning by disguising both," and remarks that Virgil was denied by the "severity of the Roman language" the advantage of having his shepherds speak a rustic dialect, an advantage that Theocritus enjoyed and in which he was followed by Tasso.[41] Elsewhere Dryden indicates how much Virgil owed to Theocritus,[42] but all he says of Creech is that he "has translated that Greek poet, which I have not read in English," i.e., that he had not read Creech's translation.[43] Years later Francis Fawkes translated the *Idyllia* and added "notes critical and explanatory" (1767); in his preface he reviewed previous translations of Theocritus and found them all wanting in one respect or another, especially Creech's, whose rustic language and lack of "an ear for numbers" exercised his scorn for some three pages.

If the choices of the anonymous translator of 1588, Sherburne, Dryden, and William Bowles can be considered one criterion of prevailing taste, then the favorite idyllia were the sixteenth, the eighteenth, the twentieth, the twenty-seventh, and the thirtieth. Fawkes did not translate the twenty-seventh because, as he put it, it "is by the commentators generally attributed to Moschus" and because "it is of such a nature that it cannot be admitted into this volume." While it is what modern editors of Theocritus label one of the erotic poems, it is still rather innocuous. In the sixteenth, Theocritus complains of the neglect he has suffered at the hands of Hiero, last tyrant of Sicily; in the eighteenth, he celebrates the nuptials of Helen and Menelaus. Number twenty concerns a neatherd who complains of the disdain shown him by a city girl; and the thirtieth relates how Venus chides the boar that accidentally slew Adonis. Thus, it can be seen that the subjects themselves are not really of the pastoral or bucolic kind, and one gets relatively little poetic diction as a result. But, as might also be expected, there is progressively more reliance upon poetic diction from 1588 to 1767.

The anonymous translator of the *Six Idillia* (1588) uses no poetic diction; Sherburne, virtually none. Creech, at least in the third, sixteenth, eighteenth, twentieth, and twenty-seventh eclogues, resorts to one of the oldest of the coronation figures, i.e., "garlands crown'd their heads"; he uses conscious in the sense of guiltily conscious, waft, flow'ry, and flood for river —and that is all. Bowles's versions are also relatively free of poetic diction, though he also uses the old coronation figure, "the board was crown'd with richest meat," and describes tears as "liquid globes." Since Mount Ida was the scene of one of Jove's dalliances, Bowles describes it as "conscious Ida." He was outdone in the use of poetic diction by the anonymous poet or poets who translated the first and twelfth idyllia in the *Miscellany Poems.* He of the first idyllium has a rising ground with "spreading mirtles crown'd" and is not above including sylvan shade, yielding boughs, a leafie train, a craggy rock, the airy tops of a mountain, vocal insects, and a nymph who "skims it o'er the plains." The translator of the twelfth idyllium is more restrained, but he has hoary mountains, fleecy dams, a feathered quire, and somebody crown'd with garlands. Dryden is quite restrained in his versions, with almost no poetic diction in the twenty-third and twenty-seventh idyllia, which do not, by their subjects, lend themselves readily to its use. But in the third, which is bucolic, and the eighteenth, the epithalamium for Helen and Menelaus, he is less restrained, using in the first of these conscious grottos, ruddy lips, a glitt'ring bribe, and steepy Othrys. In the second there is even more: a pompous palace, curious needles, purple morning, vocal souls, dewy paths, a feather'd flock, a use of augment, "animate the lyre", and two uses in the same line of generous, meaning of noble stock.

Fawkes's versions borrow some of their diction from Dryden; and, while they avoid some, they also add much of their own. In the third idyllium, for example, Fawkes's "conscious grot" comes from Dryden's "conscious grottoes"; in the eighteenth, Fawkes takes "animate the lyre" bodily from Dryden. For the most part, Fawkes, as the inheritor of almost two centuries of poetic diction, tends to depend rather heavily upon this heritage. Some part of this can be shown by comparison of the third idyllium in his version and Creech's. Creech's goatherd invites his mistress to meet him in "yonder grove"; Fawkes's recalls an earlier meeting in the "conscious grot." Creech's cave becomes a "sequester'd bower" in Fawkes's version, and his goatherd's reproach to his mistress, "all stone," becomes "flinty is your heart." Crown is elaborated to "flowery crown," trouts to "scaly fry," "yon high rock" to "a dire impending steep," and "I'll leap into the flood" to "Headlong I'll plunge into the foamy deep." And Creech's "a dainty feast"

115

takes on Homeric overtones to become "a rich repast," a phrase so frequently used in Pope's translation of the *Odyssey*. As far as Dryden and Fawkes are concerned, it is only in the eighteenth idyllium that the former exceeds the latter in the use of poetic diction.[44] Since knowledge of Greek was fairly limited in the eighteenth century and since the early English translations of Theocritus, at least up to Fawkes's version in 1767, are relatively free of poetic diction, his work is of relatively little significance in the history of this phenomenon, despite Joseph Warton's exaggerated view of his influence: "Theocritus is indeed the great storehouse of pastoral description; and every succeeding painter of rural beauty (except Thomson, in his *Seasons*) hath copied his images from him, without ever looking abroad into the face of nature themselves." Warton thought that Virgil owed much to Theocritus, but whatever the extent of that debt, and it is not inconsiderable, there is no doubt that English poets went to Virgil rather than to Theocritus. In any event, Warton himself was acute enough to see that "if the Romans excelled their Grecian masters in the graces of diction, it was owing to their exerting all their powers, in dressing up those thoughts and ideas that were ready found to their hands," since the creator "of new images, has scarce leisure to adorn them with that pomp of studied expression, which the writer that coolly copies them, can bestow upon them."[45] And then, too, as Arthos has noted, the dialogue in the Theocritan pastoral did not admit of very much poetic diction.[46]

Some part of Dryden's direct indebtedness to Virgil in the matter of poetic diction has been studied by Brower,[47] but the extent of that indebtedness is greater than Brower's somewhat limited approach would suggest. Writing of Dryden's poetry before 1697, the date of Dryden's translation of *Virgil,* Brower states that he "noted at least a score of words or phrases which can be traced to Virgil's Latin," a few being on the order of "conscious virtue" from *conscia virtus,* another group consisting of "phrases which are unmistakable translations from Virgil, though the words used are not of Latin origin" ("iron sleep" from *ferreus somnus*). In addition, before 1697 Dryden used a number of circumlocutions "identical or nearly so with expressions found in the *Virgil*" [his translation]; among these are phrases such as scaly herd, woolly care, and briny flood, which owe most, in Brower's estimation, to the influence of Virgil, as do others of Dryden's periphrases. The influence of Dryden's *Virgil* is seen in his *Fables Ancient and Modern,* especially in "the increased use of periphrases and Latinized diction." Brower's statement that "one could list an immense number of words or phrases which are bald English equivalents" for words and phrase in Virgil—adverse for *adversum* and involves for *involvere* are two of his four examples—needs some further demonstration and amplification, as do others of his suggestions.

Admittedly, Dryden may have borrowed elements of his diction from a number of sources, principally from translations of epics or of Ovid's *Metamorphoses*, rather than directly from Virgil. But then, too, these intermediate sources may have derived part of their diction from Virgil. The line of descent is difficult, if not impossible, to trace, but in what follows the primary intention is simply to suggest the further influence of Virgil's works on Dryden's diction rather than to state categorically that Dryden was specifically indebted to Virgil for this word or that phrase. One observable phenomenon is the use of a word or phrase employed by Dryden for the first time in his *Virgil* or in one of the pre-*Fables Ancient and Modern* translations from the *Metamorphoses* and then used again thereafter, both a pointer toward influence and a further indication of the individuality of the diction of the epic. Sometimes one of these words or phrases had been used once or twice by Dryden, but its frequency increased markedly with the *Virgil* in 1697 and the *Fables* in 1700. Sometimes, too, Dryden's word or phrase is a translation of the same word or phrase in the same passage in Virgil's Latin, as opposed to his use of that word or phrase in translating an entirely different passage in Virgil. Thus, where Dryden has "adverse foes" (*Aeneid* 10. 716), he may have in mind Virgil's *adversi campo* (*Aeneid* 11. 605) although, it is well to repeat, adverse had been much used as a military term in previous epics and translations of epics, being linked with words such as camp, wing, army, Greeks. The "azure Carr" with which Dryden equips Proteus in the fourth *Georgic* (l. 560) has no counterpart in Virgil's Latin where it is Proteus and not his car who is described as *caeruleus* (l. 388),[48] but there is an "azure car" in Virgil's *Aeneid*, the *caerulo . . . curru* of the fifth book (l. 819), which Dryden translated as "his [Neptune's] Azure Car" (l. 1072). Azure is, of course, a bit of poetic diction.

The use of the verb to cleave to describe the progress of deities, sea creatures, birds, and ships through air or water was already a commonplace when Dryden picked it up; it may have come from Virgil's unique use in *viam scindens* (*Aeneid* 10. 765), descriptive of Orion's stalking "through the vast pools of mid-ocean" (Loeb). Devote or devoted, meaning doomed, possibly from Virgil's *pesti devota futurae* (*Aeneid*. 1. 712) occurs nine times in this sense in Dryden's *Virgil*. He had not so used the word up to 1697, but it makes its appearance seven times in the *Fables Ancient and Modern*, a pretty clear indication of Virgilian influence. Dryden had used fleecy only once prior to its appearance in his *Virgil;* it, with wooly, and especially with "woolly care" (*Aeneid* 3. 868), almost surely owes something to Virgil's

117

curae, / lanigeros (*Georgics* 3. 286–87), *lanigerae claudit pecudes,* and *lanigerae . . . oves* (*Aeneid* 3. 642 and 660). Only twice in the canon of his poetry does Dryden use glassy and then only in the *Aeneid*—"glassy seas" (5. 998) and "the glassy deep" (10. 297)—a use probably derivative from Virgil's *vitrea . . . unda* (*Aeneid* 7. 759). Twice in the *Aeneid* Dryden used incumbent, once to describe Boreas "incumbent on the main" (12. 543) and then again to describe Turnus, "th' incumbent Heroe" (12. 1132); he had not used the word before and he used it once thereafter; Virgil was fond of the word, using it twenty-three times. The same holds true for luxuriant from *luxurio,* used twice by Virgil descriptive of horses (*Georgics* 3. 81 and *Aeneid* 11. 497). Dryden first used it in the *Virgil,* four times in the *Georgics,* and once, translating Virgil's Latin, in the eleventh *Aeneid* (749). Only once prior to 1697 did Dryden employ meditate as a transitive verb; in the *Virgil,* however, he writes of a bull that he "meditates his absent Enemy" (*Aeneid* 12. 162), a verbatim recollection of a line in his third *Georgic* (361), which in its turn may have been influenced by Virgil's *meditantem in proelia* (*Aeneid* 10. 455)—translated by Dryden as "meditate the war" (639).

Perhaps meditate deserves a digression, for the *OED* states that it is "now rare" as a transitive verb, giving as one example Dryden's post-1697 use in *Sigismonda and Guiscardo,* an epic simile which describes Sigismonda's father who, "like a Lion that unheeded lay, / Dissembling Sleep, and watchful to betray, / With inward Rage, he meditates his Prey" (ll. 242–44). This is particularly interesting as Dryden's sole pre-1697 use of meditate transitively comes in *Absalom and Achitophel,* again part of an epic simile:

> Though now his [the Duke of York's] mighty Soul its Grief contains;
> He meditates Revenge who least complains.
> And Like a Lyon, Slumbring in the way
> Or Sleep-dissembling . . .
>
> [ll. 445–48]

Incidentally, it will be remembered that in the third *Georgic* it is a bull that "meditates his absent Enemy," and it should be pointed out that in both uses in the *Aeneid* the word occurs in epic similes descriptive of Turnus, once as a bull and once as a lion. Meditate in Virgil's *meditantem in proelia* is part of the epic simile in which Turnus is likened to a lion which sees a bull from afar, and this conjunction seems to have started a minor fad. John Ozell either recalled Virgil or borrowed from Dryden for the opening couplet of an epic simile in his translation of Boileau's *Le Lutrin* (1708), for he wrote, "So two fierce *Bulls,* who Rival-Passions share / For some

118

lov'd *Heifer,* Meditate a War" (p. 92). Earlier, Blackmore, that great pick-upper of unguarded literary lumber, had written (in *Prince Arthur* (1695, Bk. I, p. 1) that Satan "meditates new War" against God, and further exploited the expression in *King Arthur, Eliza,* and *Alfred.*[49] Still earlier, and in a work known to Dryden, Waller wrote that Dido "meditates re-venge" in his and Sidney Godolphin's *The Passion of Dido for Aeneas* (1658, l. 116). Later, possibly in recollection of Sigismonda's father who "medi-tates his Prey" in Dryden's poem, Pope describes a spaniel (mock heroi-cally?) as "Couch'd close he lyes and meditates the Prey" (*Windsor-Forest,* l. 102). Christopher Pitt, who owed more to Dryden than he admitted, used "meditates his prey" in his translation of the Cacus episode in the eighth *Aeneid.* Samuel Johnson quoted "King Charles," "Some affirm I meditated a war" in his *Dictionary* (1755), wrote of the cranes in his translation of Addison's *Battle of the Pygmies and the Cranes* that they "Sharpen their claws, and meditate the war," and came back to the word many years later in a translation of some lines from Euripides's *Medea,* "Murder meditates his prey." All of which establishes meditate as another convenient piece of epic diction.[50] Virgil also used the word in his *Eclogues,* both times with *musam* (1. 2 and 6. 8); and Milton has "to meditate my rural minstrelsy" in *Comus* (l. 546) and "strictly meditate the thankless muse" in the well-known passage in *Lycidas* (l. 66), which former phrase Joseph Warton took over for his translation of the line in the sixth *Eclogue,* "I meditate the rural minstrelsy" (1753, 1. 9).

Other words Dryden may well have gone to Virgil for are obscene (ill-omened, used of birds and animals), perplex (entangle), pitchy, profound (of the sea), protend (especially of a weapon), rebellow, scaly (especially of fish and snakes), smoky, and volumes (of the folds of a serpent). Obscene occurs only once in this sense in the canon before its two uses in the *Virgil.*[51] Virgil's *rursus perplexum (Aeneid* 9. 931) is somewhere in the background of Dryden's two uses of perplex, the earlier in the "perplexing thorns" of *Aeneid* (11. 794) and the later in the "wood perplex'd with thorns" of *Sigismonda and Guiscardo* (1. 43). Milton and others had so used per-plexed, of course, but here as with the other examples adduced, Virgil appears to be the ultimate source. Dryden uses pitchy twice in the *Aeneid* and once thereafter; Virgil uses *piceus* four times. Virgil's designation of the sea as *profundo* (the deep) in the *Aeneid* (12. 263) may have prompted Dryden's "the sea profound" (*Georgics* 3. 806), for he had not so used the word before and was to use it again of the sea in "the seas profound" of his translation of the first *Iliad* (714) and in "the vast profound" of *Ceyx and Alcyone,* (423). Dryden's protended spears and lances have their ances-

119

tors in *Virgil*;[52] his use of rebellow, six times in the *Virgil* and once in the later *Palamon and Arcite,* stems probably from the five uses of *remugio* in Virgil; his "skaly Herd" in *Annus Mirabilis* (59), a direct descendant of Virgil's *squamosusque draco* (*Georgics* 4. 408), part of the passage that inspired the lines in *Annus Mirabilis,* is, with the "scaly brood" of the second part of *Absalom and Achitophel* (l. 982), the only time he used scaly before its four appearances in his *Virgil.*[53] Smoky, a seemingly common enough word, enters and leaves the Dryden canon with five appearances in the *Virgil,* with his use of the verb to describe horses, probably deriving from Virgil's *equum fumanti* and *fumantis sudore* (*Georgics* 2. 542 and *Aeneid* 12. 388).[54] Three times, each time he encountered it in Virgil's Latin, Dryden translated *volumen,* used of a serpent's folds, as volumes; only once before had he so used the word, in *Annus Mirabilis* (492), and then it was in a passage inspired by Virgil's *Georgics* (3. 423–24), as he indicated in a marginal note.[55]

A few other possible influences suggest themselves. Dryden translated Virgil's *dependent lychni* (*Aeneid* 1. 726) as "depending Lamps" (1015), one of the few such uses in his poetry, although it may in turn have influenced later English poets, for Pope has "depending Lamps" in *Statius His Thebais* (610) and Wordsworth almost surely took his "many a blazing light / Depends" in his translation of the first *Aeneid* (1001–2) from Dryden. Cowper has dependent braids and garments in his translation of the *Iliad* (2. 544 and 10. 212). Dryden's bees, in the fourth *Georgic,* "make a large dependence from the bough" (806), even though he has no warrant for dependence in Virgil's Latin at this juncture. Where Dryden writes "dissolved in sleep" in *Ceyx and Alcyone* (346) he may have in mind Virgil's *solvitur in somnes* (*Aeneid* 4. 539) or even *somno vinoque soluti* (*Aeneid* 9. 189 and 236), despite his not using that phrase at any juncture in his translation of the *Aeneid.* The use of pomp to mean a solemn procession of funereal activity of one kind or another, as in *sollemnis . . . pompas* (*Georgics* 3. 22 and *Aeneid* 5. 53) is seen in Dryden's "solemn pomp" (*Aeneid* 2. 268 and 8. 883), "funeral pomp" (*Aeneid* 6. 1208; 7. 827; and 11. 261),[56] and in four other passages in his *Virgil* where the word is coupled with some act or expression of sorrow (*Georgics* 4. 373; *Aeneid* 3. 90; 4. 970; 11. 328). Finally, although other examples could be added,[57] Dryden's unequal combats, fights, forces, fields, strifes, foes, wars, and arms (sixteen in the *Virgil*) may recall Virgil's use of *impars,* once in the *Georgics* and three times in the *Aeneid.*

In addition, there is the possibility that Dryden was influenced in other parts of his poetic diction by famous passages in Virgil. He, like Thomson and Wordsworth after him, was attracted to the description of the nightingale robbed of her young that comes in the fourth *Georgic—philomela sub umbra / amissos queritur fetus, quos duros arator / observans nido implumis detraxit* (511–13)—and so to Virgil's *implumis* we owe Dryden's four uses of callow to describe young birds. So, too, his "storm impending" (536), a translation of *vento impendente* from the famous storm in the first *Georgic* (365) of which Swift and Gay were to make so much use.[58] When one adds all the above to the examples collected by Brower (pp. 116-17) and then reads his concluding sentence, "The poetic diction which Dryden and his contemporaries innocently bequeathed to the eighteenth century may thus be traced in part to the 'best of poets,' " the only objection would be to the tentativeness of "in part," which might better read "in large part." Other Latin poets, of course, contributed their smaller part in the formation of this body of poetic diction—Lucretius and Ovid come to mind—but the figure that looms largest is always Virgil's.

There is no study of Dryden's debt to his English predecessors in the translation of Virgil's *Eclogues*, but it was considerable, especially, as with his *Georgics* and *Aeneid*, in the matter of rhyme words. Examination of these predecessors, those Dryden can be demonstrated to have known, reveals both that they used very little poetic diction and that the little that they did use left virtually no mark on Dryden's version. The predecessors in question are W. [illiam]. L. [isle], *Virgil's Eclogues Translated into English* (1628); Sir John Beaumont's version of the fourth *Eclogue* in his *Bosworth Field* (1629); John Biddle, *Virgil's Bucolicks Englished* (1634); Ogilby, in his translation of Virgil's Works (1649); Harrington's *Essay Upon Two Books of Virgil's Eclogues and Two Books of his Aeneis* (1658) the various translators of the *Eclogues* in *Miscellany Poems* (1684), "edited" by Dryden; and Maitland, to whose translation of the *Aeneid* Dryden publicly acknowledged his debt. It is curious that these various versions of the *Ecloques* should have been so free of poetic diction, although it will be recalled that examination of earlier English pastoral literature revealed much the same state of affairs. In any event, Dryden's version of the ten *Eclogues* contains about one hundred pieces of poetic diction; Ogilby's, about forty; Maitland's, about seventy; and the sum of those in *Miscellany Poems* (1684) is about fifty. Dryden's version coincides with that of one or another of his predecessors in the matter of poetic diction about twenty times, virtually always in quite unremarkable ways—mossy springs, leafy shades, briny, sylvan, downy peaches, glossy plums, for example.[59] Given the fact that there is so much dialogue in the ten *Eclogues*, one would not expect quite so much poetic diction as Dryden incorporated in his version, but he overworked the coronation figure (eleven times), made his boars tusky, his Morn rosy, his fires heapy, his pools weedy, his sheep woolly, and his streams purling. His towers are obnoxious, his woods vocal; fleece is pompous, shade is grateful, vintage is generous, eyes are dejected, and a head is devoted. Here, then, is one place where Dryden seems to pile it on a bit too heavily.

So far as Dryden's use of poetic diction in his translation of the *Georgics* is concerned, he is most likely to have been influenced by Ogilby. Mrs. Hooker's conclusions about Dryden's use of Ogilby, based almost entirely on rhyme words and on occasional verbatim or near-verbatim borrowings, is that the "greater translator's labors" were speeded by the "pedestrian poet."[60] This, of course, is true, but if, as Mrs. Hooker states, one hundred and five rhyme words in Dryden's four *Georgics* "clearly derive" from Ogilby's version,[61] Dryden's fairly extensive use of the pedestrian poet is clear. Ogilby goes back to Thomas May's version of the *Georgics* often, but he too borrows mostly rhyme words, and since May's version, unlike his translation of Lucan, is relatively innocent of poetic diction, neither Ogilby nor Dryden was influenced by him. A glance at Mrs. Hooker's parallels between May's and Dryden's translations shows that poetic diction is not involved. One slight indication of how Dryden may have been influenced by Ogilby can be seen from an example cited by Mrs. Hooker in a footnote[62] in which Dryden is said to be borrowing from May. While this borrowing is apparent, it is worth noting that in the passage in question where May has "seed," Ogilby, who is also much indebted to May's version of this passage, has "genital seed," and Dryden has "genial seed," the bit of poetic diction clearly prompted by Ogilby. Mrs. Hooker states that Lauderdale, Addison, Sedley, and others "often used Ogilby as a base, easily improving on what they found. In his turn, Dryden later used the improvements."[63] This statement holds true for poetic diction as well as for rhyme words, the aspect of these borrowings which are of most interest to Mrs. Hooker.

Further indication of the possible influence of Ogilby's version of the *Georgics* upon the poetic diction of Dryden's translation of these same poems can be seen in a few other places. Thus, where Ogilby has "annual cessation" (165) Dryden has "better'd by Cessation" (1. 109) in a line followed by a couplet whose rhyme words are also taken from Ogilby. A few lines further both have sleepy poppies. Also, in the first *Georgic*, Ogilby has bright stars that shoot headlong through the skies (the rhyme word is arise, p. 79); Dryden's stars fall headlong from the skies (the rhyme word is arise, 11. 501–2). In the second *Georgic* both translate Virgil's *non sua poma* (82) as "Apples not her own," although neither here nor in any other of these examples does May coincide with them. Ogilby, within a space of five lines in the second *Georgic,* has both fleecy Sheep and crystall Springs (p. 98); in the same passage Dryden has fleecy Flocks and Crystal Streams (11. 270 and 276). They also share the rhyme words for one couplet that comes between the two phrases, further evidence of Dryden's awareness of Ogilby's version at this juncture. Dryden's lines (420–21) of this *Georgic,* descriptive of a flame, read "At length victorious to the Top aspires, / Involving all the Wood in smoky Fires," clearly derived, with its two Latinisms, from Ogilby's "A Victor strait from bough to bough aspires, / And the crown seiz'd, involveth all with Fires" (p. 103). Dryden's "wanton Kids" (2. 765) owe something to the "wanton Sport" of Ogilby's kids (p. 112), and his resorting to the old coronation imagery in "provoke his health in Goblets crown'd" probably derives from Ogilby's "Goblets crown" (p. 112) rather than May's "the cups are crown'd." The last two words of this *Georgic* in Dryden's version are "smoaking Horse"; they come from the "smoaking Steeds" of the last line in Ogilby's translation. While the "hoary Beards" of goats (3. 485) are perhaps even more commonplace than the parallels already quoted, Ogilby's "hoarie Chin" in the same passage (p. 127) probably prompted Dryden to have recourse to the phrase. This may be true of his "Is wool thy care?" (3. 590), for Ogilby has "Is Milk thy care?" (p. 131) in a passage close to that which Dryden translates. And it should be noted that in Ogilby's next line he has "salt Herbage," as has Dryden at line 606. Both describe the lesser bees in the fourth *Georgic* as "the Vulgar" in the same passage (1. 94 and p. 143); both describe the fall of bees in battle as headlong (1. 116 and p. 143), as does May here. While these examples are not numerous, they do show where some of Dryden's poetic diction came from.[64]

Dryden, according to Professor Hooker, took "sixteen rhyme words, three identical lines, and one line nearly identical"[65] from the anonymous translator of verses 209 to 285 of Virgil's third *Georgic.* This translation, entitled *Amor omnibus idem,* published in 1693 in *Examen Poeticum,* is praised by Dryden in the Postscript to his *Virgil,* and is, hence, of more than passing interest. As far as parallels or borrowings in poetic diction are concerned, in the nearly identical line Dryden took from the earlier version his "And rough in the flinty Rock he lies" (373), deriving from "Rough on the flinty Ground all Night he lyes," the use of flinty qualifies as poetic diction. Both translators use war to mean battle; both use the Latinism infuse. Dryden has a lioness which "scour's o'er the plain" (382); his predecessor has horses which "scour amain." And Dryden's "slimy Juice" (441) comes directly from his predecessor's "slimy, pois'nous juice." Dryden also knew and borrowed from Addison's translation of the fourth *Georgic, except the story of Aristaeus.* Specifically, and solely in the matter of poetic diction, Dryden's "painted Lizard" (16) comes from Addison's "the Lizard's painted brood" (18), his "clammy Juice" (58) from Addison's "clammy dews" (46); and his bees "skim the Floods" (76), while Addison's "skim the brook" (66). Addison has "airy ramblings" (125), and Dryden has "airy march" (86); Addison has the "watry sign" (304), and Dryden has "watry Scorpion" (341). Finally, Addison's triplet, "Oft broods of Moths infest the hungry swarms, / And oft the furious Wasp their hive alarms / With louder hums, and unequal arms" (318–20), provides Dryden with the rhyme words for his couplet, "Or Wasps infest the Camp with loud Alarms, / And mix in Battel with unequal Arms" (358–59), as well as the Latinism infest (attack) and the epic "unequal arms."

Part of Virgil's 4th Georgick, Englished by an Unknown Hand appeared in *Sylvae* and was attributed to Creech in the fourth edition of *Dryden's Miscellany.* Professor Hooker points out that the passage appears in Lauderdale's edition and hence assumes it was his,[66] but Margaret P. Boddy reattributes it to Creech in the belief that Lauderdale simply took the passage bodily for his edition, just as he had with previously published translations of parts of the *Aeneid* by Dryden and John Stafford.[67] The translation, whether by Creech or Lauderdale, is of the Aristaeus and Proteus episode, and Dryden may have recalled its "scaly Flock" in his own "finny Flocks" (621) and its use of provoke in "the hungry Wolves provoke" in his "Provoke the prouling Wolf to nightly War" (630). His line "For near the confines of Etherial Light" (706) comes from "For near the Confines of Aetherial Air." If Dryden was influenced in the poetic diction of his version of the *Georgics* by others of his predecessors—Knightly Chetwood, Henry Sacheveril, or John Sheffield, Earl of Mulgrave—the traces of such influence are slight indeed.

While Dryden's translation of the *Aeneid* is a storehouse of poetic diction, much—indeed most—of that diction can be found either in a previous English translation of the *Aeneid* or in earlier English poetry of one genre or another. Few of his -y adjectives are original with him, as has been seen, and he does not lean to the usual Latinism; he has no *agrestick* (Ogilby), *coinquinate* (Gorges), or *ingeminate* (Vicars), nor any word quite so inkhornish. He does the predictable, often following squarely in the footsteps of his predecessors in translations of Virgil, in the heavy use of monosyllabic rhyme words which, with their accompanying and often almost formulaic adjectives, were so useful to writers of heroic couplets. Band, breed, care, train, race are some of these words, and these are num'rous, martial, virgin, chosen, or one or another of several favored adjectives, depending upon the contexts in which they appear. Sometimes Dryden takes these and other words or phrases or usages directly from his predecessors—i.e., in translation of the same passages—more often the influence is of a more general kind. In what follows, except where Dryden's borrowing extends to more than just a word or phrase, the intent is solely to show the availability of most of the vocabulary of poetic diction to Dryden or any other poet writing in the last decade of the seventeenth century.

When Dryden writes "And after him the *Daucian* Twins were slain, / *Laris* and *Thimbrus,* on the *Latian* Plain" (10. 545–46) and follows this with "the Sword decides / The nice Distinction" (549–50), he owes both his rhyme words and his Latinate "Distinction" to Ogilby, who had written, "And you bold *Ducian* Twins were also slain, / *Laride,* and Thymber, on th' *Ausonian* Plain," followed by "But *Pallas* now a sad distinction made" (p. 479, 1654 ed.), where, as in Dryden, distinction means the act of distinguishing between the twins. Virgil has *discrimina* (393). Here, then, is one example of Dryden's taking a bit of poetic diction directly from a predecessor. Another example is Dryden's "Conscious of the audacious Deed" (11. 1185), where conscious means guiltily conscious, which has as its ancestors Vicars's "conscious of the deed" (11. p. 370) and Ogilby's "conscious of so bold a wickedness" (11. p. 543), but which owes most to John Stafford's "Conscious of the audacious bloody deed." By the time of Stafford's translation of the death of Camilla the word conscious had become *de rigeur* in the line in question. Now Virgil's Latin here is *conscius audacis facti* (812), and Dryden may simply be translating literally, but he is close to Stafford in enough other ways, including identical rhyme words in the next couplet, to arouse the belief that in this line as in others, he was deliberately following him. And Dryden also follows his predecessors in the translation of Book 4, the very popular story of Dido and Aeneas, in the use of conscious, three of the seven uses in his *Aeneid* coming in that book. So, too, with his two uses of devoted,—i.e., doomed, descriptive of Dido—for which he had precedent in Waller's version of the episode. Dryden's use of sable to describe the troop of ants in Book 4 derives from Godolphin's "sable armye" and Harrington's "sable troop." His "frequent funerals" (2. 491) may owe something to Vicars's use of the identical phrase (6. p. 186, 1632 ed.) and is, with his earlier use in *Annus Mirabilis* (1. 1069), probably somewhere in the background of Pope's "frequent herses" in the *Elegy to the Memory of an Unfortunate Lady* (1. 38). Dryden is translating Virgil's *plurima inertia corpore* (2. 364) in both places.

When Dryden uses invest to describe the putting on of Priam's armor in

125

Book 2 he may have Denham's use of the word in the same context in mind. The same holds true for his "humid Shades" in Book 4, for Sir Robert Howard had been beforehand with him, both of them translating literally Virgil's *umentibus umbris* (351), for which Loeb gives *"dewy* shades." Ross, the translator of Silius Italicus, also has a "humid Shade" (3. p. 64). For Dryden, in Book 4, the mountain, Atlas, is crowned with "piny Forests" (4. 364), the only use of that adjective in the *Virgil;* before him it had been used of Atlas in their translations of Book 4 by Stapylton, Fanshawe, and Harrington (Atlas's "piny crown").[68] Both Vicars and May also use piny to describe mountains. Similarly, "snowy Fleeces" appears but once in the *Virgil* and then in Book 4; again Dryden's predecessors in the translation of that book (Stapylton, Waller, Harrington, Howard) all use the phrase. Dryden, whose reliance upon Ogilby's *Virgil* has never been fully explored, takes his line, "Of a rough *Lybian* Bear, the Spoils he wore" (5. 49) from Ogilby's "Clad in rough Spoyls of a huge *Libyan* Bear" (5. p. 293) and his "Starry Frame," at least, in the line, *"Atlas,* whose Head sustains the Starry Frame" (8. 181) from Ogilby's *"Atlas,* they say, supports Heav'n's starrie frame" (8. p. 406).[69] And when Dryden, again in the popular fourth book, writes that "The Hearer on the Speaker's Mouth depends" (113), he may have recalled the "depends on what he says" of the anonymous *Didos Death* (A4ᵛ).

Some idea of how much of the poetic diction in Dryden's *Virgil* was already available to him can be had in the following admittedly incomplete analysis. Many words and phrases already had a history of extensive use, chiefly in epics and translations of epics but in other genres as well, including the drama.[70] Among these are: abodes (used chiefly of the Gods), aetherial, aspire (of flames and smoke), auspicious, callow (of the young of birds), craggy (of cliffs and rocks), cut (of progress through water or air), doubtful (of the outcome of battles), impetuous (of water), involve (clouds), massy (of gold or weapons), painted (of natural phenomena), pomp (in funereal context), profound (the sea), provoke (to battle), refulgent (arms), rend (the sky with sounds, usually human voices), sable (animals, clouds, shades of night), scour (of bodies of water and air), shaggy (of lions or bears), smoke (of horses), spoils (of a lion's hide), steely (of weapons), steepy (of rocks, cliffs, mountains), supine (of persons asleep), sway (power or rule), vaulted (sky), vital (breath, air, blood), yielding (air). To these must be added the various monosyllables (train, race, etc.) mentioned earlier with their accompanying adjectives, as well, of course, as those words occurring in passages Dryden has been shown to have taken directly from his predecessors. Additionally, certain epic formulas, part of epic diction, should be included: the person Known (or unknown) to Fame, high on a . . . (the elevated position of the epic hero or heroes), the higher (taller, superior) by a head (the greater size of the epic hero), the not half so and more than mortal comparisons, the fraud or force conjunction, and the easy conquests and unequal combats.

Certain words were frequently used in certain contexts, and Dryden so uses them; again most of these are to be found in the translations of Homer, Virgil, Ovid, and Lucan. Adverse, for example, had been used in a military context, by Harington in his translation of *Orlando Furioso,* by Shakespeare, by Chapman (in his *Homer*), Gorges and May in their translations of Lucan, by Vicars, Ogilby, and Thomas Fletcher in translations from Virgil, by Ross, by Cowley and Davenant, and by Ogilby in his *Homer.*[71] Other such words, and there is no necessity to list the predecessors, are balmy (of sleep), bearded (of grain), briny (of sweat), dewy (shades or shadows of night), dire (epithet), foamy (of a boar), gloomy (of night), mow (a battle metaphor), pitchy (clouds), snaky (of hair), and speckled (of serpents).

Dryden also coincides with earlier poets in using words in unusual fashions or in certain of his conjunctions of words. Thus, he has somebody assume the reins, a use characterized by the *OED* as "Of things, *rare,*" which has a precedent in his brother-in-law Sir Robert Howard's having somebody assume a spear. He calls the earth "this goodly Ball" (*Pastorals* 6. 52), as had Sylvester before him in his translation of DuBartas, the earlier English poet describing the earth as a ball at least thirteen times. Either or both may have recalled Shakespeare's "this goodly frame, the earth" in *Hamlet.* Dryden describes a weapon as beamy; Vicars had done so before him. Three times Dryden uses clammy to describe sweat; Vicars and Ogilby had done the same. He uses damasked of flowers, and he had precedents in Shakespeare, Drayton, and Phineas Fletcher—at least. His icicles that depend are descendants of Spenser's; his downy couch similarly descends from the downy beds of Sandys and May. His dubious fight can be found in Ross (or did he go to Milton's in dubious battle?), his ductile gold in Sandys, his foamy bridle in Vicars, his milky mothers in Spenser and Phineas Fletcher, his milky dams also in Phineas Fletcher, his obscene birds in Cowley and Blackmore, plumy crests (four of them) in Vicars, his rebellow[ing] shores in Chapman, his steep of Heav'n and his swarthy Memnon in Thomas Fletcher's translation of part of the *Aeneid* (1692), his sovereign sway in Shakespeare, and his windy wings in Sylvester.

There are still more. Aetherial fire was to be found in Sandys, an auspicious Prince in both Chamberlayne's *Pharonnida* and Davenant's *Gondib-*

127

ert, with auspicious aid in Vicars. *Pharonnida* has clammy dews, Vicars has dolphins which cut the sea, and Sandys has doubtful in description of that period of time between light and darkness. Dryden uses expire to mean breathe out nine times and express to mean show or reveal three times; the former is so used by Ross, and the latter is so used by Gorges, May, and Sir Robert Howard. Ross, like Dryden, uses fallacious to mean deceitful or treacherous. Dryden's two uses of the verb glean to mean "To cut off (a remnant or straggler) in warfare" *(OED)* had precedent in the Bible and in Cowley's *Davideis.* His impetuous tides and torrents had made earlier appearances in *Pharonnida;* his leavy woods in Chapman and Vicars. A use of officious, descriptive of animals, can be paralleled in Sylvester's *DuBartas;* his officious servants can be traced to Vicars and Davenant. He and Vicars use perplexed to mean entangled, as did Milton and others, of course. His use of ruin as a noun, for example, "But down she falls, and spreads a Ruin thro' the Plain" (*Aeneid* 2. 855), although it has precedents in Spenser and Milton, is paralleled by Ross's "with a vast ruin . . . He falls" (Book 4, p. 99), and Ross's translation of Silius Italicus antedates Milton's *Paradise Lost.* Ross and Dryden have servile hands; Harrington and Dryden both use shoaly. While such bare listings are monotonous, it is only by some such method, and it is necessary to repeat that the list is not exhaustive, that one can suggest the store of poetic diction available to Dryden.

If one were to have to select the one probable major source for Dryden's poetic diction it almost surely would have to be Ogilby's translation of *Homer* and *Virgil,* and to a minor extent, his translation of Aesop's fables. Some of Dryden's direct borrowings from Ogilby have already been discussed. To these must be added the possibility that Dryden was influenced strongly by the presence of the following words and phrases in Ogilby's translations. Abodes in both are dark (14 in Dryden), blest (4), new (4), and high; light is aetherial; fire aspires; grain is bearded; sweat is briny or clammy; and the young of birds are callow, as is the down on the cheeks of a youth. These words and phrases were and had been, for the most part, common poetic property, as were most of the further examples to follow, but the present intent is to show how many were present in the translations of the man whose *Virgil* was nearest in time to Dryden's. It is no good arguing that Dryden would surely not have depended heavily on any aspect of a translation he was seeking to supersede; such considerations belong to a more modern era. To resume. Water is cut in both poets, the shades of night are dewy, clouds are dusky, hands are erected, a boar is foamy as are billows, both the sea and the deep are glassy (the only two uses in Dryden's *Virgil*), and night, shades, groves, and shades of night are gloomy. Both use

128

infuse of something medicinal or healing; the unusual pory occurs in both. Sound rends the sky in both, and the shades of night as well as the wings of night are sable. The air is scoured, poppies are sleepy (a direct steal), horses smoke, a neck is snowy, serpents are speckled, rocks (etc.) are steepy, sleepers are supine, trains are num'rous, conquests are unequal, the sky is vaulted, breath and air are vital, and the air is yielding (at least eight times in Ogilby's *Virgil*).

By 1700, then, with the death of Dryden, English poetic diction, especially in its two main divisions, epic diction and the diction of poetry of natural description, was fairly well codified, largely, but not, of course, solely because of his efforts. And largely, too, as is quite evident, as a result of his work in translation. Wherever he derived his poetic diction, and it was almost entirely derivative, it was gathered together in his *Virgil* and in the translations in *Fables Ancient and Modern*. When Dryden died, Alexander Pope was a boy of twelve, already straining at the poetic leash. For two years after Dryden's death the fourteen-year-old Pope tried his hand at translating parts of Ovid's *Metamorphoses*. And it was he, as has been said more than once, who did so much further to popularize the poetic diction that he inherited from Dryden.

NOTES AND REFERENCES

1. Reynolds, *Treatment of Nature*, p. 43 and n.

2. Ibid., p. 46.

3. Havens, "Poetic Diction of the English Classicists," in *Kittredge Anniversary Papers*, p. 442.

4. Quayle, *Poetic Diction*, p. 28; see pp. 87-8.

5. Van Doren, *John Dryden: A Study of His Poetry* (Bloomington, Ind.: University of Indiana Press, 1960), pp. 55 and 56; first published as *The Poetry of John Dryden* in 1920.

6. Loane, *Notes and Queries*, for Nov. 6, 1943, p. 280.

7. Blackmore was quick to pick up "feathered death"; see his *King Arthur* (1697), Bk. 1, p. 19.

8. Arthos, *Language of Natural Description*, p. 372.

9. Dryden was defended against Van Doren's strictures by William Frost in *Dryden and the Art of Translation* (New Haven: Yale University Press, 1955), p. 43.

10. California *Dryden* (Los Angeles and Berkeley: University of California Press, 1956), p. 293.

11. There are about 40 items of poetic diction in a poem of 1216 lines, about one in every seven or eight four-line stanzas.

12. "Fenny" appears once before the *Virgil,* twice in it; "finny" appears once in a pre-1697 translation from Ovid and then five times in the *Virgil.*

13. See, however, pp. 126-27.

14. Proudfoot, *Dryden's "Aeneid."*

15. Hooker, "Dryden's *Georgics* and English Predecessors," *HLQ* 9 (1942–43),273–309.

16. There is not, to my knowledge, any comparable studies of Dryden's reliance upon previous translators of Ovid's *Metamorphoses,* Lucretius's *De Rerum Natura,* and Theocritus's *Idyllia.*

17. Proudfoot, *Dryden's "Aeneid,"* p. 266.

18. Ibid.

19. Ibid., pp. 222–25.

20. Ibid., p. 225; see pp. 100-01 for my comments on this sentiment.

21. Tillotson, *APD,* pp. 28, 49.

22. Ibid., pp. 35, 74.

23. Arthos, *Language of Natural Description,* pp. 294–95, 156–57, and 208–9.

24. Proudfoot, *Dryden's "Aeneid,"* p. 230.

25. "Beamy" goes back at least to the "beamy black" of Stella's eyes in Sydney's *Astrophel and Stella,* 1591.

26. *OED* also quotes a 1620 work and defines the word as "chiefly as a poetic epithet of the wild boar."

27. Proudfoot, *Dryden's "Aeneid,"* p. 229.

28. *Critical Essays on Some of the Poems of Several English Poets,* 1785, p. 83.

29. He also has "erected hands" in the *Aeneid* (12. 292); Ogilby uses the phrase twice in his translation of the *Odyssey.*

30. Milton's "While smooth Adonis from his native rock / Ran purple to the sea, supposed with blood / Of Thammuz yearly wounded" (*Paradise Lost* 1. 450–52) is a splendid example.

31. Watson, 2. 24–25.

32. Ibid., 2. 26.

33. California *Dryden,* vol. 3, p. 293 n. 6; John Evelyn's translation of the first book of Lucretius influenced nobody, nor did Sir Robert Howard's version of part of the fifth book.

34. Watson, 2. 29.

35. Ibid.

36. Kinsley, *The Poems of John Dryden,* p. 1958.

37. With "air," 2. 139 and 220, 5. 542 and 1409; "sea," 1. 426, 2. 45 and 328; "waters," 1. 428; "tide," 1. 435; "flood," 2. 223; "flames," 2. 436; and "sky," 4. 183.

38. Arthos, *Language of Natural Description,* pp. 351–53; Tillotson, *APD,* p. 49.

39. This is the modern numbering of the *Idyllia;* the "thirty-first" in the 1588 translation and in Sherburne's is actually the thirtieth; the "twenty-first" in Sherburne is actually the twentieth.

40. Kinsley, *The Poems of John Dryden,* p. 1946. William Bowles, Fellow of King's College, Cambridge from 1680 to 1688, translated the second, tenth, fourteenth, and twentieth idyllia for Dryden's *Miscellany Poems* (1684).

41. Watson, 2. 30; see also 2. 268.

42. Ibid., 1. 154 and 2. 219–20.

43. Ibid. 2. 268.

44. Richard Duke, who translated the eleventh idyllium, has "a craggy cliff," the "foaming deep," the "yielding tide," and "flowers that crown each season."

45. Joseph Warton, *The Works of Virgil,* 1753, vol. 1, pp. iii and iv.

46. Arthos, *Language of Natural Description,* p. 17.

47. Reuben Brower, "Dryden's Poetic Diction and Virgil," *PQ* 18 (1939),211–17.

48. See Dryden's conflation of *caeruleus Proteus* (388) and *immania cuius / armenta et turpis pascit sub gurgite phocas* (394–95) for *Annus Mirabilis* (59–60).

49. Respectively, "meditates Delay," Bk. 8, p. 209; "meditating War," Bk. 6, p. 152; and "meditating Revenge" and "meditating new War," Bk. 11, p. 387 and Bk. 12, p. 411—all citations from the first editions.

50. Add Robert Stapylton's translation of *Aeneid* 4. 1634, 87^v; Dryden's *Of the Pythagorean Philosophy,* 1. 640; Pope in the *Episode of Sarpedon,* 11. 23 and 141, two of the fourteen uses in his *Iliad* (there are four in the *Odyssey* translation); Rowe's translation of Lucan's *Pharsalia,* 1722 ed., 2. 1056, 5. 471, and 10. 60. Broome's translation of the tenth *Iliad,* 1739, p. 102 ("meditates the war"); Thomson's *Winter,* 1746 ed., 1. 898; Pitt's translation of the *Aeneid,* 4. 692, 8. 270 ("meditates the prey"), and 11. 1066; Cowper's translation of the *Iliad,* 1791, 10. 248, 12. 368, and 23. 30.

51. *Georgics* 1. 635, translating Virgil's *obscenaeque canes importunaeque volueres,* 1. 470, and *Aeneid* 3. 341, translating Virgil's *obscenaeque volucres,* 1. 263. See also *obscenas . . . volucris,* and *obscenae volucris* at *Aeneid* 3. 241 and 12. 876.

52. Four times in Dryden's *Aeneid* and twice in translations from the *Metamorphoses* in *Fables Ancient and Modern;* for Virgil, see *Aeneid* 11. 605–6, *hastasque... protendunt.*

53. See also Virgil's *Georgics* 2. 154, 3. 426 and *Aeneid* 2. 218–19.

54. See Dryden's *Aeneid* 9. 516; 12. 510, 696 and his *Georgics* 2. 794.

55. In Virgil, *Aeneid* 2. 208; 5. 85; and 11. 753; in Dryden, 2. 286; 5. 113; 11. 1110.

56. 11. 261 translates Virgil's *haec pompa,* 11. 163.

57. Thus, Virgil's *involvit flammia* (*Georgics* 2. 308) is an ancestor of Dryden's "involv'd in Fire" (*Aeneid* 2. 476) and other involvements in fire and smoke.

58. Virgil also has *pluvia impendente* in the fourth *Georgic* (191).

59. My examination of borrowings *of all kinds* shows Dryden heavily indebted to Ogilby. Details of this dependence form part of a separate study of Dryden's practice as translator.

60. Hooker, "Dryden's *Georgics,*" p. 290.

61. Ibid., p. 287.

62. Ibid., p. 283 n. 21.

63. Ibid., p. 288.

64. Dryden's "clammy drops" of sweat in the third *Georgic* (750) may be a reminiscence of Ogilby's "clammy sweat" in a different passage in that same poem (p. 137)

65. Hooker, "Dryden's *Georgics,*" p. 301.

66. Ibid., p. 294.

67. Boddy, "The 1692 Fourth Book of Virgil," *RES,* N.S. 15 (1964),375–76.

68. Loeb translates Atlas's "pine-wreathed head."

69. OED gives Marlowe's and Nashe's *Dido* for "starry frame."

70. I use only Shakespeare's play and poems, except where I have found material from other dramatists quoted in *OED.*

71. See p. 00 for Wordsworth's similar use of the word in his translation from Virgil.

Chapter 6.

Pope

Since Pope's earliest translations were from Ovid's *Metamorphoses,* there is the possibility that in them and in his later work, both original poems and further translations, he derived some of his epic poetic diction from the Latin poet or his English translators.[1] Dr. Johnson wrote that "Homer doubtless owes to his translator"—he was summing up his views of Pope's translation—"many Ovidian graces not exactly suited to his character,"[2] but he did not stop to give any examples of these graces and his few words on Ovid make it impossible to guess what he meant. A modern critic is more specific. "The poetic diction of the eighteenth century may be said to begin," writes Tillotson, "as far as English goes, in Sylvester's translation of DuBartas." He continues, however, with the statement that "it was probably not Sylvester, but his imitator Sandys, who did most to fix the vocabulary of 'progressive' English poetry for more than a century."[3] Tillotson points to Sandys's moderate "Latinizing" of his syntax, to his imitation of "the Latin use of present and past participles as adjectives," and to his use of "verbs derived from Latin instead of composite English verbs" in his translation of Ovid's *Metamorphoses.* And he lists as Sandys's "group of favourite and semi-favourite words: anxious (often with cares), pensive, ratify, promiscuously, sad, trembling, glittering, nodding, sylvan, refulgent, pale, alternate, sings (of hail and arrows), yielding, involves."[4] The relative importance of Sandys's translation of the *Metamorphoses* can only be arrived at by a close comparison of it with the translations from the *Metamorphoses* by Dryden and Pope, always with an eye to the history of poetic diction and with Tillotson's claims for Sandys's importance in this history in mind. Golding's translation (1567) will serve as a further possible source of poetic diction.

Pope early conceived an extreme fondness for Sandys's translation of the *Metamorphoses,* led to it, he told Joseph Spence, by Ogilby's translation of Homer.[5] Among his early translations were the stories of Dryope, Polyphemus and Acis, and Vertumnus and Pomona from Books 9, 13, and 14 of the *Metamorphoses.* The editors of Volume 1 of the Twickenham *Pope* state that, for his version of the Polyphemus and Acis story, Pope "studied closely the version of two great predecessors, Sandys and Dryden," knew both the 1626 and revised 1632 Sandys translations, and "when neither edition provided him with the inspiration he sought, he had recourse to Dryden, who had also admired Sandys, and whose use of him provided an example Pope was quick to follow." They also write that Pope depended less and less on Sandys for his versions of the other two stories from Ovid.[6] Dryden's opinion of Sandys is voiced in two places. His second and final say on Sandys's abilities as a translator of Ovid's *Metamorphoses* occurs in the Preface to *Fables Ancient and Modern,* his last work. He states there that it was "the ingenious and learned Sandys, the best versifier of the former age" who had given the stories in Ovid "the same turn of verse which they had in the original."[7] Dryden had translated the first book of the *Metamorphoses* for *Examen Poeticum,* published in 1693, and it was in the dedication of that work to Lord Radcliffe that he made his first, and disparaging, remark on Sandys's abilities as a translator.[8] Despite this disparagement, however, Dryden made quite free with Sandys's version, beginning his translation with a couplet, "Of Bodies chang'd to various Forms I sing: / Ye Gods, from whom these Miracles did spring," which comes unabashedly from Sandys's opening lines, "Of bodies chang'd to other shapes I sing. / Assist, you Gods (from you these changes spring)." His other borrowings, including rhyme words, number approximately one hundred and fifty, somewhat more than the approximately a hundred borrowings in his translation of the twelfth book of Ovid's work.[9] However, the bulk of these borrowings are in rhyme words, and when they are of words or phrases they are rarely items of poetic diction. Indeed, *pace* Tillotson, Sandys's influence on poetic diction, especially as it comes down to Dryden, is very slight. Sandys has some "ayrie Mountaines"; Dryden, "on *Parnassus* airy height." Sandys has "with Fears augments his waves"; Dryden has floods "augment the Sea." There are the usual blest abodes, aspiring fire or flames, bowls or cups crowned, dire ostents, fantastic dreams or visions, generous wine or grapes, impetuous seas or floods, clouds involved, liquid air and skies, vast profounds, sable clouds, trains of one sort or another, and watery deities. Both use the Latinisms care, confess, conscious, deduce, doubtful, grateful, invest, peculiar, protend (rain in Sandys), spoils, supine, sylvan, and vital. The -y adjectives common to both are not many or remarkable: starry, flaggy, gaudy, gloomy, leavy, pitchy, plumy, ruddy, sappy, and watery. Birds cut the air, falls are headlong, eyes are humid, and the points of weapons are rebated—and that is all. Not that that is all the poetic diction in Sandys nor that Dryden could not have been influenced elsewhere in his poetry by Sandys; it is only that the sum of the coincidences in poetic diction between Dryden's translation from the *Metamorphoses* and Sandys's translation of the entire twenty-four books is small.[10]

The Twickenham editors do not mention Golding's translation of the *Metamorphoses* as in any way a model or source for any part of Pope's early translations from Ovid. There is evidence that Pope had read Golding and had declared that his translation was "a pretty good one, considering the time when it was written";[11] there is not, on the contrary, any evidence that Dryden knew Golding's version. This is all the more remarkable because the translation, first published in its entirety in 1567 (the first four books appeared in 1565), was reprinted at least seven times by 1675, and one would think that the book would have come to Dryden's notice. And yet Samuel Johnson, who knew Sandys and praised him as a poet in *Idler* No. 69, has left no recorded mention of Golding either. Possibly the lack of any edition beyond 1675 may partially account for this. In any event, Dryden's and Pope's versions of the story of Polyphemus and Acis from the thirteenth book of the *Metamorphoses* will be compared with Golding's and Sandys's for evidence of the transmission of poetic diction, as opposed to evidence of borrowing of all kinds.

Although Pope's version of the story of Polyphemus and Acis was first published posthumously in December 1749, it was written many years earlier when "he was improving himself in the Languages," as the advertisement to his *Works* (1736) states. By the time he was fourteen, the age at which he undertook this first translation from Ovid, he had read widely in poetry, classical and modern, and the translation shows evidence of that reading. Aside from the borrowings from Sandys's version of Ovid pointed out by the Twickenham editors, Pope was also under considerable debt to a number of poets who had helped in the transmission of poetic diction. This latter indebtedness does not extend to Sandys, whose *Ovid* is relatively free of poetic diction. Thus, in the 164 lines in Pope's version, in only two phrases is there the possibility that he took his poetic diction from Sandys.

Where Pope has "resounding main" (1. 47) Sandys has "far-resounding seas"; where the former has "your watry reign" the latter has "the empire where you you reign." But even in these two examples there is a good probability that Pope used the phrases he did simply because they were, and had for some time been, part of the stock language of much poetry. And, in any event, Ovid has "regnis" in the second of the passages. Pope also has warrant for his "shady cave" in Ovid's *opaca . . . caverna,* for "crystal" in Ovid's *vitro,* for "rocky caverns" in *vivo pendentia saxo / antra,* and for "shady grove" in *sylvestri nata sub umbra.* What is infinitely more important than Pope's indebtedness to previous translators of Ovid—and he owes nothing to Golding in this or in the other two translations[12]—is the extent to which he himself introduces poetic diction. Whatever warrant he may have had in Ovid's Latin, he elects, unlike previous translators of this story, to introduce the following: care, steepy, pondrous, depend, airy nest, plumy trains, rowling orb, native deeps, watry reign, reedy wreaths, azure, and crystal fountain. From Dryden's translation of the story he takes or is influenced by the following, Dryden's translation being quoted first: crystal stream, crystal brook; airy walk, airy steep; wool decks, leaves deck. Pope probably derived his "steepy height" from any one of a number of places in Dryden, for the latter uses steepy nineteen times, thirteen of these occurrences being in his *Virgil.* And Dryden also has a "steepy Height" in his translation of Ovid's twelfth book, 1. 456. The "downy cheeks" Pope gives Acis may come from those Dryden gives Corythus in his translation of Ovid's twelfth book (1. 404). Golding's version has "mossy down"; Sandys's, "scarce appearing down"; and Dryden, in his version, "doubtful down." Downy, as applied to young men, had been used by Gorges (hairs), Vicars (chin), and Ogilby (cheeks—twice). On several occasions, however, Pope avoided the poetic diction present in Dryden's version. He evidently preferred his own "all heav'n" to Dryden's "aetherial throne," his own "flocks" to Dryden's "wooly care," his own "strutting udders" to Dryden's "sweepy weight," and his own "clear lake" to Dryden's "watry glass." He avoids Dryden's use of grateful in the sense of pleasing, has only shells where Dryden has "orient shells," opts for "resounding main" in preference to "watry plains," and has no real equivalents for Dryden's "shady grove" and "watry family." One's final impression is that translations of Ovid were more and more encrusted with poetic diction from the time of Golding on, with the heaviest accumulations coming after Dryden's *Virgil* in 1697 and reaching a point of maximum use in rival versions of the *Metamorphoses* published in 1717.

Pope's translation of the Vertumnus and Pomona episode in Ovid's fourteenth book was first published in 1712, although it may have been written at the same time as the Polyphemus and Acis story. The Twickenham editors find it a better work than the earlier translation, partly because it is less literal, partly because Pope gave himself greater liberty by expanding the seventy-nine lines of the original to one hundred and twenty-three.[13] Yet, in this version as in the earlier, the intrusion of poetic diction is quite remarkable. Only once does Ovid's Latin provide a source for Pope's choice of an item of poetic diction, namely in "the luxuriant Year" (1. 10) which derives from the earlier poet's *luxuriem* (1. 629), possibly via Sandys's "luxurious twigs" (p. 407). But Pope's version includes for the first time: a sylvan train, vegetable care, flow'ry (field, garland, plant, ground), decent, sylvans (twice), frequent, trembling, crown (twice as verb), care (twice), milky, florid, refulgent, and the various God. Most of these words and phrases were already shopworn; Pope may have taken others from a particular source. Thus, "vegetable care" is sufficiently unusual, but it has antecedents in Andrew Marvell's "vegetable love" from the poem *To His Coy Mistress* (1. 11), Milton's "fruit of vegetable gold" in *Paradise Lost* (4. 220), and in Dryden's "vegetable arts" in the fourth *Georgic* (1. 178), for which, incidentally, there is no close source in Virgil. Pope's "various God," descriptive of Vertumnus, may owe something to Dryden's use of the same words to describe Proteus in the fourth *Georgic* (1. 610) and Iris in the *Aeneid* (4. 1003), with the necessary change of God to Goddess. Dryden also writes of "the various Iris" in the *Aeneid* (9. 2). Pope passes up Sandys's "vernal frost" for "no frost," and contents himself with "our Alban woods" where Sandys has "Alba's high and shady hils imbrowne."

The Twickenham editors compare the opening four lines of Pope's translation of the Vertumnus and Pomona episode to Sandys's, calling attention to the former's use of "Sylvan Train" as opposed to the older poet's "Latin Hamadryades," and to the fact that "Pope also humanizes his plants, in a way that Sandys does not, by the coupling of epithets and nouns in such phrases as nobler Race and Vegetable Care; yet it might be argued that Pope has the better succeeded in capturing the tender zeal in pastoral care which is attributed to Pomona, at least by implication, in the original. Of course Pope must have learned the use of such phrases, in part, from Sandys himself. They were a means of saying a great deal in little, and thereby a means of reproducing, in a near-equivalent number of words, the classical original. By using even more of them than Sandys, Pope was able to smooth out his lines and, at the same time, retain the substance of the original."[14] A desire to find poetic excellences even in Pope's earlier works has led the Twickenham editors too far. The effect of the poetic diction in "Sylvan train," "nobler Race," and "Vegetable Care" may be to smooth Pope's lines, but the long history of the use of these stock phrases—I exempt vegetable as adjective from this category—makes for artificiality. Possibly Golding's version will seem too primitive by comparison,

> In this kings reigne *Pomona* livd. There was not too bee found
> Among the woodnymphes any one in all the *Latian* ground
> That was so conning for to keepe an Ortyard as was shee,
> Nor none so paynefull to preserve the frute of every tree.
>
> [11. 709–12]

but there is no suggestion of the *dejà lu* that mars Pope's lines.

What is true of the two earlier translations from Ovid is also true of Pope's third, his version of the Dryope story in the ninth book, published in 1717. Besides the possible, albeit remotely possible, indebtedness to Golding in his "milky moisture," already referred to, Pope's lines, "A Lake there was, with shelving banks around, / Whose verdant summit fragrant myrtles crown'd" (15–16) come obviously from Sandys's, "A Lake there is, which shelving mergents bound, / Much like a shore; with fragrant myrtles crownd" (11. 353–54).[15] Even though Ovid's Latin reads *est lacus, adclivis devexo margine formam / litoris efficiens, summum myrteta coronant* (11. 334–35), there can be no doubt that Pope was writing with Sandys before him. Demonstration of the obvious fact that little needs inevitably be the same in translations of the same passage lies in Golding's version of these lines: "There is a certain leaning Lake whose bowing banks doo show / A likenesse of the salt sea shore. Upon the brim doo grow / All round about it Mirtle trees" (11. 403–5). For one line Pope went to Dryden again, for where the former writes "Thy branches hung with humid pearls appear" (1. 65) the latter has "And hung with humid Pearls the lowly Shrub appears" (1. 20) in his translation of Virgil's tenth *Eclogue.* Pope's "conscious Morn" (1. 98) may be a recollection of Dryden's "conscious Morn" ("The Speeches of Ajax and Achilles" from Ovid's thirteenth book, 1. 22); his "watry Plain," 1. 250, appears twice in Dryden's translations from Ovid; in Book 1. 170 and in the Acis, Polyphemus, and Galatea episode from Book 13. 61. Pope's own contribution to the poetic diction in this 103-line translation consists of: verdant (twice), flow'ry (plant and garlands), trembling (twice), sylvan (adj.), honours (i.e., branches), shady woods, latent life, crystal lakes and floods, and watry Lotos. And in the last three words of line 4, "And kindly sigh for sorrows not your own," he falls back on an epic formula which may be best remembered by his mock epic use of it to

137

close Canto 1 of his *Rape of the Lock:* "And *Betty's* prais'd for Labours not her own." Twice, however, Pope refuses to follow Sandys in a bit of poetic diction, preferring "th' unpitying pow'rs of heav'n" (1. 70) to Sandys's "the powres imbowr'd in heaven" and "my head" (1. 97) to Sandys's "my leavy top." In fairness to Pope, also, it must be said that his "watry *Lotos*" comes from Ovid's *aquatica lotos* (1. 341) and his "trembling tree" that "with sudden horror shook" (1. 30) from *tremulo ramos horrore moveri* (1. 345). But then, of course, Golding had a plain "lote tree" for the first and branches that were "shuddring horribly" in the second, again unnecessary evidence of the choices open to translators.

Pope was not alone, however, either in his reliance on Dryden's *Virgil* or in his rather extensive use of poetic diction in translating Ovid. When Samuel Croxall is remembered, if he is remembered at all, it is as the author of *The Fair Circassian,* which the *Dictionary of National Biography* chastely characterizes as "a poetical adaptation of the Song of Solomon, which too closely copies the oriental warmth of the original." The work was dedicated to a Mrs. Anna Maria Mordaunt and won its clergyman-author a certain continuing notoriety as it went through many editions. However, Croxall was sufficiently well thought of as a poet, either by Sir Samuel Garth or somebody else connected with the 1717 *Ovid's Metamorphoses: In Fifteen Books: Translated by the Most Eminent Hands,* to have been entrusted with the translation of Ovid's sixth book, three episodes in the eighth, one in the tenth, most of the eleventh, and a very brief episode in the thirteenth. Incidentally, Pope's share in this edition was his translation of the Dryope story in the ninth book. Croxall, an indifferent poet at best, affords corroborative evidence of the reliance upon poetic diction observable in translations of the more popular classical works. The opening episode in Ovid's sixth book describes the metamorphosis of Arachne into a spider, the passage chosen to be compared with Golding's and Sandys's versions.

Initially, it can be said that Croxall owes nothing to Golding, and only possibly one example of what I have termed the coronation figure to Sandys. If Tillotson's statement that Sandys "did most to fix the vocabulary of 'progressive' English poetry for more than a century"[16] is true, his influence on the poetic diction of later translators of Ovid is remarkably slight. Without any sanction in Ovid's Latin nor in Golding or Sandys, then, Croxall introduces the following in the 209 lines of his translation of the Arachne episode: peculiar care, crown (verb), toothy slay, transient, transpierced, dewy sea-god, glitt'ring spear, scaly breast-plate, airy crane, cleaves the skies, briny tide, waft, supinely, fluid gold, lambent flame, fishy form, oozy flood, depend, and suspence. Perhaps one example will suffice to show how Croxall ornamented his translation with the poetic diction at his disposal. *"Care,"* Tillotson writes, "comes straight from the *Georgics: cura* is Virgil's constant word for the job of the shepherd and farmer",[17] and peculiar comes from *peculiaris,* meaning one's own, special, peculiar. So that when Croxall writes of the nymphs leaving the "vineyards, their peculiar care" (p. 176) he expects his readers to know the Latin origins of the words and their associations. Golding's version of the line reads "their vineyards often times forsooke," and Sandys's version is equally unadorned, "oft their vines forsooke."[18]

Croxall avoids poetic diction in two or three places where it is present in Sandys. Thus, Sandys uses confessing, in the phrase "eyes confessing rage," in its meaning of manifesting; Croxall has "an angry look." Where Ovid has "filis . . . aurum," Croxall is literal with "threads of gold," resisting both Golding's "glittring golde" and Sandys's "ductil gold." And Sandys's "hoary olive" becomes "a tree pale-green with fairest olives hung" in Croxall's version. But nothing in Golding or Sandys can compare with Croxall's rendition of Pallas's curse on the boastful Arachne. Ovid writes *"vive quidem, pende tamen, improba,"* dixit (1. 136); Golding has Pallas say "lewde callet live: but hang thou still for me" (1. 170); and Sandys is even more laconic, for his Pallas simply exclaims, "Live wretch, yet hang" (p. 150). Croxall pulls out all the stops, "Live, but depend, vile wretch, the Goddess cry'd, / Doom'd in Suspence for ever to be ty'd" (p. 181). Here, an important part of poetic diction, the practice of using Latin root meanings, as exemplified by depend and suspence, is carried to a ridiculous extreme. But Croxall is small game; what is important is the fact that Ovid's *Metamorphoses,* both in Latin and in translation, is another source of English poetic diction, with eighteenth-century poets inheriting not only a body of translation of his work but also a number of Elizabethan and later Ovidian imitations.

The longest of Pope's early translations was not the extracts from the *Metamorphoses* but his 864-line version of the first book of Statius's *Thebaid.* Statius had not attracted many English translators when Pope, then about fourteen years old, translated *The First Book of Statius his Thebais,* which he revised and eventually published in Lintot's *Miscellaneous Poems and Translations, By Several Hands* in 1712. As a boy of about eight Pope had read Statius in Thomas Stephens's *An Essay upon Statius: or The First Five Books of Publ. Papinius Statius his Thebais, Done into English Verse* (1648) and enjoyed it enough so that traces of influence are discernible in his own translation.[19] Walter Harte translated *The Sixth Thebaid of Statius* when he was nineteen, as the advertisement to his *Poems on Several Occa-*

sions (1727) immediately informs the reader. In 1736 Thomas Gray, then twenty years of age, translated two passages from the sixth *Thebaid;* in this, as in his other translations—from Dante, Tasso, and Propertius—he fell into the inevitable pitfall of poetic diction. It was not, however, until 1767 that the twelve books of the epic were translated into English. William Lillington Lewis wrote in his preface: "I begun it soon after I entered at the University, at the age of eighteen . . . my chief Merit consists in having had the Patience to go through with it at a Time of Life, which is too often squandered away in a Circle of Follies and Amusements" (p. xxi). Lewis's appraisal of his work may be allowed to stand; he patiently translated the twelve books in pedestrian couplets rife with poetic diction. All four young men—Pope, Gray, Harte, and Lewis—it is clear, were serving their poetic apprenticeship; all four, Pope to an equal extent to the others, indulged themselves in poetic diction, virtually none of which goes back to Stephens's translation. Since Pope had translated Homer by the time the others turned to Statius, it is perhaps strange that they should not have had even more frequent recourse to poetic diction, since they had the reservoir of diction in Pope's *Homer* upon which to draw. In Pope's version of the first *Thebaid,* in any event, there is some item of stock diction in almost exactly one of every eight lines. He has watry, airy, dusky, brawny, starry, haily, massy, briny, beamy, and a number of other such adjectives. Among his Latinisms are exalt, prevent, servile, aspiring, undistinguished, involve—all used in unoriginal phrases. And he has liquid air, yielding air, train, vocal cave, generous, and feather'd fates among other favorites of the practitioners of poetic diction. Indeed, the evidence of this early translation points to a conscious effort to imitate the language of the epic. But whatever influence Statius's epic, both in the original and in translation, may have had on the course of English poetic diction was very slight. Indeed, the editors of the Twickenham edition state that "throughout his poem Pope seems to have remembered Virgil, particularly as he had been translated by Dryden. He also, in the turns and ingenuities of his language, often recalls Ovid, yet, as the notes reveal, he is attempting at the same time to capture some of the epic breadth and vigour he discovered in Milton."[20] One comes back again to Virgil, without whose *Aeneid* there may not have been a *Thebaid,* and to Ovid, poets whose popularity is undisputed and whose works in translation were so influential in the transmission of English poetic diction.

While the Twickenham editors, depending in part on the Elwin-Courthope edition of Pope's works, acknowledge and document the influence of Virgil in Dryden's translation upon Pope's *Status his Thebais,* they do not

140

realize the extent to which the older poet influenced the younger in his choice of poetic diction. Actually, of course, Dryden, both poet and translator, is everywhere in Pope's early work: in the pastorals, the *Messiah, Windsor-Forest,* as well as in the translations. Specifically, in his version of Statius's first book, Pope probably went to Dryden's *Virgil* as his readiest source for abodes (blest, dark, proud), brown Horrors, Tutelary Care (see Dryden's "the shepherd's tutelary God," in the first *Georgic,* 1. 19), confess'd the God, cut the yielding Skies, depending Lamps, dusky Pinions (of a Fury), gen'rous Juice (three times in the *Virgil*), her Second Hope,[21] a Robe obscene (Dryden has "his obscene Attire" in *Aeneid* 6. 417), Birds obscene, popularly bow'd (i.e., bowed to the people),[22] remurmur, (Night's) sable Wings, *Nemea's* dreadful Spoils (i.e., a lion's skin),[23] the Steep of Heav'n, stormy Main, vocal Caves (Dryden has vocal woods, tree, grove, oke), watry (main, Reign, War), yielding (Air, Skies). Even more common items of poetic diction—briny, brood, crown, devoted—could as easily have come from Dryden's *Virgil,* although there is no need to belabor such a point. It is also of interest to note that Pope went back to his translation of Statius when he was translating Homer in later years, for both contain airy Height, aspiring Piles ("aspiring Wall" in *Iliad* 12. 368), peculiar Care, the Consistory crown'd (verbatim in *Iliad* 10. 232), etherial Height,[24] exalt their Scepters, feather'd Fates, gloomy Rein, grateful Smoke, headlong Fury, remurmur, (lion's) Spoils, starry Train, the Steep of Heav'n, the Sylvan Shade, vocal Caves,[25] watry Reign. Here, as before, it is obvious that in most of these examples Pope need not have had a specific prior use, his own or Dryden's—or somebody else's—in mind. What is important is that Dryden's influence upon the young Pope was almost surely strongest in the matter of poetic diction rather than in other kinds of verbal borrowings or than in identical rhymes.

With the publication of volumes 7–10 of the Twickenham Pope, the translations of the *Iliad* and the *Odyssey,* Pope's already heightened modern reputation got another boost. The editors of these four volumes lavished somewhat over two hundred pages on their introduction and almost two hundred more were given over to Appendixes. These translations, which had been censured by classicists and poets alike from their first publication until well into the twentieth century, were tried in various balances and rarely found wanting. Such a reappraisal got under way in 1951 with Douglas Knight's work.[26] In his discussion of "the style of a heroic poem" Knight, later one of the editors of the Twickenham edition of these translations, writes about certain similarities between Pope's *Iliad* and Milton's

Paradise Lost and between Pope's *Iliad* and Dryden's *Aeneid.* He compares the death of Euryalus in *Aeneid* (9. 581–84) with that of Gorgythio in *Iliad* (8. 371–74) and shows how indebted Pope was to Dryden's translation.

It is clear that this poignancy emerges so vividly in good part because of a skillfully generalized diction. But the very fact that the language is derivative, if it is also fully functional in the later poem, helps greatly to strengthen the importance to the reader of the point which the poem is making. Not only has he been in the poem's world before, but he knows that it is a world of permanently and supremely important human experience. The generalized style guides us to the crux of an individual action, but the properly used derivative style emphasizes the great recurrent crises of human life. This is evident in its most emphatic form when we consider the derivative nature of Pope's treatment of the formulas of Homer, formulas which, to repeat a remark of C. S. Lewis, "emphasize the unchanging human environment, . . . The permanence, the indifference, the heartrending or consoling fact that whether we laugh or weep the world is what it is." This pressure of unchanging reality explains in good part phrases like "watery field," "watery way," "wat'ry track," "the Main," "the Deep" (used where Homer would use "the wine-dark sea"), "the purple Morn," "the vulgar Dead"—all of them shared in some form by Dryden and Pope, and by them with other English heroic poets and translators. But in the English *Aeneid* and *Iliad* the striking thing is the consistency with which the phrases are used for precisely those aspects of the poems which depend upon recurrence and lack of change. Not only persistent nature beyond and around man but the persistent demands of human life are caught up by these formulas; and their sharing by a group of poets serves above all to emphasize the fact that these basic forces are not the private property of even the greatest single poem. The conventionalized style is a way of building the immutable powers of the universe into the action of an individual poem, and at the same time a way of saying through the style how much a whole group of poems shares in attitude.[27]

While much of what Knight suggests may be true of the passages being compared, his statements about phrases such as watery field, watery way, wat'ry track, the Main, the Deep, the purple Morn, and the vulgar Dead, all examples of poetic diction (although he prefers to call them and think of them as "derivative" language or "skillfully generalized diction"), are open to question. What, in essence, it comes down to is whether these phrases, "all of them shared in some form by Dryden and Pope, and by them with other English heroic poets and translators," have the allusive power that Knight attributes to them, or whether, having passed through so many poetic hands, many of them neither skillful nor heroic (i.e., not writers or translators of heroic poetry), they have lost much of their allusive quality along with their freshness. Indeed, of the examples given by Knight, only "the vulgar Dead" could, by 1697, be considered almost exclusively part of epic diction, the other phrases, whatever their remote origins, having been used by too many poets in too many different genres to qualify as that.

Maynard Mack, principal editor of the Twickenham edition of Pope's *Homer,* writes that "Pope's years of mining in the common vein of epic diction gave him a second language. Its heaviest incidence occurs not unexpectedly in the *Rape of the Lock* and the *Dunciad.* "[28] He lists a number of words and phrases in those two mock epics that derive from the translation of Homer and then proceeds to give examples of the influence of the translation on others of Pope's poems. While most, not all, of the examples adduced for the *Rape* and the *Dunciad* are epic diction, and while one or two of those adduced for Pope's other poetry are epic diction, some of the former and most of the latter are either from the larger area of poetic diction in general or are similarities that do not fall into either category. Thus, the use of the coronation figure in Pope's *Epistle to Bathurst* (327), wherein John Cutler's "rev'rend temples" are crown'd with a few grey hairs, need owe nothing to the *Homer,* its use in this manner cutting across generic lines.[29] The "juice nectareous" of the grape (*Essay on Man* 1. 136) comes from the periphrastic mania that afflicted all manner of poets, not merely the writers and translators of epics, its presence in the *Homer* being another manifestation of poetic diction. Mack, in his capacity as editor of the *Essay on Man* for the Twickenham edition, noted John Philips's use of "nectareous Juice" in *Cyder* (1708), but did not cite Philips's source, Milton's "nectareous draughts" and "nectareous humour" (*Paradise Lost* 5. 306 and 6. 332), the draughts being "from milky stream, / Berry or grape." All of which is meant to suggest that Pope's vocabulary in these later poems and in the examples adduced by Mack does not necessarily derive from epic sources of one kind or another. And here it will be well to repeat that Milton's use of nectareous in the two periphrases quoted is but one more example of poetic diction, not of epic diction. After all, all the words, phrases, and locutions to be found in epics, or any given epic, must not be thought of as epic diction, especially when they are also found in nonepic poetry. So very much, too, of Pope's diction in the *Homer* comes from predecessors, all manner of predecessors, that sweeping critical pronouncements about that diction and its importance must be made with extreme caution.

Yet the fact remains that Pope's predecessors in the translation of Homer's epics exerted great influence upon him. Thus, Dr. Johnson—with full access to Pope's preface to the *Iliad* in which Chapman's version of Homer's epic is said to be "involved in Fustian, a Fault for which he was remarkable in his Original Writings"—wrote that "with Chapman, whose work, though now totally neglected, seems to have been popular almost to the end of the last century, he [Pope] had very frequent consultation, and perhaps never translated any passage till he had read his version, which indeed he has been sometimes suspected of using instead of the original."[30] Certainly the existence of Pope's "markings and marginalia" in his copy of Chapman's *Iliad* (TE 10. 474–91), although not known to Johnson, lends credence to his statement. And yet, William Frost, the Twickenham author of the section entitled "Pope and His English Predecessors," tells us that "parallels to Ogilby occur oftener than parallels to Chapman or Hobbes" because the former is "generally closer to the Greek" than either of the latter two, because he used couplets, and because "his couplets are several decades closer to the end-stopped, epigrammatic, neo-classical kind" (*TE* 7. cxii). Curiously enough, Pope was quite brutal in his remark, in the same preface to the *Iliad,* on the poetry of Hobbes and Ogilby, which he described as "too mean for Criticism." Still more curious, perhaps, is Pope's remark about Dryden's translation of the first book of the *Iliad,* a translation which he admired, although Dryden, according to him, "seems to have had too much Regard to *Chapman,* whose Words he sometimes copies, and has unhappily follow'd him in Passages where he wanders from the Original" (*TE* 7. 22). Since Frost later writes that "Close study shows not only that many lines are strikingly parallel in Pope's and Dryden's versions [of Book 1], but even that Pope hardly runs on for more than ten or twenty lines together at any point in the book without some sort of echo, parallel, or contrast to Dryden" (*TE* 7. cxl), one's conclusion would be that Pope is also quite close to Chapman, at least in the first book. This is belied by the table of parallels in Appendix F of volume 10 of the Twickenham edition, for there Chapman is overshadowed by Ogilby, Dryden, and Arthur Maynwaring. Nor are the parallels particularly striking. Thus, Pope's lines, "For *Chryses* sought with costly Gifts to gain / His Captive Daughter from the Victor's Chain" (*Iliad* 1. 15–16) is marked as parallel to Chapman, whose version reads "Chryses, the Priest came to the fleets to buy, / For presents of unvalued price, his daughter's libertie" (11–12).[31] Arthur Maynwaring is also cited as a parallel; his lines read, "For *Chryses,* charg'd with boundless Treasure, came / To free from servile Bonds a Beauteous Dame" (17–18). Dryden's version of these lines is plainly modeled on Chapman's: "For venerable *Chryses* came to buy / With Gold and Gifts of Price, his Daughters Liberty" (17–18). Even more remarkable is the Twickenham

144

editor's citing Dryden's "on the woody plain / Of Hippoplacus" (*The Last Parting of Hector and Andromache*, 11. 34–35) as a parallel to Pope's "The Queen of *Hippoplacia's Sylvan Lands*" (*Iliad* 6. 539) and ignoring Chapman's "in sylvane Hypoplace" (1. 462). This is compounded by a similar failure to note Chapman's use of sylvans to mean trees at *Iliad* 16. 705, for Pope, in the same passage, uses the word in the same very unusual way (1. 926).[32] One cannot, then, be sure of the closeness of parallels, except when typographically signaled as verbally very close by the Twickenham editors.

It is possible, however, to chart with some greater degree of precision Pope's dependence upon epic poetic diction, to show, that is, from what sources he drew his vocabulary, not only in the *Iliad* and in the *Odyssey* but also in the earlier translations, those from Ovid, Statius, and Homer. As far as the two early Homeric fragments, the episode of Sarpedon from the twelfth and sixteenth *Iliads* and the arrival of Ulysses in Ithaca from the thirteenth *Odyssey*, are concerned, they passed without significant change in poetic diction into the completed translations of Pope's later years.

The Twickenham edition lists Pope's English predecessors in the translation of Homer's two epics, both the complete translations as well as versions of particular parts. What are described as "the several fragmentary *Iliad* translations in heroic couplets" are said to "have a special interest as constituting the immediate tradition in which he worked." All of these, except that by John Denham, fall in the period from 1693 to 1707 (*TE* 7. cxxxvi). When it is recalled that Pope's first attempt at Homeric translation, the Sarpedon-Glaucus passage, was published in 1709, close in time to these previous translations, it is easier to understand the claims for the importance of these fragments in his version of the *Iliad*. The ensuing discussion of these fragments will demonstrate that from all but one of them Pope got very little of that poetic diction for which his *Iliad* (and his *Odyssey*, too, though it is less his) became famous and infamous, whether one chooses to align himself with Dr. Johnson on the one hand or with Wordsworth and Coleridge on the other.

Frost writes that "at no point in the *Iliad* is Pope's relationship to his predecessors more active than in Book I [as translated by Dryden] and in the crucial parts, translated by Congreve, of Book XXIV . . . throughout the 220 lines where Congreve has preceded him, evidence of Pope's acquaintance with the dramatist's version occurs, I think, in more than one line out of three" (*TE* 7. cxl). Congreve is very little given to poetic diction in his translation of these passages, partly because much of the first section is given over to the speeches of Priam and Achilles; the same holds true of

Pope's version, although he manages to introduce somewhat more poetic diction than Congreve does. John Denham, whose 1668 translation of the few but famous lines of Sarpedon's speech to Glaucus in Book 12, is credited with having begun "the entire tradition of English Augustan Homer translation" (*TE* 7. cxxvii) had even less to offer by way of poetic diction, his one extravagance being the periphrasis "the sparkling Tears / Of the rich Grape" for wine. Whatever the influence of Denham's translation upon the versification and the point of view of English Augustan Homer translation, no part of this influence was felt in the area of poetic diction. A later translator of the Sarpedon speech, P. A. Motteux, whose version was published in 1707, two years before Pope's own version of that speech appeared in print, has nothing by way of poetic diction that Pope saw fit to use.

Thomas Yalden, who translated the words of Patroclus to Achilles in Book 16 in 1694 for the *Annual Miscellany* of that year, has been praised for his skill in certain parts of his translation. (*TE* 7. cxxxviii) His version of this short passage, relatively unadorned by poetic diction, certainly was not a source for what diction Pope has in his translation of the same lines. Conceived solely in terms of epic poetic diction, then, Pope has a "martial Band" (17), Peleus is hoary, (21), there is a dire Oracle (54), and an "o'er labour'd Train" (62). What is more, "good *Menoetius* breathes the vital Air" (20), for which Yalden has "good Menoetius he is yet alive" (p. 260); and Pope also has "*Greece* respire again" (63), for which there is no equivalent in Yalden.[33] Where Pope's Patroclus charges Achilles that his "Breast alone no Lenitives appease" (39), Yalden's Patroclus says that Achilles's "Breast alone remains implacable" (p. 262). But then Yalden has "generous [noble] Breast" (p. 262) where Pope simply has Breast (31); he has Achilles's "distinguish'd [distinctive, distinguishable] Arms" (p. 264) for which Pope has "dreadful Arms" (58); and he rings in both an "unequal Fight" and "an easie Conquest" (p. 264), for which there are no equivalents in Pope's version.

Knightly Chetwood translated the popular Hector-Andromache passage in the sixth book for the *Collection of Poems,* published in 1693, which went through a number of editions. Although his translation, with that of Arthur Maynwaring's translation of the first 412 lines of the first book, published in Tonson's *Miscellanies V* in 1704, was not important for Pope, it is of some slight interest to note that he too exerted no influence, for his 130 lines are quite bare of poetic diction. He has a "Beauteous Train" and "her Princely Care" (both p. 94), "our vital Breath" and a use of officious (both p. 100) —and that is all. Pope takes 170 lines to cover the same ground; he has "th' Attendant Train" (478). "*Ilion's* steepy Tow'r" (480),[34] "the doubtful Day"

(481), "his only Hope" (i.e., his only child, 1. 497), "*Jove's* Sylvan Daughters" (532), "snowie Flocks" (536), "Sylvan Lands" (539), and a use of decent in a funereal context, "And lay'd him decent on the Fun'ral Pile" (529). Pope, it is clear, derives none of his poetic diction from Chetwood and has more of it in this passage than his predecessor. Maynwaring's version of the first two-thirds of Book 1 is fairly derivative, his source being Dryden's version of that book. Maynwaring's version and Pope's coincide only in the phrase "th' AEtherial Host," with a few other similarities being traceable to Dryden's influence.

Frost devotes some fourteen pages to a comparison of the obscure poet Charles Tooke's translation of "Part of the 14th Book of Homer. In this is Described the Contrivance of *Juno* to lull Jupiter to Sleep, that *Neptune* the mean time may assist the *Grecians*" with Pope's version of that same incident to show the latter's indebtedness to the former. Tooke's translation first appeared anonymously in *A Collection of Poems* in the 1701 and 1702 editions; his name first appeared in the 1716 edition. While Pope's indebtedness is clearly demonstrated—he even partially acknowledged this himself by taking a line verbatim from Tooke and placing it in quotation marks— that indebtedness, with the possibility of one or two exceptions, did not include poetic diction. Both poets have "remote abodes" twice in the same lines, and while abodes appears twenty-six times in Pope's *Iliad* the only two uses of it with remote are where he coincides with Tooke.[35] Despite the evidence of other borrowings, one can only conclude that Pope derived virtually none of his poetic diction from Tooke. Indeed, Tooke offered him some opportunities in this direction, none of them particularly novel and none of which he took—i.e., a Crystal flood, refulgent Stars, exalted state, flow'ry Lap, and an unusual use of introduce in the lines, "So thick a Cloud I'll cast around, no Ray / Of light shall introduce th' unwelcome Day."[36]

The longest *Iliad* fragment in heroic couplets available to Pope was Dryden's version of Book 1, first published in 1700 in *Fables Ancient and Modern.* Parallels between the two are catalogued, with quotation, in Appendix F of the Twickenham *Pope,*[37] as are parallels between the entire *Iliad* and Dryden's *Aeneid* and other works, including *Paradise Lost* and the Bible.[38] Such an appendix is, of course, invaluable, but there are one or two areas of weakness.[39] What seems an obvious parallel, one that involves poetic diction but which is ignored, is Dryden's "T'involve the lean [meat] in Cauls" (*Iliad* 1. 632), which Pope followed in his "double Cawls involv'd with Art" (*Iliad* 1. 604 *and* 2. 506). For further example, although parallels between Dryden's and Pope's versions of Book 1 are listed, there is no attempt to ascertain whether there are further parallels, parallels between

147

Dryden's Book 1 and the other twenty-three books of Pope's translation. Thus, when one comes to Pope's Book 15 and reads, of Juno, who "sullen took her Place" (1. 108) "While on her wrinkled Front, and Eyebrow bent, / Sate stedfast Care, and low'ring Discontent" (112–13), he would be unaware that the lines derive from Dryden's "and *Juno* took her Place: / But sullen Discontent sate lowring on her Face" (*Iliad* 1. 719–20). Behind these lines there is a history of personified attributes sitting, resting, or otherwise taking up a position on the face, brow, or cheeks of some person,[40] but the verbal similarities between Dryden's use of this old figure and Pope's are too close for coincidence. Whether Pope still had Dryden in mind when he wrote in Book 9 that Fear, Flight, and Horror "Sate on each Face" (11. 2–4) is less sure, even though Dryden has "Scorn sate on his Brows, and sour Disdain" in the *Aeneid* (7. 896). However, it is in some of these possible earlier influences on Pope's use of epic diction in the *Iliad,* and later in the *Odyssey,* as the Twickenham editors have realized of other kinds of influence, that one can appreciate the longevity and endurance of some of these words, phrases, and images.

Dryden's version of the first *Iliad* may also have influenced Pope's use of diction in a few other places in the *Iliad.* The latter's *"Greece* respir'd again" (11. 424) and *"Greece* respire again" (11. 933, 16. 63) could not, one supposes, have been written entirely without knowledge of the former's *"Greece* respir'd again" (1. 626). Dryden's "The Skies with dawning Day were purpled o'er" (651) is almost surely the source or model for Pope's " 'Till rosie Morn had purpled o'er the Sky" (623). And while Pope's use of "sov'reign Sway" four times in the *Iliad* (2. 648, 5. 1076, 10. 140, and 14. 104) need not reflect Dryden's use of the same phrase three times (11. 227, 312, 389) any more than his "imperial Sway" (24. 678) need reflect its use by Dryden (1. 406), the numerous resemblances between their versions of the first book, both those listed in the Twickenham edition and the few added here, make the possibility of such reflection very real. A commonplace in Homeric translation such as "heaps on heaps," with twenty-four appearances in Pope's *Iliad* (none, however, in the first book) had already made two appearances in Dryden (11. 16 and 530). Dryden's use of intercept, in the rather rare sense of prevent, stop, hinder, in the line "E'er Evil intercept thy tardy Flight" (1. 40) is taken over almost bodily by Thomas Tickell in his translation of Homer's first Book, "Begone, ere evil intercept thy way" (1. 43), and these usages are paralleled in Pope's "And intercept his hop'd return to *Troy*" (10. 414). Even closer is Pope's "sable crows with intercepted flight" in the *Odyssey* (14. 342). Dryden has "servile Race" (1. 191) and "servile Bands" (fetters, 1. 611); Pope has "servile, second Race"

(15. 223) and "servile Bands" (21. 527). Achilles's famous vow, as translated uniquely by Dryden, "That while my Nostrils draw this vital Air" (1.
131), is surely behind Pope's "Long as *Achilles* breathes this vital Air" (1.
112) and almost equally surely behind "Thy good *Menoetius* breathes the
vital Air" (16. 20) and "For *Peleus* breathes no more the vital Air" (19.
356). Previous translators of Achilles's vow had stuck fairly close to Homer's "while I live and have sight on the earth" (Loeb translation). And,
of course, Pope pressed Dryden's line into service in a more famous context,
Baron Petre's vow, "while my Nostrils draw the vital Air," in *The Rape of
the Lock* (2. 137). Possibly, too, for one is now treating largely of possibilities, Dryden's lines, "His pensive Cheek upon his Hand reclin'd, / And
anxious Thoughts revolving in his Mind" (11. 458–59) helped Pope to his
"Pensive she sate, revolving Fates to come" (24. 113). Pope's lines about
the "Goddess with the charming Eyes" (14. 373; the rhyme word is replies)
may derive from Dryden's *Aeneid*, "the Goddess, with the charming Eyes"
(10. 862; the rhyme word is replies) but it may also owe something to that
same "Goddess with the charming Eyes" in Dryden's first *Iliad* (1. 741; but
with Skies as the rhyme word). And when the Twickenham editor parallels
Pope's "The moving Squadrons blacken all the Strand"[41] to Dryden's "With
Trojan Bands that blacken all the Shore" (*Aeneid* 4. 579), he forgets the
line in *Absalom and Achitophel*, "Cov'ring the Beach, and blackning all the
Strand" (1. 272). That Dryden's version of the first *Iliad* made itself felt
in Pope's *Odyssey* as well can be concluded from, among other similarities,
the use of the rare word obtend meaning oppose. The *OED* gives *only*
Dryden's *Aeneid* 10. 126, "obtend an empty Cloud" and Pope's *Odyssey* 22.
88, "obtend these ample boards," overlooking Dryden's "obtending
Heav'n" (1. 161). Curiously enough, Pope has "obtests the Skies" twice in
the *Iliad* (15. 426 and 22. 45), and "obtesting Heav'n" occurs in Broome's
translation of the twelfth book of the *Odyssey* (1. 436), another unusual
word also employed by Dryden in the *Aeneid* (11. 151). In the ninth book
of the *Aeneid*, Dryden describes warriors who, "drunk with wine, supinely
snore (1. 424); Polyphemus, in Pope's *Odyssey*, also drunk with wine,
"snoring lay supine" (9. 440). It may be well to record here that Dryden's
The Last Parting of Hector and Andromache from the sixth *Iliad* may have
provided Pope with his *"Ilion's* steepy Tow'r" in the same book (1. 480;
Dryden has "the steepy Tow'r of Ilion," 1. 5) and the Latinism of hope for
son (1. 143 in Dryden and 11. 487 and 497 in Pope). It will be remembered
that Dr. Johnson wrote that Pope's "chief help" in translating the *Iliad*
"was drawn from the versions of Dryden. Virgil had borrowed much of his
imagery from Homer, and part of the debt was now paid by his translator.

Pope searched the pages of Dryden for happy combinations of heroic diction, but it will not be denied that he added much to what he found. He cultivated our language with so much diligence and art that he has left in his *Homer* a treasure of poetical excellences to posterity."[42] Johnson was referring to Dryden's translation of Virgil; he could with equal justice have included the translation of the first *Iliad*.

Pope's predecessors who translated both the *Iliad* and the *Odyssey* were Chapman, Hobbes, and Ogilby, in that chronological order. The possible influence of Chapman's *Homer* on Pope's in the matter of poetic diction can be seen in certain words and phrases which the later poet almost surely took from his predecessor. In what follows, unless otherwise noted, Hobbes does not use any of the items of poetic diction in which Chapman and Pope coincide. Reference is to the *Iliad* of both men, unless otherwise stated. The following are common to both translations: blest abodes, adverse powers, azure goddess, azure eyes, crown (hills), crown (with conquest), crown (bowls, cups, or goblets with wine), that firste embrude the field,[43] gulphy Xanthus,[44] headlong,[45] refulgent arms, inglorious flight, inglorious hands, massy bowl, massy gold, provoke (war or fight), scour (the field), and vital spirits. Chapman's "adverse champion" is paralleled in Pope's "adverse Chief" and his "Satnius's silver flood" in Pope's "Satnio's silver Shore." Chapman's unusual use of implide in "thy false wrists implide" (15. 18) and "old Limbes implide / In warm Sheep-fels" (*Odyssey* 20. 222–23) is echoed in Pope's "implicit Hands." Chapman's "shadie shields" (4. 104) may have suggested Pope's "A shady Light was shot from glimm'ring Shields" (4. 324) and his "shaggie roofe" of Achilles's tent (24. 402) may have similarly suggested the "shaggy Carpets" spread for Priam in Achilles's tent in Pope's version (24. 813).

In addition, there are a few similarities between Chapman's *Odyssey* and Pope's *Iliad* and *Odyssey*. The "abhord abodes" of Chapman's translation appears in Pope's *Iliad;* the former's "circumfluous Ile," in the fourth book of Pope's *Odyssey,* one of the books translated by Fenton. Fenton also has a "fishy flood"; Chapman had written of the "fishy maine." Both Pope and Fenton use gulphy in their parts of the *Odyssey,* as had Chapman. Chapman has recourse to sea-girt three times, and it also appears in Pope's *Iliad.* Chapman's "refluent Oceans" may be in the background of Pope's "refluent Waters" in the *Iliad;* the same is true of respire (to breathe), ruddy wine, and sandy Pylos. Pope and Chapman agree in using sable to describe a bark or barks (five times in the latter, while the former also uses it with ships and vessel), blood (both twice), clouds (twice in both), Jove's brows (twice in Pope), wine (three times in Pope), and sea or seas (four times in Chapman).

Of the above, Dryden has only "sable clouds" (twice) in his *Virgil*. Chapman has "vital spirits" in the *Iliad* and in the *Odyssey,* as does Ogilby, incidentally, in the *Odyssey* (3. 37); Pope uses the phrase four times in the *Iliad* and once in the *Odyssey*.

Pope owed very little in the matter of poetic diction, if indeed he owed anything, to Thomas Hobbes's translation of *Homer*. The following parallels are few enough and sufficiently commonplace to warrant the view that, for the most part, he ignored Hobbes's version. Spence records Pope as saying in 1739 that there were "several passages in Hobbes's translation of *Homer* which, if they had been written on purpose to ridicule that poet, would have done very well."[46] Both Hobbes and Pope link Zephyr with the sea and the curling motion produced by wind over water, the latter in both epics, the former in the *Iliad* alone.[47] In parallel passages, where Hobbes has a falcon flying "dexter" (*Odyssey* 15. 473) Pope has "Yon bird that dexter cuts th' aerial road" (*Odyssey* 15. 573).[48] Hobbes has massy spears and massy gold, sedgy river, and sooty Vulcan; the first two occur in Pope's *Iliad,* and there are sedgy Reeds (*Iliad* 21. 406) and a reference to Vulcan as the sooty workman, also in the *Iliad*. Hobbes's "The Greeks did for a little while respire" (*Iliad* 16. 298) is echoed in Pope's three uses of "Greece respire [d] again" (*Iliad* 11. 244, 933; and 16. 63), but Dryden has the same phrase and Pope may have got it from him, if indeed he took it from anybody.

While Pope could say that Ogilby's poetry was "below criticism," the numerous parallels between his translations of Homer's epics and Ogilby's prompted Gilbert Wakefield to write, at one such parallel, that the earlier writer's poetry may have been "below criticism, perhaps, but not imitation."[49] Part of Pope's dependence upon Ogilby's *Homer* may have been in the form of the poetic diction he found there, a poetic diction which he echoed.[50] Thus, Ogilby refers to the eagle's "callow young" (Book 16, p. 231); only twice in the *Iliad* (2. 377; 17. 848) (and once in those books of the *Odyssey* he translated) did Pope use callow and then it was to refer in one of these two to the cranes' "callow young" (17. 848). Pope uses the verb to disembogue once in his *Homer* at *Iliad* 17. 311, and while the word was certainly not peculiar to Ogilby it appears three times in his *Odyssey* (Book 5, p. 65; Book 12, pp. 166 and 175).[51] Both use to exalt to mean to raise an object on high; Ogilby of an axe (Book 3, p. 37), Pope of a sceptre (*Iliad* 10. 379); the word is not used in this way anywhere in Dryden's *Virgil,* some indication of its relative rareness in the above sense. Of only three uses of glassy in Pope's Homeric translations one is his "glassy deep" for the ocean (*Odyssey* 15. 510); it occurs in Book 12 of Ogilby's *Odyssey* (p. 168). Twice Ogilby describes fish as "scaly fry" in the *Odyssey* (Books 4 and 12, pp. 50 and 170);

"scaly fry" appears in Pope's *Iliad* (21. 414).[52] Ogilby has a "Virgin-Train" (6. 80) and a "female train" (19. 273); Pope has both (*Odyssey* 21. 8 and *Odyssey* 15. 24). Ogilby is so fond of the phrase "waterie world" that he employs it at least ten times in the *Odyssey;* Pope finds occasion to employ the same phrase twice in his part of the *Odyssey* (5. 376 and 503). As always, it is well to be reminded that some of these words and phrases were much handled, and Pope could, therefore, have got them elsewhere, but some were relatively rare, and since Pope had delighted in Ogilby's *Homer* as a child of about eight he may have gone back to his early favorite.

It may have been Ogilby's "Full Goblets brought with sparkling Nectar crown'd" (*Iliad* 1. 30) which prompted Pope's "The double Bowl with sparkling *Nectar* crown'd" (*Iliad* 1. 753),[53] and his "foaming Bowls with gen'rous Nectar crown'd" in the early translation of the Sarpedon episode (1. 31). The former's "Scarce did the Down his rosy Cheeks invest" (11. 287) may look back to the latter's "Beaded-invested Chin" (1. 26); even more probable is it that Pope's "The Nod that ratifies the Will Divine" (1. 680) owes something to Ogilby's "Jove ratifi'd this Sentence with a Nod" (17. 379). But it will be better to list the slightly more unusual words and phrases of poetic diction which they have in common, commenting only on the most remarkable similarities. Both use bossy to describe shields; both use the rather rare word commutual, Pope twice with death, Ogilby with javelins and with gore.[54] Both write of the "aetherial breed" of horses; Ogilby's "dexter part" is echoed in Pope's two uses of dexter, although one or both may be recalling Hobbes's *Homer*. Ogilby's "distinguish'd Regiments"—i.e., distinct from one another—is echoed in Pope's "distinguish'd Bands." Although the word, in the same sense, occurs in Dryden's *Virgil*, it is not in the same kind of military context. Both use effusion in sanguinary contexts, enamel'd to describe natural phenomena, fleecy to describe snow, flow'ry to describe a river's side, gulphy to describe a river, infuse with balm, and ignipotent (twice in Pope's *Iliad* and twice in Ogilby's *Aeneid*). Ogilby is fond of rebate, to blunt the edge or point of a weapon, with at least five occurrences in his *Iliad;* Pope also employs this rather rare word. Ogilby has two "starry mansions" in the *Iliad;* there is one in Pope's version. And a rather unusual use of the verb to serene appears in Ogilby's *Aeneid* and in Pope's *Iliad*.

Pope would also have found in Ogilby's *Iliad* what he could of course have found in others of his predecessors, and what he used himself in his *Iliad*, such more common locutions as "aetherial skies" and flames that aspire, as well as a slight partiality for briny. Both use pomp in a funereal context. "Dire events" and presages occur in both; and, as with so many

152

of their predecessors and contemporaries, dire is employed as an epithet. Distain is joined with blood or gore; clouds are dusky; steeds are inevitably gen'rous. Shade is gloomy; weapons are glutted with blood; storms impend; and to infest means to attack. Goblets and bowls are massy and weapons and stones are invariably pond'rous. To provoke is to challenge to battle and purpled means bloodied. Horses scour over the ground.

Much of the poetic diction of Ogilby's *Iliad* finds its way into his *Odyssey*. Over and above what Pope may have taken, or remembered, or been in some way influenced by in Ogilby's *Iliad* he could similarly have been influenced by certain words and phrases in Ogilby's *Odyssey*. In what follows it must be remembered that while Pope translated only Books 3, 5, 7, 9, 10, 13, 14, 15, 17, 21, 22 and 24 of the *Odyssey* he had the supervision of the entire translation and exercised editorial powers over Broome and Fenton. Hence, there is no need to identify the translator for each example in this short catalogue of borrowings or parallels. Indeed, there is little need for comment. Both translators share the somewhat unusual absterse, assiduous, dissipate, erected, florid, impale, intercept, retorted.[55] There are "azure plains" (the sea) in both as well as the "spiry tops" of mountains.

While it is manifestly impossible to determine where Pope got a particular word or phrase of poetic diction, it is possible to suggest to some slight extent what other writers and works may have contributed to his store. Quotations are solely from his translation of the *Iliad:*

TABLE 2

Possible Sources of Pope's Poetic Diction

Pope's Iliad	*Possible Source*
aetherial texture	Manilius[1]
aetherial throne	Sylvester, Dryden's *Ovid*[2]
aetherial flame	Ozell's *Lutrin,* Dryden's *Ovid*
airy way	Godolphin
airy height	Dryden's *Ovid*
animate my shade (of the dead)	the animated air, Harrington
assume (of objects)	Sir Robert Howard, *Achilleis*
balmy (of sleep)	Shakespeare, Fanshawe *(Aeneid 4)* Chamberlayne
beamy lance	Vicars
bristly boar	Dryden's *Georgics*
brown (shade, shadow)	Sylvester
callow young	Dryden's *Ovid*
congregated (of troops)	Vicars (at least 3 times)
conscious of the deed	See p. 124.
curl (of Zephyrs)	Drummond of Hawthornden
dire contagion	Sandys, Ross, Ogilby's *Aesop*

dire debate	Phineas Fletcher
dire alarm	Ross
dire portent	Davenant
disembogue	Dryden's *Ovid*
mazy error	Milton
feathered (of weapons)	Fanshawe *(Aeneid 4)*, Ogilby's *Aesop*, Harrington, Dryden's *Ovid*
flaggy wings	Dryden's *Ovid;* flaggy pinions, Dryden's *Georgics*[3]
flamy	Sandys, Vicars, Harrington
forky (lightning)	Dryden's *Ovid*
genial bed	T. Randolph's *Amintas*, Ogilby's *Aeneid*, Dryden's *Ovid*
glean (as a military term)[4]	Bible, Fanshawe *(Aeneid 4)*, *Davideis*, Garth's *Dispensary*, Dryden's *Aeneid* and *Ovid*, Addison's *Campaign*
solid globe	Shakespeare
honours	See pp. 109–10.
humid (of eyes)	Shakespeare, Sandys, Dryden's *Ovid*
ignipotent	Vicars, Ogilby's *Aeneid*
implicit	Milton
intercept	Ross, Davenant
meditate (as transitive verb)	See pp. 117–18.
missile (weapons)	May, Ross
missive (of weapons)	Blackmore
paints (morning paints the sky)	Sandys
precipitates (flight)	Dryden's *Ovid*
retorted (eyes)[5]	J. Philips, *Blenheim*
revert (eyes)	Sandys, Chamberlayne
scud (*OED:* "To sail or move swiftly on the water.")	Stanyhurst, *Aeneid;* Sylvester, Sandys, Hobbes, Manilius
sluicy	Dryden's *Georgics*
submiss	Sylvester, Milton
sweepy	Dryden's *Ovid*
tawny (of a lion)	Dryden's *Aeneid*
towery	Ogilby's *Virgil* and *Homer* (at least 6)
tribute (of water)	Fairfax, Sylvester, Milton
undistinguished ("Sons, Sires, and Wives, an undistinguish'd Prey," 5.596)	"Flocks, Folds, and Trees, an undistinguish'd Prey," Dryden's *Aeneid* 2. 412
viny	Ogilby's *Iliad, Aeneid*
visionary (*OED:* "Seen only in a vision . . .")	Addison, *Metamorphoses 3*, Ozell's *Lutrin*

[1]Edward Sherburne, *The Sphere of Marcus Manilius Made an English Poem*, 1675.
[2]I so designate Dryden's various translations from the *Metamorphoses*.
[3]Gorges, Sandys, and Vicars use "flaggy" of plants.
[4]See p. 127.
[5]Sandys and Vicars use it of weapons, i. e., thrown back; Milton, of scorn.

Pope knew most, if not all, of the writers and works in this list, but it would be very difficult, except if the evidence were overwhelmingly clear to the contrary, to demonstrate specific indebtedness to any one of them. Pope had prepared himself for his career as poet by steeping himself in earlier English poetry, as well as in the poetry of Greece and Rome, and when he came to write his own translations and original poetry it was natural for him to draw upon a poetic diction that was ready to hand. What is more, and this is especially true of the translations of Homer and Ovid, the *Rape of the Lock* and the *Dunciad,* and the four *Pastorals,* Pope could count upon his readers to provide the original contexts or frames of reference necessary for a full understanding and appreciation of the effects for which he was working, precisely by having recourse to a poetic diction which his readers had encountered time and again.[56]

NOTES AND REFERENCES

1. In Pope's translation of Ovid's Epistle, *Sapho to Phaon,* there is little poetic diction and little influence of Sir Carr Scrape's 1680 translation of that same epistle. See the Twickenham *Pope,* vol. 1, pp. 339–43.

2. Johnson, *Lives,* vol. 3, p. 239.

3. Tillotson, *On the Poetry of Pope,* pp. 64 and 66.

4. Ibid., p. 67.

5. Joseph Spence, *Observations, Anecdotes,* p. 14.

6. Twickenham *Pope,* vol. 1, pp. 332, 336, 338.

7. Watson, 2. 270.

8. Ibid., 2. 164.

9. I have been gathering materials for a study of Dryden's practice as a translator vis-à-vis his predecessors.

10. So, too, is the possible influence of the imitators of Ovid; see, for example, the selections in *Elizabethan Minor Epics,* ed. Elizabeth S. Donno (London: Routledge and Kegan Paul, 1963).

11. Spence, *Observations, Anecdotes,* p. 181.

12. In his version of the story of Dryope from *Metamorphoses 9,* Pope has "milky moisture," where Golding has "not a whit of milke nor moysture," the nearest thing to a remotely possible parallel. And "milky moisture" is not all that felicitous or inventive; Dryden has "milky freight" and "milky Juice" (*Met.* 13. 128; 15. 300).

13. Twickenham *Pope,* vol. 1, p. 336.

14. Ibid., p. 337.

15. I quote Sandys from the note in the Twickenham *Pope,* vol. 1, p. 386.

16. Quoted on p. 131.

17. Tillotson, *APD*, p. 35.

18. See pp. 80 for "peculiar care."

19. Sir Richard Howard had translated *Statius His Achilleis,* published in his *Poems* (1660), and Christopher Pitt had expended about a hundred couplets in a translation of part of the second book of the *Thebaid.*

20. Twickenham *Pope,* vol. 1, p. 352.

21. Compare *Windsor-Forest,* 1. 81, "his second Hope."

22. This comes from *Absalom and Achitophel,* 1. 689, "bowing popularly low."

23. Dryden uses "spoils" of the skin of a bear, wolves, and foxes in *Aeneid* 5. 49; 7. 952; and *Georgics* 3. 17.

24. While this is quite common, it does not appear in Dryden's *Virgil.*

25. See "Vocal Hill" in *Iliad* 16. 287, "vocal Hills" in the *Messiah,* 1. 31, and "vocal Shore" in *Winter,* l. 59.

26. Knight, *Pope and the Heroic Tradition, a Critical Study of his "Iliad"* (New Haven: Yale University Press, 1951).

27. Ibid., pp. 61–62.

28. Twickenham *Homer,* vol. 7, p. ccxxv.

29. While "rev'rend" is frequent in both the *Iliad* and *Odyssey,* no "rev'rend temples" are "crown'd" therein.

30. Johnson, *Lives,* vol. 3, p. 115.

31. Loeb gives "For he had come to the swift ships of the Achaeans to free his daughter, and he bore with him ransom past counting."

32. *OED* gives the following "? A forest tree, shrub, etc. *rare"* and quotes examples from 1632 and 1787 only.

33. Compare Dryden, Book 1 of the *Iliad:* "Unbent his bow and *Greece* respir'd again," 1. 626.

34. Dryden has "the Steepy Tow'r of *Ilion"* in his version of this passage, 1. 5.

35. Dryden has one use of "remote abodes" in the *Aeneid* 1. 492, and T. Ross uses it in his translation of Silius Italicus, 1661, Bk. 3, p. 70.

36. Page 224, I have used the 1702 edition; the translation is on pages 216–24.

37. Twickenham *Pope,* vol. 10, p. 496.

38. Ibid., vol. 10, pp. 500–6.

39. See pp. 150–1.

40. Milton has "care / Sat on his [Satan's] faded cheek," *Paradise Lost* 1. 601–2, and, again of Satan, "deep on his front engraven Deliberation sat and public care," *Paradise Lost* 2. 203–4. The figure is long-lived, with William Golding using it in *Lord of the Flies,* "authority sat on his shoulder" (New York: Capricorn Books, 1959), p. 138.

41. Twickenham *Pope,* vol. 2, p. 971.

42. Johnson, *Lives,* vol. 3, pp. 237–38.

43. Chapman's spelling, 14. 425 in his version and 14. 602 in Pope's, a parallel unnoted in the Twickenham edition.

44. Note, too, Pope's "And *Xanthus* foaming from his fruitful Source; / and gulphy *Simois,* rolling to the Main," 12. 20–21. Chapman also has "the deep sea's gulphie breast" (13. 33) and "the gulfie flood" (21. 16), as well as the metaphorical "gulfie mouth of warre" (10. 7).

45. Used 22 times in Chapman and 33 times in Pope, as opposed to only 6 in Hobbes; there are 7 uses in Chapman's *Odyssey* and 8 in Pope's.

46. Spence, *Observations, Anecdotes,* p. 193.

47. Respectively, *Iliad* 23. 693 and *Odyssey* 4. 390–91; *Iliad* 7. 72.

48. Hobbes also has "an eagle dexter flew" in the *Iliad* 19. 780 and in the *Odyssey* 15. 137; Pope also has "a dexter Eagle flew" in the *Iliad* 14. 1039.

49. Quoted in Twickenham *Pope,* vol. 7, p. cviii n.

50. Some of this body of diction descended from Ogilby to Dryden, from whom Pope may have taken what he needed. See pp. 121–2

51. Fenton also uses it in the *Odyssey* 4. 480.

52. See also pp. 118–19

53. The references in what follows are to the *Iliad* translations of the two men unless otherwise noted.

54. Fenton was to use it twice in the *Odyssey* 4. 241 and 19. 223.

55. Pope's three uses of circumfuse may owe something to Ogilby's use in his *Aeneid.*

56. See Earl Wasserman, "The Limits of Allusion in *The Rape of the Lock,*" *JEGP* 65 (1966), 425–55.

Chapter 7.

Thomson

The great gathering place for all that was worst, as well as all that was best, in the language of poetry of natural description was James Thomson's *The Seasons* in the final 1746 version. It is a tribute to Thomson's poetic gifts that his poem is as good as it is despite the prevalence of poetic diction.[1] That it was so popular in the eighteenth and nineteenth centuries—and Wordsworth was among its admirers—has little direct bearing on its excellence as poetry, although perhaps some slight significance may be attached to the relative dearth of editions of the poem[2] and of Thomson's poetry as a whole in the twentieth century. So far as critical attention is concerned, Ralph Cohen has more than redressed the balance in favor of Thomson by his two books on *The Seasons*.[3] Patricia Meyer Spacks has written another book-length study of Thomson's poem;[4] it, however, receives short shrift at the hands of Professor Cohen. Since Cohen has reviewed the criticism of Thomson's poem from its beginnings to the 1960s there is no need to repeat that entire history. As the present concern is almost solely with the matter of poetic diction, a few comments from critics, those who condemn and those who commend Thomson's use of that diction, may be quoted.

Pride of place, mistaken though he is in part, goes to Dr. Johnson, who wrote that Thomson's "mode of thinking, and of expressing his thoughts, is original. . . . His numbers, his pauses, his diction, are of his own growth, without transcription, without imitation,"[5] a remark which, so far as originality of diction is concerned, is belied by the researches of Otto Zippel and W. P. Mustard, who show how much Thomson was indebted to Virgil and other poets. But Johnson could not be mistaken in the quality of Thomson's diction, which he labeled as "in the highest degree florid and exuberant. . . . It is too exuberant, and sometimes may be charged with filling the ear more than the mind."[6] Joseph Warton, more than two decades before Johnson, had written that "the diction of the SEASONS is sometimes harsh and inharmonious, and sometimes turgid and obscure."[7] To these strictures should be added some of Hazlitt's remarks in his lecture on Thomson and Cowper in *Lectures on the English Poets*. Hazlitt writes that Thomson

is frequently pedantic and ostentatious in his style, because he had no con-sciousness of these vices in himself. He mounts upon stilts, not out of vanity, but indolence. He seldom writes a good line, but he makes up for it by a bad one. He takes advantage of all the most trite and mechanical commonplaces of imagery and diction as a kindly relief to his Muse, and as if he thought them quite as good, and likely to be quite as acceptable to the reader, as his own poetry. He did not think the difference worth putting himself to the trouble of accomplishing. He had too little art to conceal his art: or did not even seem to know that there was any occasion for it. His art is as naked and undisguised as his nature; the one is as pure and genuine as the other is gross, gaudy, and meretricious.—All that is admirable in the Seasons, is the emanation of a fine natural genius, and sincere love of his subject, unforced, unstudied, that comes uncalled for, and departs unbidden. But he takes no pains, uses no self-correction; or if he seems to labour, it is worse than labour lost. His genius "cannot be constrained by mastery." The feeling of nature, of the changes of the seasons, was in his mind; and he could not help conveying this feeling to the reader, by the mere force of spontaneous expression; but if the expression did not come of itself, he left the whole business to chance; or, willing to evade instead of encountering the difficulties of his subject, fills up the intervals of true inspiration with the most vapid and worthless materials, pieces out a beautiful half line with a bombastic allusion, or overloads an exquisitely natural sentiment or image with a cloud of painted, pompous, cumbrous phrases.

But Hazlitt is as alive to Thomson's excellences as he is to his faults. Two of the best critics of English literature, then, are agreed in finding grievous faults in Thomson's style or diction.[8]

Modern critics, for the most part, or at least in significant number, appear to find it necessary not only to defend Thomson's heavy use of poetic diction but even to find hidden excellences where in other poets they might find faults, a critical error already shown to be at work in the criticism of the poetry of Spenser and of Milton. Among these critics are Tillotson, in a passage already quoted (page 17); Deane, also quoted (pages 16–17); and Bateson, who sees the use of "finny tribe" by Thomson and others as motivated by the same purpose "that led chemists to create a word like 'phogiston' (first used in 1733)," i.e., "by restricting a general notion to a particular field they represented a gain in precision."[9] John Butt explains Thomson's Latinisms as natural "to a lowland Scot writing Southern English,"[10] and suggests that "his periphrases were used not to escape vulgarity, but precisely and evocatively." His defence of these periphrases may be seen in his interpretation of "their brittle bondage" for birds' eggs and of "the fearful race" for certain game birds. Mrs. Spacks finds that "the condensed and conventional phrase 'The vocal Grove' [Summer, A, 1. 368], hints at a wide range of meaning: the physical reality of the grove [would it be less real without birds in it?], the presence in it of animate inhabitants [hardly a hint], and—most important of all—the idea that the works of nature attest their creator in toneful or expressive terms [the idea is present elsewhere in *The Seasons,* but not in "The vocal Grove"]." Vocal, as applied to a plant, had been used by John Biddle in his translation of Virgil's eighth *Eclogue,* "vocall Pines" (1634, B7ᵛ); notably by Milton in the "vocal reeds" of *Lycidas* 86 (Dryden has "vocal reeds" in his translation of the first book of the *Metamorphoses* 940 and Gay has a "vocal reed" in *Cephisa*); by Dryden in the "vocal grove" of the eighth and tenth *Pastorals* of Virgil (11. 31 and 10), in the "vocal woods" of *Pastoral* 4. 4, the "vocal tree" of *Pastoral* 6. 14, and the "vocal oke" of the second *Georgic* (1. 21); Pope has "vocal hills" in *Messiah* 31 (echoed in the "vocal hill" of the *Iliad* translation, 16. 287); and Catcott has a "vocal forest" in his translation of the thirteenth book of the *Metamorphoses* (1717, p. 469 in the collaborative translation edited by Sir Samuel Garth). By the time of Thomson, vocal, as he used it, was somewhat conventional, if not downright stale—and this is to omit the vocal shells, shores, and so on in poetry before *The Seasons.*[11] John Chalker reconsiders the influence of Virgil's *Georgics* on Thomson's poem, but also offers a variation on the discovery of hidden depths in *The Seasons.*[12] He quotes part of the hunt supper in *Autumn* as an example of Thomson's mock-heroic style. The drinkers at the hunt supper are sinking beneath the table one by one:

> Before their maudlin eyes,
> Seen dim, and blue, the double tapers dance,
> Then, sliding sweet, they drop. O'erturned above

160

Lies the wet, broken scene; and stretch'd below,
Is heap'd the social Slaughter . . .

[1744, ll. 550–55]

Chalker comments that "the last phrase *(social slaughter)* is an interesting one. The word *social* is a very important one for Thomson and it occurs with exceptional frequency in the poem. It connotes the integration of different elements, the unity in variety which, it is suggested, is one of the central themes of the work as a whole, and its use here consequently has a good deal of ironic force."[13] In the quoted passage "social Slaughter" means simply, albeit in Latinate form, the slaughter of a number of comrades *(socii);* it is intended, with the whole of the rest of the passage, to be humorous not ironic. What is more it is an afterthought (the 1730 edition has "drunken slaughter") possibly designed to heighten the burlesque (see page 174). Thomson almost invariably uses social in its sense of comradely, as did many of his predecessors.[14] Whatever relevance social may have for Thomson's major themes does not reside in the "social Slaughter" passage.

Thomson's greatest champion is, of course, Cohen. Indeed, the loving, although to many minds excessive, care he has lavished on *The Seasons,* explicating, interpreting, defending, praising, has forced Thomson back into the scholarly arena. Any detailed criticism of Cohen's efforts would require a book in itself, but it may be enough to give an extended example of the sort of thing he does. One of the earliest and ablest of Thomson's critics was John Scott of Amwell, one of whose longest essays in his *Critical Essays on Some of the Poems of Several English Poets* (1785) is on *The Seasons.* Cohen gives Scott somewhat his due,[15] characterizing him as an "intelligent and careful critic."[16] Nevertheless, he disagrees with much in Scott's essay. In his comments on Thomson's "vernal shower" (*Spring,* ll. 155–76) Scott had written

Where a subject occupies any considerable number of lines, it is commonly necessary to mention it repeatedly, either in the same terms or in others. The permitting one word to recur frequently has been justly termed a slovenly practice; and writers, to avoid it, often have recourse to a kind of metonymical, or rather catachrestical expressions which are mostly either improper or inelegant. Thomson has a great number of these quaint phrases of his own construction. . . . the single circumstance of rain, is described by no less than seven different appellations; it is called "falling verdure," "lucid moisture," "promised sweetness," "treasures of the clouds," "heaven descending in universal bounty," "fruits and flowers," and lastly, "milky nutriment."

161

Cohen comments:

> The reason given by Scott for the use of these images—the avoidance of
> repetition of "rain" or "shower"—seems in the light of eighteenth-century
> descriptive poetry as well as of *The Seasons* to be inadequate. These terms
> were considered "improper," "inelegant," and "catachrestical" because, for
> the most part, they were extravagant comparisons. But "falling verdure,"
> "promised sweetness," "treasures of the clouds," "heaven descending in uni-
> versal bounty," "fruits and flowers," and "milky nutriment" are instances of
> the consequences of the shower. [Scott was aware of this; he writes that "it
> is also as violent a substitution of effect for cause, to call the rain 'verdure,'
> and worse still, by the addition of a previous and totally inapplicable epithet
> to term it 'falling verdure' " (p. 301).] In this language of Thomson, the future
> appears *in potentia* in the present, and the shower is described by the products
> it will bring forth. "Lucid moisture" is not an image but a factual description,
> and in the language of growing nature there was a distinction between "falling
> verdure," "treasures of the clouds," and "milky nutriment." The first was an
> example of the falling shower seen in terms of its natural product—the second
> part was part of a formal contrasting with an informal image and "milky
> nutriment" was scientific terminology. Each of these functioned in a special
> way to achieve poetic meaning, and it was an unfortunate reaction to attribute
> one function to all these images.[17]

At an earlier point Cohen had invoked the work of Alan D. McKillop,
writing that "material thus became available illustrating the scientific language of the poem and refuting the view that it was an artificially con-
structed poetic diction."[18] Not so. McKillop wrote that Thomson's "con-
sciousness of scientific process strews his lines with *pseudopoetic paraphrase
of technical terms*"[19] (my italics). Nor is Thomson's cause helped by Mrs.
Spacks's attempt to defend the "falling verdure" of the quoted passage.
Writing of Thomson's periphrastic "feathered kind" for birds, she states
that Thomson "reminds his reader, in passing, of the great pattern of
universal order, of the way in which individual species are differentiated
within it, of the importance of considering one *kind* of creature in relation
to other kinds. The poet accustomed to this sort of diction can use a phrase
like 'falling verdure' to describe—not visually but metaphysically—the
spring rain which will, given the universal order, inevitably produce the rich
foliage of summer."[20] My own opinion of the matter is that the seven
variations are bad whether they describe rain *or* "the consequences of the
shower."

It is restorative, after reading much modern criticism of Thomson and of other poets of the eighteenth century to have one of these poets giving his forthright opinion of aspects of the poems of some of his predecessors. A cento of John Scott's remarks on what he considered faults in *The Seasons* would include the following. "He often, in attempting energy and dignity, produces bombast and obscurity; and in avoiding meanness, becomes guilty of affectation."[21] "To say that the floods seem forgetful of their course, '*through delusive lapse,*' is to talk nonsense."[22] Cohen attempts to clear Thomson of the charge of writing nonsense, on page 324 of his *Art of Discrimination.* "Fancy seems indeed here to have run wild."[23] "Writers often have recourse to a kind of metonymical, or rather catachrestical expressions, which are mostly either improper or inelegant. Thomson has a great number of these quaint phrases of his own construction."[24] " '*Dewy murmurs,* is a vicious expression: the epithet '*dewy,*' can relate only to an object of feeling or sight, consequently it is absurdly joined with '*murmurs,*' an object only of hearing."[25] "There is a perverse tendency in men to admire what they do not understand. Not only hearers, but readers, are often best pleased with nonsense. This passage [part of the story of Celadon and Amelia] has undoubtedly been thought very fine by many who knew not its meaning."[26] There are many more such strictures, but they are balanced by an equal number of passages of great praise. Thus, although Scott could speak disparagingly of a passage in the story of Celadon and Amelia, he could also write, of another passage in the same story, "This is a beautiful passage: there is perhaps no finer instance of attributive allusion in our language."[27] Scott, like eighteenth-century editors of Shakespeare and un-like too many modern critics and scholars, was not unwilling to "point out the nature" of the "beauties and defects" of the work under consideration.

Most critics of Thomson's diction are agreed that its most prominent feature is, in Havens's words, "his use of uncommon words derived from the Latin." The same critic adds that "Thomson also follows Milton in giving to a word a meaning or an application which it had in Latin or Greek but has lost in English."[28] In an introductory essay on Thomson's poetry for an edition of *The Seasons* Edmund Gosse wrote

Mr. Saintsbury has . . . declared the Latinisms of Thomson to be neither a crutch nor a staff to him, but "a mere clouded cane which, as he mistakenly thinks, is an appropriate ornament." This is an acute apology, but hardly does justice to an inherent vice in Thomson. It is difficult not to believe that he was in reality afraid to trust to a simpler diction, and that, dealing, as he did, with rural subjects, a certain intellectual snobbishness led him to try to cover their rusticity with an excess of gentility in diction. The result is sometimes down-

163

right ludicrous, and at all times blurs or deadens the effect of the poetry. Fortunately it does not occur so frequently as it does in the verse of the minor Thomsonians, where it continually mars our pleasure, but it is prominent enough to be a tiresome element.[29]

What Saintsbury, Gosse, Havens, and others have not stressed, or thought it unnecessary to stress, is that in the latter usages Thomson often falls into predictable phrases. A few examples will suffice here. Thus, he has cities aspiring, clouds congregated, a conscious heart, a devoted wretch, the dubious day, "In cheerful error let us tread the maze" (the conjunction of error and maze was of long standing), ethereal arch (or bow), the generous lion, natural phenomena "invested," two "irriguous" vales (taken, of course, from Milton), luxuriant herbage, and pendent icicle.[30] The same holds true of Thomson's -y adjectives; he has many, few of them original with him or used in original contexts. He has airy rings, the balmy power (i.e., sleep), the billowy plain, the briny deep, craggy mountains, the downy peach, the finny race, gaudy spring, massy gold, ruddy fire, spiry towns, and a tusky boar—to list but a few.[31] Equally true is his employment of certain words favored by poets and poetasters, some of them writers of epics. Abodes are blest, black, or dark (*Winter* 293, *Summer* 951 and 898) veins are azure (*Summer* 215), the young of birds are callow (*Spring* 670), sea fowl cleave the clouds (*Winter* 147), there is a high cope to heaven (*Autumn* 25), hills are wood-crowned and mountains forest-crowned (*Summer* 559 and 459) water is crystal (*Summer* 1245), places of habitation are domes (even the bees have their "honeyed domes," *Autumn* 1182), enlightened means to be illuminated (*Spring* 1036), torrents are headlong (*Spring* 817), as are descents of various kinds (*Summer* 1249, *Winter* 341 and 637), clouds sail in heaps on heaps (*Spring* 149), clubs are ponderous (*Winter* 822), spears are protended (*Autumn* 462), the Thames is silver (*Summer* 1416; also see page 63), scenes are sylvan (*Autumn* 1044), both sky and earth are vaulted (*Summer* 1093, *Autumn* 78), and the air is yielding (*Summer* 789). While it is difficult to be precise, because of the lack of a concordance to *The Seasons,* most of Thomson's favorite words in the reservoir of poetic diction are those favored by earlier poets also. While it is true that he has some unusual favorites—amusive and gelid are examples —his preferences run to words such as aerial, azure, balmy, dewy, etherial, liquid, pour (in a metaphorical sense), verdant, and vernal—a few examples among many possible. And despite his writing in blank verse rather than in heroic couplets where monosyllabic rhyme words are so necessary, he nevertheless is fond of those convenient generic words race (18), train (15), and tribe (10).

The preceding, it is mandatory to repeat, are but a few examples of the lack of originality in Thomson's use of poetic diction. (It may be well to add, however, that some of the parallels between Thomson and Milton listed by Havens are misleading in that they include items of poetic diction that antedate Milton's poems. The "parallel" use of involve is one such example.) Here, as elsewhere in this chapter and in this study as a whole, the appearance of somewhat tarnished items of poetic diction in a poem is held to militate against the overall excellence of that poem, unless there are overriding considerations of context. The deliberate use of poetic diction for one purpose or another is one thing; the unconscious or indiscriminate use of it is something else entirely. Thomson, it is already clear and it will become clearer, was unaware that he was using or avoiding poetic diction. Indeed, he piled it up, not only in single lines ("The uncurling floods, diffused / In glassy breadth, seem through delusive lapse," *Spring* 159–60.) but in long passages. For example, one can hardly do better, or possibly worse, than when Thomson went excavating (see *Autumn* 773–835). Thus, one can open an edition of *The Seasons* haphazardly and be sure that he will find some, if not much, poetic diction at that opening. This is even true of the very popular interpolated stories. Of course, as has already been suggested, the attempt either to explain away or to find hidden beauties in Thomson's poetic diction has stretched the ingenuity of some critics almost to the breaking point.[32]

With Thomson, as with a number of other poets of the eighteenth century, there is the problem of the effect of his revisions on the poetic merit of *The Seasons*. Dr. Johnson, who is usually quoted on this point, wrote that he thought the revisions improvements in general but that he regretted the loss of "race; a word which, applied to wines in its primitive sense, means the flavour of the soil."[33] More than one critic has preferred the original, 405-line version of *Winter* to any of the four revised and enlarged versions, but there is little total agreement as to the merits or shortcomings of what is after all, a formidable body of revisions. For the considerable additions made to *The Seasons*, the final version (1746) containing almost 1,100 lines more than the first edition (1730), the decision rests on such considerations as the excellence as poetry of the various additions, their consonance with the context into which they are introduced, and their place in the larger scheme of the poem and in Thomson's thought. Where Thomson omits matter, which he does but infrequently, the decision is more difficult. But it is when Thomson changes a word, a phrase, a line, or several lines that the possibility of assessing the merits or shortcomings of the changes becomes greatest. The change of one word for another, or the rejection of three or four choices in favor of the word that appears in the final text, limits the area of conjecture open to the student of such revisions. And it is, of course, in those revisions in which Thomson changes a word or phrase taken from the reservoir of poetic diction to something else, or vice versa, that the student of poetic diction is interested.

First of all, it is quite apparent that in many of his revisions Thomson increased the number of personifications in the poem. Cohen gives a few examples of the revision in *Winter* from the second to the third editions, separated in time by about four years, and concludes that "the changes predominantly created a personified nature."[34] Examination of some of the revisions closest in time, those between the first and second editions of *Winter,* published in March and June 1726, leads to no such clear-cut conclusion, either as to personification or as to Thomson's possible avoidance of poetic diction. In Table 3, line references are to the first edition; the revisions can most easily be seen in context in the Oxford *Thomson.* More extensive revisions are quoted after analysis of the changes listed in the table.

TABLE 3

Changes Between 1st and 2nd Editions of *Winter*

1726 (1)	*1726 (2)*
44 Sad *Philomel*	some widowed songster
76 hoary Caves	prophetic Glooms
83 vapoury, Prey	moist captives
88 radiant	brightening
98–99 silver o'er / The Face of Mother-Earth	impearl / The face of mother-earth
112 *Winter* . . . confest	[revision omits *confest*]*
116 The dreary Plain	unsightly
163 th' uncertain Main	passive
306 Brighten'd	Radiant
327 a weeping Thaw	trickling
348 the troubled Sky	gelid

*In 1730 the line takes its final, perfected form: "Then comes the father of the tempest forth" (1. 72).

166

The first three revisions offer a choice between kinds of poetic diction, although the personifying tendency emerges weakly in the change from "hoary Caves" to "prophetic Glooms." Whatever one thinks of the fourth change, from "radiant" to "brightening" must be tempered by the change at line 306 from "Brighten'd" to "Radiant." To "silver o'er" is less precious an item of poetic diction than to "impearl," and a "troubled" sky is more acceptable than a "gelid" one, especially when there is already a sufficiency of ice and frost in that particular passage. But then Thomson rights the balance somewhat by omitting the Latinism confest, meaning stands revealed, and by exchanging the lachrymose thaw of line 327 for one that trickles. The differences between "dreary" and "unsightly" plains and "uncertain" and "passive" mains is slight, although some preference may be expressed for the less poetic "uncertain" main.

Thomson made more extensive changes. The first edition has:

> Prone, on th' uncertain Main, passive
> Descends th' Etherial Force, and plows its Waves,
> With dreadful Rift: from the mid-Deep, appears,
> Surge after Surge, the rising, wat'ry, War.
> Whitening, the angry Billows rowl immense,
> And roar their Terrors, through the shuddering Soul
> Of feeble Man.
>
> [163–69]

And the second edition has:

> Prone, on the passive Main,
> Descends th' Etherial Force, and plows its Waves,
> In frightful furrows: from the brawling Deep,
> Heav'd to the Clouds, the watry *Tumult* comes.
> Rumbling, the wind-swoln Billows rowl immense,
> And, on th' evanish'd vessel bursting fierce,
> Their Terrors thunder thro' the prostrate Soul
> Of feeble Man.

Besides the change from uncertain to passive, there is the revision of "With dreadful rift" to "In frightful furrows" to sustain the image in the preceding line's "plows its Waves," an image that disappears, incidentally, in 1746. The "brawling Deep" of the second edition is another example of the personifying tendency at work, as is "rumbling." But Thomson makes his billows "wind-swoln" rather than "angry," a movement in the opposite

167

direction. The "wat'ry, War," a tired phrase, gives over to the "watry *Tumult,*" but then Thomson spoils whatever good he has achieved by introducing that "evanish'd vessel," only to get rid of it in 1746. Evanished is a word sufficiently rare as to merit noting that the *OED* shows it used largely in prose, as well as noting that Wordsworth introduced it in revising his translation of the episode of Orpheus and Eurydice from Virgil's fourth *Georgic.*[35] Allan Ramsey's use of the word in his *Gentle Shepherd* (1728) is quoted in the *OED* as one of the rare appearances in poetry. Johnson defines the word in his *Dictionary* but gives no examples, either in the 1755 edition or in the 1773 revision. The rest of the changes in this passage, with the exception of "prostrate" for "shuddering"—i.e., the introduction of another Latin word, do not fall within the limited sphere of this discussion.

A few lines further the first edition reads

> But hark! The *Almighty* speaks:
> Instant, the chidden Storm begins to pant,
> And dies, at once, into a noiseless Calm.
>
> [ll. 192–94]

The second edition substitutes

> Till Nature's King, who oft
> Amid tempestuous Darkness dwells alone,
> And on the Wings of the careering Wind
> Walks dreadfully serene, commands a Calm:
> And strait Earth, Sea, and Air are hush'd at once.

Thomson wisely gets rid of the somewhat ludicrous figure of the storm, a dog chidden by his master panting into silence, and puts in its place a biblical image, derived from 2 Samuel 22: 10–11: "He bowed the heavens also, and came down; and darkness was under his feet. And he rode upon a cherub, and did fly: and he was seen upon the wings of the wind" (repeated in Psalm 18: 9–10),[36] and from either Psalm 107: 29, "He maketh the storm a calm" or from the story of Christ's rebuking the wind and the water of a storm until they cease and are calm, as told in the gospel according to Matthew (8: 26), Mark (4: 39), and Luke (8: 24), and from other biblical passages. The text of this revision persists through all subsequent editions.

The third change of any extent comes at lines 224–26, with the first edition reading

See! sudden, hoar'd,
The Woods beneath the stainless Burden bow,
Blackning, along the mazy Stream it melts;

and the second reading

Blackening, they melt
Along the mazy Stream. The leafless Woods
Bow their hoar Heads. And, ere the languid Sun
Faint from the West emit his evening Ray,

Here there is not much upon which to comment, except that Thomson's electing to get rid of the awkward "hoar'd" gave place to the "hoar Heads" of "the leafless Woods," which would, one imagines, have been bald, and his introducing a "faint" and "languid" Sun. He refused to give up his "mazy stream," although he finally changed it in 1746 to a "mazy current," and, one is happy to add, dropped "leafless" from "woods," thus allowing "hoar head" to remain. But the sun continued "faint" and "languid."

The most often discussed revision in *Winter* is an addition of twelve lines, coming after line 292 of the first edition, which read, in part,

the Bear,
Rough Tenant of these Shades, shaggy with Ice,
And dangling Snow, stalks thro' the Woods, forlorn.

The bear makes his bed "beneath the inclement Wreath" in this addition. In 1730 the bear is described as follows:

There thro' the ragged woods absorpt in snow,
Sole tenant of the shades, the shaggy bear,
With dangling ice all horrid, stalks forlorn
[ll. 370–72]

and he "makes his bed beneath the drifted snow" (374). In 1744 the passage reads

There thro' the piny Forest half-absorpt,
Rough Tenant of these Shades, the shapeless Bear,[37]
With dangling Ice all horrid, stalks forlorn
[ll. 827–29]

and he "makes his Bed beneath th' inclement Drift" (831).

Disregarding major additions to the text which make the changes from "Rough" to "Sole" tenant and then finally back to "Rough" understandable, one has a bear originally "shaggy with Ice / And dangling Snow" making his bed "beneath the inclement Wreath," revised in 1730 to one "absorpt in snow" and shaggy "With dangling ice all horrid" making his bed "beneath the drifted snow." "Absorpt" and "horrid" are Latinisms; *absorbere* means to swallow up and *horridus* is rough, shaggy, bristly (so defined in Cassell's dictionary).[38] Inclement is also a Latinism; it means unmerciful, not clement, harsh, rough (Cassell again). No one today would do other than applaud the substitution of "drifted snow" for "inclement Wreath" as the place beneath which the bear makes his bed. The changes in the physical description of the bear are something else entirely. Not only is he "swallowed up" in snow but he becomes *"horrid* with dangling ice"; i.e., "shaggy" or "rough," the first of which is a redundancy, since he has already been described as "shaggy" or "bristly." Since he is swallowed up in snow, he has presumably lost all shape; but he is still bristly with ice. That this is what these lines mean seems manifest from the revisions that took place in 1744. Now the bear is "half-absorpt," only half swallowed up, he is no longer "shaggy," but he is now "shapeless" although still "horrid" with dangling ice. Thomson appears not to know exactly what to do with this ursine creature—make him entirely swallowed up in snow, hence shapeless, but still with a bristly shape made up of dangling icicles? Or make him half swallowed up, still shapeless (a contradiction in terms?), and yet still with the bristly coat of dangling icicles? One must note, too, that Thomson discards the perfectly good "drifted snow" of the 1730 version for a poor compromise between it and the "inclement Wreath" of the second edition, with the unsatisfactory "inclement Drift" as a result. And it should be pointed out that the bear's habitat in the second edition is "the Woods"; in 1730 it is the "piny woods," thus introducing one of the -y adjectives of poetic diction. All in all, one wishes Thomson had kept his original description of the bear and had not cluttered it up with absorpt or half-absorpt (an epithet) and horrid. The woods could have remained as they were, neither ragged nor piny. Only that "inclement Wreath" should have made way for "the drifted snow." Incidentally, there is no reason, given the source in Virgil, for Cohen to drag in the myth of the mother bear licking her formless cubs into shape in a comment on "the shapeless Bear" in this passage.[39]

Some further insight into the quality of Thomson's changes, whether they be of poetic diction or not, may be had in an analysis of the revisions in the hunting scene and the somewhat mock-heroic hunt supper that follows.[40]

A "thick-thundering" gun gives way to a "fast-thundering" one, presumably because the latter word more properly describes the rapidity with which the gun is fired[41]—and incidentally gets rid of an unpleasant alliteration. The "useless wings" of birds "caught in the meshy snare" become "idle wings," even though one sees that the wings *could not* be used rather than were voluntarily "idle." And birds driven "else-disperst," an awkward and harshly sibilant epithet, are driven "wide-dispersed." Now Thomson turns to "the peaceful muse" who is "most delighted when she social sees / The whole mixed animal creation round / Alive and happy." In 1730 the muse "smiling" sees the "whole mixed animal creation round," and the change to "social," i.e., "in fellowship," reinforces one of the themes of the poem, unity in nature, that was not only not there originally, but which was actually contradicted by the phrase "the whole *mixed* animal creation round." Here, then, is a very important, if seemingly innocuous, change. And when beasts of prey who had "roamed the dark" become those who had "ranged the dark" the suspicion arises that Thomson was seeking *le mot juste:* to range, used of persons and animals "(*esp.* of hunting dogs searching for game)" *(OED)* as opposed to to roam, which the *OED* defines as "To wander, rove, or ramble; to walk about aimlessly; esp. over a wide area." What is more, roamed appears five lines below, having itself been revised from howled, an intransitive verb used transitively in 1730, which has a monster howling "the waste."

When "rage" is revised to "wrath" (1. 392) one might query the necessity for such a meaningless change, but four lines later the 1730 reading, "Upbraid us not, ye wolves, ye tigers fell," is revised in the direction of generality to "Upbraid, ye ravening tribes our wanton rage," getting rid of the quasi-archaic fell but also prompting the revision of rage to wrath to avoid repetition. Thomson sometimes seems conscious of his personifying tendency, for in this same passage he has man pursuing "the cruel chase" in preference to his taking up "the cruel Tract." One comes now to a revision that has attracted some critical attention. "Poor is the triumph o'er the timid hare! / Shook from the corn," wrote Thomson in 1730, only to revise the unusual and very striking "Shook" to "Scared" in 1744. Robertson, editor of the Oxford *Thomson,* having cited Johnson's remark on the loss of "race" as a result of the revisions, writes "that the loss of raciness is chiefly seen in the substitution, for example, of so comparatively tame a line as—'Then scale the mountains to their woody tops,' for 'Then snatch the mountains by their woody tops' in the description of the fox-hunt; or in the exchange of 'Shook from the corn' for 'Scared from the corn' in the hare-hunt."[42] G. C. Macaulay, author of the English Men of Letters *Thomson,* writes that "the idea of scaling mountains rapidly is rather absurdly expressed by the line,—'Then snatch the mountains by their woody tops,' and with reference to the startled hare, 'Shook from the corn' is not more expressive than 'Scared from the corn,' and it is less grammatical."[43] Cohen comments:

> The difference in expressiveness between "scale" and "snatch" or between "shook" and "scared" depends upon the context of pertinence which is considered. For example, "shook" referred to the action of the hunters, implying their elementary efforts, not even requiring force or resistance. "Scared" referred to the behaviour of the hare and emphasized his timidity, creating a feeling of sympathy for him instead of disrespect for the hunters. The difference attributed to "expressiveness," therefore, was a difference in expressive implication, not a difference between vigour and its absence.[44]

I am not sure by what authority in the text Cohen finds that "shook" refers "to the action of the hunters, implying their elementary efforts, not even requiring force or resistance." To be sure, the immediately preceding line reads: "Poor is the triumph [man, the hunter's] o'er the timid hare!" a complete sentence in itself. Then there is a long description of the hare "shook" or "scared" from the corn and retired "to some lone seat" (1. 402) hearing the pack of hounds and the shrill horn (1. 421), the neighing steed (1. 422), and the loud hunter's shout (1. 423)—all of which is after the fact of being "shook" or "scared." The hare hears "the coming storm" (1. 417) and "springs amazed" (1. 419), thus exposing herself completely to the dogs, which may already have scented her. Therefore, it is quite possible that the impending "tempest" (1. 429) first "shook" or "scared" her and not the hunters. Eventually, a decision on the comparative merits of "shook" and "scared" in this passage resolves itself into a matter of individual preference, *teste* Robertson and Macaulay.

Thomson was evidently satisfied with the rest of the hunted hare passage, for he leaves lines 403–25 untouched and goes on to describe the stag hunt. Here, too, the revisions are few, the epithet "fear-aroused" which had persisted up to the 1744 edition becomes "roused by fear," the "tract" becomes "track," and, more importantly, the rather flat and prosaic "went" in a description of forest glades "Where in kind contest with his butting friends / He went to struggle" becomes "wont"—"He wont to struggle." When the hunted stag seeks the herd, they "With quick consent avoid the infectious maze"—so read the editions prior to 1744, but Thomson changed the line so that it suggested a parallel with human beings, the herd "With

172

selfish care avoid a brother's woe." This is a particularly interesting revision, for it brings the whole passage more closely in line with its model or source, the stag hunt in Sir John Denham's *Cooper's Hill,* for there

> the herd, unkindly wise,
> Or chases him from thence, or from him flies.
> Like a declining States-man, left forlorn
> To his friends pity, and pursuers scorn.
>
> [ll. 271–74]

The reasons for the above revision are clear; less clear are the reasons for changing the lines immediately following from

> His once so vivid nerves,
> So full of buoyant soul, inspire no more
> The fainting course; but wrenching, breathless toil
> Sick seizes on his heart

to

> His once so vivid nerves,
> So full of buoyant spirit, now no more
> Inspire the course; but fainting, breathless toil
> Sick seizes on his heart

The change from "buoyant soul" to "buoyant spirit" may have been prompted by the desire for greater consonance, that is, spirit and inspire are closer than soul and inspire, but some would argue, among them almost surely Dr. Johnson, that the change made for mere repetition. Thomson did, however, get rid of a personified "fainting course," albeit at the expense of the more expressive "wrenching" which should never have been abandoned.

Fourteen lines later, having completed his account of the stag hunt and gone on to suggest that if "sylvan youth" must hunt let them hunt the fiercer animals such as the wolf, "for murder is his trade," which last phrase is revised to "and let the ruffian die," Thomson reverses his decision in an earlier revision which saw the adjective "fell" omitted (l. 396) by changing "the brindled boar / Grins near destruction" to "the brindled boar / Grins fell destruction." Here, as with "shook" and "snatched" in the passages discussed by Macauley and Robertson and with "wrenching," one regrets the substitution of a tamer, more conventional word for a more daring,

173

more expressive—"Grins *near* destruction" must mean that the hunter was so terribly close to the dreaded boar.

The next passage describes the fox hunt and introduces a radical change in tone; now one is in the realm of the mock heroic, and the fox, originally described as "the sly destroyer of the flock," becomes "the nightly robber of the fold." It may be remembered that it is in this passage that Thomson changed the line "Then snatch the mountains by their woody tops," meant to suggest the speed with which the mounted hunters ride up the mountain, to "Then scale the mountains to their woody tops." When the fox is caught it is

> by an hundred mouths
> Relentless torn: O glorious he beyond
> His daring peers, when the retreating horn
> Calls them to ghostly halls of grey renown

for which Thomson originally had written

> by an hundred mouths
> At once tore relentless. Thrice happy he!
> At hour of dusk, while the retreating horn, etc.

The changes do away with the ungrammatical "tore" and the more traditional epic formula "Thrice happy he" and reinforces the contrast between the one hunter who is in on the kill and his "daring peers." Incidentally, Thomson had already characterized the hunter as "happy he" in line 487, another reason to change the "Thrice happy he" of line 492. As the passage continues, the contrast is emphasized, and Thomson adds a line in 1744 to enhance the mock-heroic tone of the passage, having the hunters boast of "feats Thessalian Centaurs never knew."

The scene is now set for the hunt supper. There is a smoking sirloin, "on which," the 1730 text reads, "with fell intent / They deep incision make." In 1744 Thomson had second thoughts about the making of incisions armed only with "fell intent" and provided the hunters and the passage with a "desperate knife," also banishing "fell" again. With the sirloin there is also a game pasty into which the hunters plunge, "Relating how it ran and how it fell"—so the 1730 text. Again Thomson saw that he had committed an absurdity, for the pasty it was that ran and fell, and so he revised the line to read, "Relating all the glories of the chase." After revising "reviving" to "delicious" and "not ashamed" to "not afraid," both minor improvements, Thomson changes the order of a line (524) in order to make the verb "to vie" the intransitive verb it should have been. "Whist," the eighteenth-century predecessor of modern-day bridge, "a while / Walks his grave round beneath a cloud of smoke," Thomson having finally settled for "grave" after having discarded "gentle" (1730–1738) and "dull" (1744), showing that in little things as well as greater he knew what he was doing, as one now sees the hunters, deep in drink, gravely, not gently (certainly not gently) nor dully, concentrating on their cards.

Now the hunters "set ardent in / For serious drinking," and nothing is "to the puking wretch" of little prowess "indulged apart," this last word having been substituted for "askew," which must have meant something like indulged with contempt, the indulgence, incidentally, meaning to be let off from one or more rounds of drinks. In successive revisions Thomson changes the quite rare "vociferate . . . by" to "vociferous . . . from" in the lines, "the talk / Vociferous at once from twenty tongues" and also "every kindred soul" to "each congenial soul," evidently feeling that the Latinate "congenial" was a weightier word than "kindred" and hence better for his mock-heroic purposes. Inexplicably, as the drunken celebrants "slide" to the floor, their descent is described as "sweet" in the original edition, a word that is changed to the understandable "soft"—"Then, sliding soft, they drop." In "Confused above," another Latinism is introduced, for originally it had been "O'erturned above." Now Thomson adds two lines, "Glasses and bottles, pipes and gazetteers, / As if the table even itself was drunk" then describes how the "social Slaughter," still another Latinism in place of the original's "drunken Slaughter," is heaped below.[45] The demon Drink, described as "the lubber Power," which had originally sat, "himself triumphant," now sits "in filthy triumph," one of the rarer lowerings of mock-heroic tone in the passage (although much more expressive), and steeps the hunters "drenched in potent sleep till morn," a change from "silent all in potent sleep," Thomson remembering belatedly that surely one of this group of drunken men might emit the occasional snore. There is an addition of five lines which end the scene:

> Perhaps some doctor of tremendous paunch,
> Awful and deep, a black abyss of drink,
> Outlives them all; and, from his buried flock
> Retiring, full of rumination sad,
> Laments the weakness of these latter times.

175

These lines strike the proper elegaic-heroic note as they recall Homer's description of the "Rocky Fragment" wielded by "fierce *Tydides*," "Not two strong Men th' enormous Weight could raise, / Such Men as live in these degen'rate Days" (5. 371–72 in Pope's translation of the *Iliad,* a couplet repeated verbatim at 12. 539–40 and a formula widely imitated by poets before and after Pope's translation).

For the most part, then, analysis of the revisions in the passages quoted above leads to an agreement with Dr. Johnson's statement that Thomson's revisions were, in general, improvements.[46] Absurdities were corrected, both of grammar and of meaning, and many of the substitutions of one word or phrase for another were felicitous, although there is enough evidence to warrant the conclusion that Thomson was unaware, particularly in the matter of poetic diction, that he was going from good to bad or from bad to worse in some of his revisions. Cohen, who approves of most of Thomson's revisions, concludes of the language in *The Seasons* that "it provides a unifying force in the sense that, for all its variations of tone—burlesque, comic, eulogistic, elegiac, beautiful or sublime—it incorporates Biblical, classical and scientific meanings with current usage. To this extent, illusive allusions, Latinate words, periphrases and personifications, participles and hyphenated terms [in short, poetic diction] belong to the procedure of making the past simultaneous with the present or adding present implications to past meanings and acts. Yet such words and procedure are selective, for not all fragments of the past function effectively."[47] Such a sweeping statement, if I have completely understood it, leaves no room for adverse criticism, for poetic diction is defended on seemingly philosophical or thematic grounds, and the assumption throughout is that Thomson's "delusive" lapses (see page 162) can be explained and given final approval.

A more salutary view of Thomson's poetry is expressed by Bonamy Dobrée in his final assessment of *The Seasons*.

> But it is not such revisions that make it difficult for us to grasp the poem as an entity; it is the extravagant amount and variety of material inserted. Thomson is a perfect magpie; he goes about making finds, and adding them to the treasures he hoards in his nest. He is so charmingly eager in his discoveries, from the Psalms to Maupertuis, that he has to tell us everything, and the man who tells everything becomes a bore.[48] Thomson incurs the danger of being such, even to those naturalized in his idiom. . . . The fact is that he confused the "kinds"; and "the confusion of kinds", as Henry James remarked, "is the inelegance of letters and the stultification of values". . . . Try as we will the poem obstinately resolves itself into separate morsels,

many of them indubitably fine, others touching; some, it would be foolish to deny, either emotionally or poetically unworthy. Here and there the work is intolerably slack; Dr. Johnson could read passages aloud omitting every other line, to the "highest admiration" of Shiels, and G.C. Macaulay gave an example of how this might be done. Yet if it is not a poem of the first order, it is one that we would not do without.[49]

Dobrée admits, as must everyone, Thomson's excellences and the importance of *The Seasons,* but he quite properly touches, in his summary, upon most of the shortcomings of the poem and its author. That he does not name poetic diction among these faults is understandable in view of his earlier pronouncement on the subject.[50]

Thomson and his fellow Scotsmen, A. M. Oliver suggests, "acquired English as Wordsworth acquired Greek and Latin. His [Wordsworth's] view of the process, and its results, is relevant and illuminating," and he then quotes the passage from *The Prelude* beginning, "In fine, / I was a better judge of thoughts than words" (6. 105–14).[51] Wordsworth had contemplated a biography of Thomson to be "prefixed to a Volume containing The Seasons, The Castle of Indolence, his minor pieces in rhyme, and a few Extracts from his plays, and his Liberty." He spoke of Thomson "as a real poet, though it appeared less in his 'Seasons' than in his other poems. He had wanted some judicious adviser to correct his taste." And he praised him in an often-quoted passage as the only poet to offer new images of external nature from the time of Milton to the publication of *The Seasons*—with the exception of the Countess of Winchelsea's *Nocturnal Reverie* "and a passage or two in the *Windsor Forest* of Pope."[52] Wordsworth, like Thomson, was a real poet, but he too, like Thomson seemed unable to distinguish between his "vicious style" and that style which makes the *Lines Composed a Few Miles Above Tintern Abbey* an almost flawless poem.[53] As will be seen he, too, like Thomson, seems not to have been very discriminating in revising his poems. Unlike Thomson, however, most of his revisions cannot be described as improvements. Both men, to use Wordsworth's term again, were real poets, but this was despite the frequent poor judgment about words which sprang from their greater preoccupation with thoughts.

NOTES AND REFERENCES

1. For discussions of the extent of poetic diction in *The Seasons,* see Leon Morel, *James Thomson: sa vie et ses oeuvres* (Paris: Hachette, 1895) or G. C. Macaulay, *James Thomson* (London: Macmillan, 1908) or R. D. Havens, *The Influence of Milton.*

2. My authority for the dearth of editions of *The Seasons* in this country is Ralph Cohen's bibliography in *The Art of Discrimination, Thomson's "The Seasons" and the Language of Criticism* (Berkeley and Los Angeles: University of California Press, 1964).

3. Cohen, *The Art of Discrimination* and *The Unfolding of "The Seasons"* (London: Routledge and Kegan Paul, 1970).

4. Patricia Meyer Spacks, *The Varied God,* 1959.

5. Johnson, *Lives,* vol. 3, p. 298. Robert Shiels in his life of Thomson (1753) had made similar remarks on Thomson's diction, arousing the faint suspicion that he was influenced by Johnson who had a hand in *The Lives of the Poets,* nominally edited by Theophilus Cibber. See Cohen, *The Art of Discrimination,* pp. 317–18.

6. Johnson, *Lives,* vol. 3, pp. 298, 200. Zippel edited *The Seasons* with full apparatus in 1908; Mustard devotes six pages of his "Virgil's Georgics and the British Poets," *American Journal of Philology* 29 (1908), 1–32 to Thomson's debt to Virgil in *The Seasons.*

7. Joseph Warton, *Essay on the Genius and the Writings of Pope,* vol. 1 (1756); I quote from the 5th ed., 1806, vol. 1, p. 41.

8. Bonamy Dobrée, in the *Oxford History of English Literature,* vol. 7, p. 494, finds that in Thomson's revisions "abstractions, personification, metaphor, and classical reference have ousted objectivity and sensitiveness."

9. F. W. Bateson, *English Poetry and the English Language,* 2nd ed. (Oxford: Clarendon Press, 1961), p. 69.

10. D. N. Smith had made this point at some length in the chapter on "Thomson-Burns" in *Some Observations on Eighteenth-Century Poetry* (Toronto: University of Toronto Press, 1937), pp. 63–64. It is repeated in A. M. Oliver, "The Scottish Augustans," in *Scottish Poetry: A Critical Survey,* ed. James Kinsley (London: Cassell, 1955), p. 121.

11. See Cohen, *The Art of Discrimination,* chap. 6, for the above critics and others. The quotation from Mrs. Spacks is from pp. 103–4 of *The Varied God.* For another attempt to find recondite excellences in Thomson, see Mrs. Spack's introduction to *Eighteenth-Century Poetry* (Englewood Cliffs, N.J.: Prentice-Hall, 1964), pp. xl–xliii.

12. Chalker, *The English Georgic, A Study in the Development of a Form* (London: Routledge and Kegan Paul, 1969).

13. Ibid., pp. 136–37.

14. Only once, however, in Milton, *Paradise Lost* 8. 429. For Thomson, see *Summer,* 11. 24, 370, 754, 1384, 1605, 1764; *Spring,* 11. 305, 322, 1017, 1174; *Autumn,* 11. 144, 381, 561 (social slaughter), 834, 1029, 1289, 1347; *Winter,* 11. 356 (2), 358, 552, 975; there may be others; I have no concordance.

15. Cohen, *The Art of Discrimination,* passim.

16. Cohen, *The Unfolding of "The Seasons,"* p. 158. It is of interest to note that Scott praised, as "poetry indeed" (p. 370) Thomson's lines on Cairo and Mecca (*Summer,* 11. 977–80), one of the few passages Wordsworth singled out for praise. See *Critical Opinions,* p. 370. Joseph Warton may have been the first to praise the passage in print; see his *Essay on the Genius and Writings of Pope,* 5th ed. (1806), vol. 1, p. 46.

17. Cohen, *The Art of Discrimination,* pp. 327–28.

18. Ibid., p. 71.

19. McKillop, *The Background of Thomson's "Seasons"* (Minneapolis: University of Minnesota Press, 1942).

20. Editor, *Eighteenth-Century Poetry*, p. xlvii.

21. Scott, *Critical Essays*, p. 296.

22. Ibid., p. 300.

23. Ibid., p. 301.

24. Ibid., pp. 303–4.

25. Ibid., p. 318.

26. Ibid., p. 339 n.

27. Ibid., p. 339.

28. Havens, *The Influence of Milton*, p. 135.

29. Gosse, introduction, *The Seasons*, ed. Henry D. Roberts (London: G. Routledge and Sons, 1906), p. xxxi.

30. Respectively, *Summer* 1099, *Winter* 55, *Spring* 1001, *Winter* 194, *Winter* 53, *Autumn* 626 (see *MLR* 67:745–51), *Autumn* 1214 and *Spring* 204, *Winter*, 406, *Summer* 763 (one of some six such uses), *Spring* 495 and *Autumn* 751, *Summer* 706 and *Winter* 1750

31. Respectively, *Spring* 621, 1049, *Autumn* 327, *Summer* 167, *Spring* 814, *Autumn* 676, *Spring* 395, *Autumn* 146, 124, *Winter* 430, *Spring* 955, and *Autumn* 59.

32. See pp. 158–61.

33. Johnson, *Lives*, vol. 3, p. 301.

34. Cohen, *The Art of Discrimination*, p. 22.

35. *Poetical Works*, ed. E. de Selincourt, vol. 1, p. 284.

36. And see Psalm 104: 3: "who walketh upon the wings of the wind." Zippel mistakenly gives *Paradise Lost* 2. 263–67 as the "model" or "source" for this passage.

37. From Virgil's *Georgics* 3. 247–48, *tam multa informes ursi stragemque dedere / per silvas*, unnoted by Zippel.

38. "Absorpt" in its primary sense of swallowed up is relatively rare in English poetry. Samuel Johnson quotes only one example, from "Phillips" (presumably John Phillips's *Cyder*) in his *Dictionary*.

39. Cohen, *The Art of Discrimination*, p. 25; Cohen's interpretation of the total revisions is on pp. 25–26. Bonamy Dobrée has also commented on the passage in the *Oxford History of English Literature* (1959), vol. 7, p. 492.

40. The scenes occupy pp. 146–53 of the Oxford *Thomson;* the inclusive lines are 360–569.

41. *OED*, however, gives the following as one definition of thick: "Of actions: Occurring in quick succession, rapid, frequent . . . *Obs.*" Quotations range from c. 1450 to 1665. See Dryden, *Annus Mirabilis*, 478: "And his loud guns speak thick like angry men."

42. Oxford *Thomson*, p. vi.

43. Macauly, *James Thomson*, pp. 247–48.

44. Cohen, *The Art of Discrimination*, p. 67.

45. See p. 160.

46. See too Macauly, *James Thomson*, the Appendix on Thomson's revisions.

47. Cohen, *The Unfolding of "The Seasons,"* pp. 328–29.

48. Compare Oliver, p. 121 (see note 10): "The temptation to write about it and about it is overwhelming: many words will surely include the right one. Sometimes they do so, but the result is usually tiresome and distracting overpainting."

49. *Oxford History of English Literature,* vol. 7, pp. 494–95.

50. See p. 17.

51. Pp. 123–24; see note 10.

52. See *The Critical Opinions of William Wordsworth,* ed. Markham L. Peacock, Jr. (Baltimore: Johns Hopkins University Press, 1950), pp. 367 and 368.

53. "Vicious style" is also Wordsworth's and descriptive of *The Seasons; Critical Opinions,* p. 369.

Chapter 8.

Wordsworth

When thinking of Wordsworth and poetic diction, one naturally thinks of the 1802 appendix to the preface to *Lyrical Ballads, with Pastoral and other Poems,* as there Wordsworth writes that he is "anxious to give an exact notion of the sense" in which he used "the phrase *poetic diction,*" for in the preface he had written of "the distinction of metre" as "regular and uniform, and not like that which is produced by what is usually called poetic diction, arbitrary, and subject to infinite caprices upon which no calculation whatever can be made."[1] Wordsworth's view of the development of poetic diction, reduced to barest terms, is that "the earliest Poets of all nations generally work from passion excited by real events" and therefore "their language was daring, and figurative." Later poets, aware of the "influence of such language," strove to emulate it without, however, having "the same animating passion"; and thus they produced a language "differing materially from the real language of men in *any* situation." The earliest poets "superadded" meter "of some sort," separating "the genuine language of Poetry still further from common life," with the result that hearers or readers felt themselves moved emotionally. Later poets also added meter to their "unusual language" and so "perverted" the taste of men that "with the progress of refinement this diction became daily more and more corrupt, thrusting out of sight the plain humanities of nature by a motley masquerade of tricks, quaintnesses, hieroglyphics, and enigmas" (pp. 63–65,

181

passim). Wordsworth then refers to his analysis of Gray's sonnet on the death of Richard West, states that with the exception of lines 6–8 and 13–14 the poem "consists of little else but this diction, though not of the worst kind," condemns Pope's *Messiah,* and then compares verses six through eleven of the sixth chapter of Proverbs, "Go to the ant, thou sluggard," etc. with Samuel Johnson's poetic version of those same verses, which he characterizes as a "hubbub of words." Finally, he analyzes two stanzas of William Cowper's *Verses Supposed to be Written by Alexander Selkirk,* brands the first as "vicious poetic diction" and praises the second as "admirably expressed," an example of "natural language so naturally connected with metre" (pp. 65–67, *passim*).

What is immediately apparent is that Wordsworth's definition of "poetic diction" has little in common with modern definitions of that term, although it has affinities with what Groom means by the phrase. Thus, his dismissal of nine of the lines in Gray's sonnet is because the words do not follow the order of prose, a consideration that does not enter into modern discussions. And about all one can gather from Wordsworth's comparison of Johnson's poem and the verses from the sixth chapter of Proverbs is that the poem is a good example of poetic diction, because, one assumes, it is a bad poem. With the two stanzas from Cowper's poem one is on relatively firmer ground. Here are the two stanzas and Wordsworth's comments on them:

> Religion! what treasure untold
> Resides in that heavenly word!
> More precious than silver and gold,
> Or all that this earth can afford.
> But the sound of the church-going bell
> These valleys and rocks never heard,
> Ne'er sighed at the sound of a knell,
> Or smiled when a sabbath appeared,
>
> Ye winds, that have made me your sport,
> Convey to this desolate shore
> Some cordial endearing report
> Of a land I must visit no more.
> My Friends, do they now and then send
> A wish or a thought after me?
> O tell me I yet have a friend,
> Though a friend I am never to see.

182

I have quoted this passage [writes Wordsworth] as an instance of three different styles of composition. The first four lines are poorly expressed; some Critics would call the language prosaic; the fact is, it would be bad prose, so bad, that it is scarcely worse in metre. The epithet "church-going" applied to a bell, and that by so chaste a writer as Cowper, is an instance of the strange abuses which Poets have introduced into their language till they and their Readers take them as matters of course, if they do not single them out expressly as objects of admiration.[2] The two lines "Ne'er sigh'd at the sound," &c. are, in my opinion, an instance of the language of passion wrested from its proper use, and, from the mere circumstance of the composition being in metre, applied upon an occasion that does not justify such violent expressions; and I should condemn the passage, though perhaps few Readers will agree with me, as vicious poetic diction. The last stanza is throughout admirably expressed: it would be equally good whether in prose or verse, except that the Reader has an exquisite pleasure in seeing such natural language so naturally connected with metre. The beauty of this stanza tempts me here to add a sentiment which ought to be the pervading spirit of a system, detached parts of which have been imperfectly explained in the Preface,—namely, that in proportion as ideas and feelings are valuable, whether the composition be in prose or in verse, they require and exact one and the same language.

Wordsworth is not really discussing "three different styles of composition" in these stanzas; he is, rather, reacting violently and perhaps justifiably to the triteness of the sentiment poorly expressed in the first four lines of the excerpt. The last four lines would, understandably, appeal to him, because the word order is almost wholly that of prose. And while one might agree with his strictures on the last four lines of the first stanza, because of the pathetic fallacy therein, it is difficult to see why Wordsworth should have spared the first four lines of the second stanza. Not only are the winds invoked but there is still, in "cordial," the practice of harking back to the primary meaning of Latin words.[3] Clearly, then, Wordsworth's theory of poetic diction has no relevance for this study; equally clearly demonstrable is the fact that both in his early poetry, where examples are rife, as well as in his later poetry, he much offended in the matter of poetic diction. Critics have been at some pains to point out Wordsworth's faults in the early *Descriptive Sketches* and *An Evening Walk* and to trace them to their eighteenth-century sources. Emile Legouis catalogued these in 1921; later Ernest de Selincourt wrote that Wordsworth "took over all the stylistic vices" of "the latest exponents" of the heroic couplet, "overgoing them in preciosity of language, in meaningless personification of the abstract, in

183

harsh transference of epithets and forced constructions," and thus offering "an extreme example of that false poetic diction against which he was later to tilt."[4] Wordsworth himself described the two poems as "juvenile productions, inflated and obscure," at the same time that he claimed they contained "many new images, and vigorous lines."[5]

Wordsworth is a poet more remarkable for what he says then for how he says it. In Book 6 of *The Prelude,* "Cambridge and the Alps," he tells us

> —In fine,
> I was a better judge of thoughts than words,
> Misled in estimating words, not only
> By common inexperience of youth,
> But by the trade in classic niceties,
> The dangerous craft of culling term and phrase
> From languages that want the living voice
> To carry meaning to the natural heart;
> To tell us what is passion, what is truth,
> What reason, what simplicity and sense.[6]

He is, of course, referring to his early reading, but he writes in lines 99–100, "And yet the books which then I valued most / Are dearest to me *now,*" and it is this greater sensitivity to thoughts rather than to words which underlies much of his criticism of poetry. Indeed, the prefatory sonnet he wrote for the album of *Poems and Extracts* he chose as a Christmas gift for Lady Mary Lowther in 1819 clearly shows this principle at work

> Lady, I rifled a Parnassian Cave
> (But seldom trod) of mildly-gleaming ore;
> And cull'd, from sundry beds, a lucid store
> Of genuine crystals, pure as those that pave
> The azure brooks where Dian joys to lave
> Her spotless limbs; and ventured to explore
> Dim shades—for reliques, upon Lethe's shore,
> Cast up at random by the sullen wave.
> To female hands the treasures were resign'd
> And lo! this work—a grotto bright—and clear
> From stain or taint, in which thy blameless mind
> May feed on thoughts tho' pensive not austere;
> And if thy deeper spirit be inclined
> To holy musings, it may enter here.[7]

184

His selections are "pure as those that pave / The azure brooks where Dian joys to lave / Her spotless limbs" (his intentions are manifestly good, although his poetry offends), and Lady Mary can be sure there will be no "stain or taint, in which [her] blameless mind / May feed on thoughts tho' pensive not austere." Lady Mary, the last two lines state, will also find poetry of a religious bent in the collection. Wordsworth's preferences are revealed to be for poetry of natural description, for moral and didactic poetry, for religious poetry, and for melancholic-meditative ("pensive") poetry. His admiration for Anne Finch, Countess of Winchelsea, results in his devoting to her poetry thirty-two of the ninety-two manuscript pages of the album. Others whose poetry he cherished were John Dyer, James Thomson, John Langhorne, James Beattie, and nineteen more, ranging in time from Sir John Beaumont to William Cowper. Even a cursory reading of the poems and extracts in the album confirms the statement that Wordsworth continued to be "a better judge of thoughts than words." Some of his critical opinions equally confirm this conclusion. He writes, for example, of John Langhorne's "Poem of the Country Justice" that "it is not without many faults in style from which Crabbe's more austere judgment preserved him—but these are to me trifles in a work so original and touching." Of Thomson's poetry in *The Seasons* he could write that "not withstanding his high powers, he writes a vicious style; and his false ornaments are exactly of that kind which would be most likely to strike the undiscerning," although he admired the poem so greatly for what it says. His high, and to me incomprehensible, opinion of John Dyer's merits as a poet—"In point of *imagination* and purity of style, I am not sure that he is not superior to any writer in verse since the time of Milton"—is based, it is clear from the quoted sentence, both on what Dyer says and how he says it, an opinion that also holds true for the poetry of Anne Finch, for to him her "style in rhyme" was "often admirable, chaste, tender, and vigorous; and entirely free from sparkle, antithesis, and that overculture which reminds one by its broad glare, its stiffness, and heaviness, of the double daisies of the garden, compared with their modest and sensitive Kindred of the fields."[8]

Coming closer in time to his own period, one finds that Wordsworth thought highly of William Crowe's "excellent loco-descriptive Poem, 'Lewesdon Hill,' " first published in 1784 and read by Wordsworth in 1795,[9] an opinion he shared with Coleridge, Moore, Rogers, and Bowles.[10] The reviewer for the *Gentleman's Magazine* was fulsomely adulatory, writing that the piece was "one of the first pieces of poetry, in many points of view, which modern times have seen" (1788, Part 1, p. 151). A more recent admirer of Crowe's "hill poem" attributes Wordsworth's praise to a number of aspects of the poem: its topographical nature, its treatment of the past, and "the vein of meditation, the touches of political and philosophical comment, perhaps the attack on the doctrine of Necessity, with which Wordsworth was himself at the moment wrestling, and certainly, not least of all, the diction, which, although not quite purged of the conventional phrases of the time, is yet the diction of a scholar whose vocabulary has at once been refined by scholarship and vitalized by contact with the life of a country parish."[11] If Wordsworth was indeed attracted by the diction of the poem, and Maclean can only conjecture this, there was more than a little of what Maclean describes as "the conventional phrases of the time" in the poem, which actually, should be emended to "the conventional phrases and devices of poetic diction." Crowe, as the reviewer for the *Monthly Review* remarked, "discovers a peculiar partiality for double epithets," and while he, the reviewer, admired "the scanty-pastored sheep" and "thy furze-clad summit," he withheld his approval from "phosphor-seeming waves," "the minion-kissing King," "false-measured melody," "toy-taking fancies," and "earthy-rooted cares."[12] The reviewer disliked "hill" poems but allowed Crowe "evident marks of genius." He might have mentioned Crowe's "dew-fed vapours," "seemly-coloured cloak," "a look consumption-bred," "reed-roof'd cottage," "wide-branching oak," and "richliest-laden ship." Crowe's quite unoriginal use of another phenomenon of poetic diction, -y adjectives, can be observed: in a hill's wintry garb, hoary frosts, flowery hawthorn, a wavy fold of verdant wreath, a hill's airy top, this earthy stage, flowery vesture, spongy turf, milky treasure, chalky bourne, Neptune's foamy jaws, spicy Ternate, massy gold, branchy trees, palmy shade, towery shape, vasty mole of the sea, Neptune's watry reign, hoary pile, and downy soft wings. His Latinisms are not many, but they include verdant, vested, fantastical, vital, undistinguished, grateful, and adverse. From Milton he may have remembered tufted, sequestered, embowered, and mazes serpentine. And there is the pervasive if not too obtrusive personification which has natural pheonomena clad, garbed, cloaked, mantled, vested, robed, drest, decked in livery, skirts, dress, vesture, and a cap of flowery hawthorn. Nor is the poem without its personified Beauty, Youth, Courage, Love, Liberty, and Virtue —among others. The poem would have appealed to Wordsworth because of the strongly religious note as well as because of a certain revolutionary feeling exemplified, to cite but one example, in a tribute to General Paoli, the brave Corsican whose home was in the hands of "ambitious France." Again Wordsworth proves "a better judge of thoughts than words," although *Lewesdon Hill* is not without poetic merit.

The excesses of poetic diction in Wordsworth's earliest poems are understandable; they result from an unthinking imitation of earlier eighteenth-century models. A surer way to analyze the extent to which Wordsworth had recourse to poetic diction, knowingly or unknowingly, throughout his career is to study the revisions of three of his longest poems, revisions that span, in one instance, fifty years. The first of these poems is that which was finally entitled *Guilt and Sorrow*. Wordsworth himself is authority for 1791–92 as the date of composition of the poem in its earliest form. Of four extant manuscripts, one preserves the poem as first conceived, a second contains a significantly revised version, and the other two date from 1842, the year of publication. The first manuscript contains 61 stanzas, thirty of which were published under the title *The Female Vagrant* in *Lyrical Ballads* in 1798 and reprinted in 1800, 1802, and 1805, as well as in *Poems,* 1820–1836. Wordsworth revised the poem constantly, being dissatisfied with it from the beginning and admitting that "the diction is often vicious, and the descriptions are often false, giving proofs of a mind inattentive to the true nature of the subject on which it was employed."[13] Other critics have been concerned to examine the development of Wordsworth's thought as revealed by the thoroughgoing revisions over a period of fifty years, but some light can also be thrown on Wordsworth's use or avoidance of poetic diction. De Selincourt, for example, notes at one point that in the lines in the first manuscript that correspond to lines 199–216 of the final version "the 'poetic diction' of the phrases 'finny flood,' 'fleecy store,' 'snowy pride' [is] not found in later published text" (1. 337).

Initially, it can be said that Wordsworth seems conscious, even in the early revision stages, that he has lapsed into poetic diction. Thus, the first manuscript (Ms. 1) contains these readings that are entirely omitted in later versions: "By laughing Fortune's sparkling cup elate," "Hence where Refinement's genial influence calls," and "wintry sleep." "Wintry lustre" of Ms. 2 proves equally distasteful (pp. 335, 336). The following readings, also in Ms. 1, also disappear by 1842: gulph profound,[14] naked steep, th' etherial field, the hoary desart, ye glittering dews of youth, the fleecy train, snowy kerchiefs, glittering table store, balmy air (twice), chequered the yellow mast, the lucid mist, tears his weather-beaten cheek impearled (pp. 100–14, *passim*). And there was also the excision of finny flood, fleecy store, and snowy pride noted by de Selincourt. The "meads of green" of Ms. 1 become "meadows green" in 1842 (1. 517) and the line, "The groves resound the linnet's amorous lays" is revised to "The dripping groves resound with cheerful lays" (1. 519), Wordsworth possibly recalling and wishing to avoid any resemblance to the "amorous descant" of Gray's sonnet on the death of Richard West. Stanzas from Ms. 1 that have "no counterpart to the poem as published" contain a "kindly train" and a "frozen main" (pp. 338–39) as well as a "sleety shower" (p. 97). One line in Ms. 2, descriptive of smoke rising, "One volume mingles every various wreath," becomes "Rise various wreaths that into one unite" (1842, 1. 462). Both Ms. 1 and Ms. 2 have the line, "Or desert lark that pours on high a wasted stain," for the 1842 "Or whistling thro' thin grass along the unfurrowed plain" (1. 36). Certain readings of *The Female Vagrant,* the poem in its 1798 published form, also were dropped or changed. "The neighboring flood" (1. 3) was part of a whole stanza omitted in 1802, as were uses of "dewy prime," "deck'd" and "obtrude" (11. 25, 33, and 123). The "balmy" in "balmy air" (1. 161) disappears; "the wild brood" of 1. 215 becomes "the travellers"; and the line, "For them, in nature's meads, the milky udder flowed" (1. 225), is much revised to "In every field, with milk their dairy overflowed"—all in 1802.

Some of the poetic diction is kept, however, or restored, or added. Wordsworth retained, for his final version (to which line references are given in what follows): "a poor devoted crew" (297), the "watery load" of eyes (310), the "glittering main" (336), "the wind that hardly curled / The silent sea" (355–56),[15] and June's "warm and genial moon" (414). He restored the use of "deck'd," in "myself I deck'd," which had been cut out in the 1802 version, and he added a use of "chequering" in "Chequering the canvas roof the sunbeams shone" (542). And the line, " 'Twas dark and void as ocean's watery realm" (138), he changed from the less poetic reading of Ms. 1, " 'Twas dark and void as ocean's barren deep." One must suppose that Wordsworth was alert to rid his poem of some of the -y words rife in poetic diction and some of the Latinate words also connected with that diction. And so it is that he dispenses with finny flood, fleecy store, snowy pride, fleecy train, dewy prime, balmy air, snowy kerchiefs, wintry sleep, wintry lustre, watery load, hoary desart, milky udder, sleety shower. And so, too, it is that elate, genial, volume, and obtrude are dropped, although one use of genial persists in 1. 414. Devoted in the Latinate sense of doomed escapes revision, however (1. 297). The "pendent grapes" of line 16 are a final choice, the other alternative being the Ms. 2 reading, "the grapes hung."[16] A use of smoking to describe rain is retained from Ms. 2. Examples of poetic diction that appear for the first time in the 1842 version are "heaven's darkening cope" (1. 39), "hoary" walls (1. 115), and reference to a "rivulet" as "the flood" (1. 543).

Wordsworth's excision of a number of -y adjectives suggests his suspicion of them, yet Henry Cecil Wyld can write of "the last flickerings of eighteenth-century diction in Wordsworth's early poems, written before he had said 'good-bye to all that' in his famous Preface," and concludes, more elegantly than accurately, that "the 'feathered quires' have fled away for ever' the 'scaly breed' and 'finny droves' have retreated, along with the 'sea stallions' of a still earlier day, to the remotest depths of ocean; the 'fleecy store' bleats no longer from a thousand hills. Yet if the old clichés are out of fashion, and if later poets are but little solicitous to invent new figures on the old models, this is not to say that they have given up the use of metaphors."[17] This statement is not true of Wordsworth's poetry nor of that of many of his contemporaries, good poets and bad, as recourse to the Wordsworth and Keats concordances as well as to the poetry pages of periodicals such as the *Monthly Magazine* will amply demonstrate.

One has only to glance at—there is no necessity to read—the poems in the first few volumes of the *Monthly Magazine,* begun in 1796, to realize that virtually all the elements, as well as the very words and phrases and images, of poetic diction had not only survived to this time but had actually flourished. Robert Mayo was able to demonstrate convincingly that in form, themes, and meters *Lyrical Ballads* paralleled popular tastes and attitudes as reflected in poems in contemporary magazines;[18] the same demonstration is possible as far as poetic diction is concerned. Marjorie Barstow quotes a few verses from the *Monthly Magazine* for the first six months of 1797 to show the kind of poetry against which Wordsworth was reacting. The following, quoted as an example of "the heroic couplet and all the periphrastic elegances associated therewith," is a translation from Lucretius that appeared in the February issue; the poet is Gilbert Wakefield:

> For thee the fields their flowery carpet spread,
> And smiling Ocean smooths his wavy bed;
> A purer glow the kindling poles display,
> Robed in bright effluence of ethereal day,
> When through her portals bursts the gaudy Spring,
> And genial Zephyr waves his balmy wing.
> First the gay songsters of the feather'd train
> Feel thy keen arrows thrill in every vein.[19]

As far as the diction of these eight lines is concerned it is possible to parallel or duplicate much of it in Wordsworth's poetry, early and late. While he has no flowery carpet, he has a hill's flowery platform (*Ecc. Sonn.* 1. 6.13), with twenty-four other uses of the adjective listed in the concordance; and although he never uses wavy, his Ocean can be joyless ("When, to the attractions of the busy world," 1. 84) or angry (*Ecc. Sonn.* 1. 37.14). In

The Excursion one finds "Ocean's liquid mass in gladness lay" (1. 202). Wordsworth was fond of ethereal, using it thirty-two times, and there are two appearances of effluence in his work. He, too, falls into the personification implicit in the employment of verbs of dressing to describe natural phenomena, and as a result we have "the undaunted Rill / Robed instantly in garb of snow-white foam" (*River Duddon Sonnets* 4. 10) and "nature's pleasant robe of green" (*The Excursion* 7. 997)—to stay only with robe. And there is also the "white-robed waterfall" of *The Excursion* (3. 48). Spring's "portals" of the poem are paralleled in "the gates of Spring" of *The Recluse* (1. 188) and the "genial Zephyr" which "waves his balmy wing" of the former finds counterparts in the latter's twelve uses of Zephyr, not with genial it is true, although that is a word Wordsworth links with Spring four times in the old meaning of procreative. Balmy occurs seven times in the Wordsworth canon, never with wings, however. Wordsworth has his songsters and his songstresses and he has his feathered task-master, tenants of the flood, progeny, Lieges, and kinds. There are even parallels with the last line of the quoted poem, for there are real "keen" arrows in *The Highland Boy* (107), and Wordsworth writes of "sorrow's thrilling dart" in *The White Doe of Rystone, Ded.* 11 and of "every thrilling vein" in the second line of the *Sonnet, On Seeing Miss Helen Maria Williams Weep at a Tale of Distress.* Much the same sort of comparison could be successfully undertaken with the other short selections quoted by Barstow.

Possibly the best comment on the kind of poetry being written for the *Monthly Magazine,* a periodical that printed poems by Coleridge, Southey, and Lamb, is the bare quotation of a few stanzas from two poems that appear on succeeding pages of the April 1797 number. The first, by a "J.C.E.," is entitled "To***."

> See, fairest of the nymphs, that play
> In vernal meadows, blooming May
> Comes tripping o'er the plain:
> Lo! all the gay, the genial powers
> That deck the woods, or tend the flowers,
> Compose her smiling train.
>
> See, softer, rosier hues adorn
> The glowing cheek of blushing morn,
> When first the wakes the light:
> Behold! a thousand gentle shades

Attend the evening o'er the glades,
   And glad the sullen night.

What sweets perfume the balmy air!
While Flora bids her glittering care
   In all their beauty shine.
See Nature round, beneath, above,
All big with joy, all breathing love
   And gratitude divine.

[p. 296]

The second poem is "To the Primrose," by "the Rev. J. Bidlake (Author of the Sea, a Poem)."

Pale visitant of balmy spring,
   Joy of the new-born year,
That bidst young Hope new plume his wing,
   Soon as thy buds appear:
While o'r the incense-breathing sky
The tepid hours first dare to fly,
   And vainly woo the chilling breeze,
That bred in Winter's frozen lap,
Still struggling chains the lingering sap
   Within the widow'd trees.

Remote from towns, thy transient life
   Is spent in skies more pure;
The suburb smoke, the seat of strife,
   Thou canst but ill endure.
Coy rustic! that art blooming found
Where artless Nature's charms abound,
   Sweet neighbour of the chanter rill;
Well pleased to sip his silv'ry tide,
Or nodding o'er the fountain's side,
   Self-gazing, look thy fill.

[p. 297]

William Prideaux Courtney's account of Bidlake in the *Dictionary of National Biography* ends with the statement that he was "a man of varied talents and considerable acquirements, but his poetry was imitative, and the interest of his theological works was ephemeral." This, then, was the state of popular poetry in April 1797.

191

Wordsworth, to come to the second of his revisions of long poems, "continually went back to *The Prelude,* retouching and revising" it over a period of thirty-five years, and he is himself authority for the care and seriousness, even meticulousness, with which he undertook the revision of his work. Of certain poems he wrote that though they were not very good, "in justice to myself I must say that upon the correction of Style I have bestowed, as I always do, great Labour."[20] At another time, in a letter to Robert Gillies of December 22, 1814, he wrote, "my first expression I often find detestable; and it is frequently true of second words as of second thoughts, that they are best," remarks which hold true for the revisions in the much less remarkable *Guilt and Sorrow.* Helen Darbishire wrote of the revisions in *The Prelude* "these revisions, and Wordsworth was an inveterate reviser, follow a familiar course: bald simplicity gives way to a more decorative, more conventionally literary form (An innocent, flat line, 'The day before the holidays began,' is lifted into 'On the glad eve of those dear holidays'). Rough and crude expression is smoothed and clarified; faults of ambiguity and loose repetition carefully amended."[21] De Selincourt had made much the same comment in his edition of *The Prelude,* using such terms as "abstract and artificial language," "a more definitely literary flavour," and "pompous phrase-making" to characterize the revisions in the poem.[22] Unfortunately, the scholar who studied these revisions most closely came to the opposite, untenable conclusion. Mary Burton, both in an article in *College English* for 1944 and then in her book, *The One Wordsworth,* published the following year, finds the revisions improvements.

Present concern is with changes in poetic diction, some of which changes Miss Burton had described as "words richer in poetic association,"[23] but which, in almost every instance, are changes from a simple word to a more poetic one. In the following examples from Miss Burton's book the second word or phrase is the revision: see, behold; sticks, cleaves; stuck, adhered; ice, glassy plain; residence, abode. She writes also that Wordsworth "abandons a poetic word for an everyday term when he changes *clad* to *clothed,*"[24] clearly betraying in these and other examples her quite naive conception of what is poetic. In the following analysis of the poetic diction in *The Prelude* in its 1805–1806 and 1850 versions the emphasis is largely on the omissions, additions, and changes, i.e., revision, but a preliminary word or two should be said about the poetic diction that survived thirty-five years of "retouching and revising," to use de Selincourt's words again. Thus, one finds that Wordsworth did not see fit to revise very many Latinisms, for he kept vernal (promises, thrush, heat of poetry), vital breeze, instinct with (twice), boyish sport less grateful, latent qualities, intervenient (Nature), impervious crags, obsequious (twice), incumbent o'er the surface, aboriginal vale, vagrant tent, attractive head (i.e., with the power to attract) genial (South wind, sun), circumambient world, sagacious (a shepherd, of a storm's approach),[25] fulgent spectacle, monumental writing, the congregating temper, circumfused, thin umbrage, and cordial transport. Of -y adjectives he retained fleecy clouds, pillowy (minds), spiry (rocks, rock), leafy trees, streamy Morven, rimy trees, balmy (time, springtime), sleety rain, grassy hills, and craggy ways.

Wordsworth's additions to *The Prelude* did not include much poetic diction. He added a protending staff, an impetuous stream, an aerial Down, sylvan meditation, Winter's hoary crown, sylvan shades, briny weeds, pebbly shore, sapient priests, genial faith, the ethereal vault, the billowy ocean, the vocal streams, and the dewy grass. There are fewer omissions of poetic diction than there are additions, Wordsworth dropping only six phrases: a rocky Steep, a vital breeze, an aerial island, a pendant area of grey rocks, every pervious strait, and with liquid gold / Irradiate. The changes in poetic diction, while not very many, may best be seen in a Table.

Poetic Diction Changes in The Prelude

1805–06	1850
1. 478 the ice	1. 452 the glassy plain[1]
1. 593 steady clouds	1. 566 impending clouds
1. 665 this mood	1. 637 this genial mood[2]
2. 118 that Valley	2. 111 that sequestered valley
3. 361 delicious rivers	3. 357 crystalline rivers
4. 413 I could mark	4. 397 I could ken
6. 209 Dovedale	6. 193 Dovedale's spiry rocks[3]
6. 478 two brother Pilgrims	6. 548 two social pilgrims
8. 627 the pulse of Being	8. 480 a vital pulse
8. 717 the roof	8. 566 the massy roof
8. 741 A Spectacle	8. 588 Strange congregation
10. 150 a stream	10. 170 a fluent receptacle

[1]Wordsworth had been guilty of an earlier "glassy plain" in a skating passage from *Influence of Natural Objects* (1. 52).

[2]Unless I grossly misread this passage, genial here means procreative, as it does when Wordsworth writes of the "genial sun" (10. 515, both versions).

[3]De Selincourt notes "spiry rocks" as a "phrase found in Dyer's *Fleece* I. 658, used by Wordsworth in a note to *Descriptive Sketches* (v. note to 1. 70)" and points to a rejected Ms. s use of "spiry rock" in Book VI of *The Prelude*, p. 198. Spiry was hardly fresh when Dyer used it.

All in all, as far as the above passages are concerned, it would have been better if Wordsworth had stuck to his first words, whatever the possible improvement of second thoughts over first may have been.

Table 4 shows the revisions in poetic diction between one or more manuscript versions of the third long poem, *The Excursion,* and its final, published form serves further to emphasize the point that in so many of his revisions Wordsworth fell back on much-handled words and phrases.

TABLE 4

Poetic Diction Changes in *The Excursion*

Mss.	Published Poem
in his childhood	1. 406 in docile childhood
on the Bench he lay	1. 438 Supine the Wanderer lay
that tall slender shrub	1. 452 that aspiring shrub
grass	1. 462 plumy ferns
to catch the motion of the earth	1. 467 to respire
the grass	1. 526 the dewy grass
By speaking voice	4. 653 by vocal utterance
dismal rocks	4. 923 impending rocks
in plenteous folds	7. 180 in decent folds
upon	7. 203 chequering
the lake, though bright	9. 421 The silvery lake
the peaceful flood	9. 441 the crystal flood
with a strenuous arm	9. 489 with arms accordant
clear water	9. 491 crystal water
the crystal	9. 508 the glassy flood
shyest of plants	9. 544 the [lily's] pensive beauty
ethereal mould	9. 598 ethereal texture
this spacious Mere	9. 701 this crystal Mere

Much of the poetic diction of the final version of *The Prelude* is paralleled in *The Excursion,* sometimes quite closely. Indeed, the later poem is literally dense with poetic diction. First of all, it shares with the 1850 *Prelude* vernal (6 times in *The Excursion*), vital (8), instinct with, impervious (2), grateful (at least 7 times in its meaning of pleasing), impending (5, three times of rocks), obsequious, aboriginal ("And mantled o'er with aboriginal turf," 6. 609—note also mantled), vagrant (3), attractive (3, meaning with power to attract), genial, circumambient (present only in these two poems), monumental (4), cordial ("Of cordial spirits and vital temperament," 7. 313), and umbrage (and leafy umbrage at that, 4. 1067). Of -y adjectives the two poems share craggy (6), glassy (2), grassy (5), fleecy ("In fleecy folds voluminous [more poetic diction], enwrapped," 2. 860, an example of double or treble tautology), and leafy (6). It must be understood that the parallel uses of poetic diction in this brief comparison are far from exhaustive, most of them being of words and phrases taken from Wordsworth's revision of *The Pre-*

lude. A complete comparison would reveal many more similar parallels, of which a few examples would be in the use of social with some reminiscence of the meaning comradely (14 in *The Prelude,* 16 in *The Excursion*), supine (only in these two poems in the canon), respire, ethereal vault (2 in *The Excursion*), fluent, airy, aerial—there is no need to list others.[26] J. S. Lyon writes that "there is really a surprising resemblance between many phrases in *The Excursion* and the 'poetic diction' of eighteenth-century poets that Wordsworth denounced in the famous Preface and Essay Supplementary to the Preface of *Lyrical Ballads*" and documents his statement by examples of "flowery circumlocutions," Wordsworth's "choice of modifiers," and of his Latinate words.[27] Lyon's statement is not entirely accurate, especially in his reference to Wordsworth's theory of poetic diction, and in a complimentary bow in the direction of Miss Burton's study of the revisions in *The Prelude*[28] he seeks to link the revised *Prelude* with *The Excursion* in terms of competent craftmanship. It is worth repeating, as a corrective, that the excesses of poetic diction in *The Excursion* are akin to the unfortunate lapses in taste in the revisions in *The Prelude* and that Wordsworth evidently sinned in this matter without knowing it. As far as the poetic diction in the revisions of *Guilt and Sorrow,* of *The Excursion,* and of the *Prelude* is concerned it is of a piece with that in *An Evening Walk* and *Descriptive Sketches.*

In her brief survey of the history of poetic diction Marjorie L. Barstow states that "Dryden became the creator of the elegances and flowers of speech so dear to the heart of the eighteenth century, so obnoxious to the taste of the nineteenth." She then quotes approvingly this passage from Myra Reynolds:

> For instance, there is the adjective "watery." To him [Dryden] the ocean is a "watery desert," a "watery deep," a "watery plain," a "watery way," a "watery reign." The shore is a "watery brink," or a "watery strand." Fish are a "watery line," or a "watery race." Sea-birds are a "watery fowl." The launching of ships is a "watery war." Streams are "watery floods." Waves are "watery ranks."[29]

Mrs. Barstow goes on to say that "to call fish the 'finny race' is not to say anything new or interesting about them; to vary the expression to the scaly tribe is only to make matters worse. Yet is it easy to see that all these atrocities might be produced, with no intention of thus distinguishing poetry from prose, by any man who was trying to write well without knowing

195

what he was talking about."[30] Now, Wordsworth probably recognized that he had lapsed into poetic diction and so omitted the "finny flood" of the first manuscript of the poem that finally became *Guilt and Sorrow*. The concordance of his poetry lists no use of the offending adjective in his published work, but he did use precisely the phrase, "scaly tribes," at which Mrs. Barstow rightly points the finger of scorn.[31] And, what is even more revealing in light of the pejorative listing of Dryden's uses of "watery," is Wordsworth's own fairly frequent recourse to it—nineteen times, according to the Lane Cooper concordance. Nor is there anything particularly novel about his watery phrases, as he links that adjective with lights, plains (twice; did he remember Dryden?), realm, load (for tears), globe, glade, gleam, cove, bog, vale, surface, storm, rocks, element, duplicate (image). It is instructive to note that Pope was as fond of that adjective as Dryden, for in his translation of the *Iliad* he uses it twenty-two times, with such words as reign (twice), plain, race, store (twice), main, way, waste (twice), bowers, and mountains (twice, to describe waves). As far as Wordsworth's use of watery is concerned, he is squarely in the tradition of Dryden's translation of *Virgil*, where most of his uses of the word occur, and of Pope's translation of the *Iliad*.

Ironically enough, Wordsworth was extremely harsh in his judgment of both Dryden's *Virgil* and Pope's *Homer*. Of Dryden he wrote in a letter to Sir Walter Scott, "That his cannot be the language of imagination must have necessarily followed from this, that there is not a single image from Nature in the whole body of his works; and in his translations from Virgil, whenever Virgil can be fairly said to have his *eye* upon his object, Dryden always spoils the passage." In another letter to Scott, on the matter of translation, he wrote, "I have a very high admiration of the talents both of Dryden and Pope. . . . But thus far . . . their writings have done more harm than good. It will require yet half a century completely to carry off the poison of Pope's Homer."[32] But twenty years after the first publication of *Lyrical Ballads* Wordsworth began and continued for three or four years a translation of parts of the *Aeneid*, and in an advertisement to the translation acknowledged that "three or four lines, in different parts, are taken from Dryden" (*Poetical Works*, 4. 286). And, among his juvenilia, there is a translation of the story of Orpheus and Eurydice from lines 467–527 of Virgil's fourth *Georgic* in which he borrows Dryden's line, "The mighty heroes more majestic shade."[33] In the same translation, his "And strew'd his mangled limbs the plain around" (1. 72) very probably comes from Dryden's line, "And strew'd his mangl'd limbs about the field" (759).

196

Wordsworth had another translator of Virgil in mind, or before him, when in another piece of juvenilia, a translation of the description of a horse from the third *Georgic,* lines 75–94, he writes that he "with neighings shrill / Fill'd all the shaggy round of Pelion high" (11. 22–23), for Joseph Warton (1753) had written, "And pierc'd with neighings shrill hoar Pelion's piny head" (1. 134). Wordsworth follows or coincides with Warton in: generous breed, stately, easy, threatening flood (Warton—"threatening wave"), din of distant arms (Warton—"the battle's distant din"), erected ears (Warton—"erects his eager ears"), his mane redundant (Warton—his redundant mane), solid horn, Such Cyllarus, steeds of Mars (Warton—"the steeds . . . That . . . bore the god of war"), all in a passage of twenty-three lines.[34]

Wordsworth's admission that three or four lines of his *Aeneid* translations came from Dryden, his reliance on Warton's translation of the *Georgics* and on Pitt's of the *Aeneid* in their joint edition of 1753 for word and phrase, and his dependence on the Pitt *Aeneid* for about one-fifth of his rhyme words[35] raises the question of a further probable influence, that of the poetic diction in Dryden and Pitt-Warton. One must always bear in mind that Pitt and Warton are themselves heavily indebted to Dryden's *Virgil.* Poetic diction in the two short pieces from the *Georgics* consists of: lonely main, leafy bower, torpid flood, aerial rocks, shaggy prospect, callow in the Orpheus and Eurydice episode, and foal of generous breed, threatening flood, luxuriant, his mane redundant in the description of a horse. Generous meaning of noble birth and flood for river were used too often by poets earlier than Wordsworth, and Dryden, for that matter, to count for very much; the same is true of main for ocean. All three occur, however, in Dryden's and Warton's versions of the *Georgics.* Dryden has: leafy bow'rs in the fourth *Georgic* (1. 75), aerial honey also in the fourth (1. 2), shaggy in the third (1. 452, but used of animals), and three uses of callow in as many *Georgics* (1, 2, 4); of five uses of luxuriant in the *Virgil,* four are from the *Georgics,* and the only use of redundant is in *Georgic* 1. 129. Warton uses leafy five times; has an aerial hill (G. 3. 508) and aerial Alps (G. 3. 579); describes horses or their attributes as generous three times; has three uses of luxuriant; and is the source for Wordsworth's redundant mane. He, like Dryden describes animals (goats) twice as shaggy, and writes of the callow young of birds (G. 1. 486). One reading, leavy grove, a manuscript variant in Wordsworth's version of the Orpheus and Eurydice story, finds a counterpart in the leavy woods of Dryden's first *Georgic* (1. 491), the only occurrence of that adjective in the *Virgil.* Wordsworth has plaintive shell and plaintive note in the Orpheus and Eurydice story; of two uses of plaintive in Dryden's *Virgil,* one is from the fourth *Georgic* (1. 473). All in all, this is pretty good evidence that the young Wordsworth was not unaware of Dryden's and Warton's versions of the *Georgics* when he translated the two episodes.

The two early translations from the *Georgics* taken together extend to only 101 lines of poetry, while the translations from the *Aeneid* run to exactly 3,000 lines. What is more, the mature Wordsworth, although he wrote that he began the translation of the *Aeneid* "by accident," had evidently given some thought to Virgil's style in his epic, for he wrote to Lord Lonsdale in 1819, the year he began, that "Virgil's style is an inimitable mixture of the elaborately ornate and the majestically plain and touching. The former quality is much more difficult to reach than the latter, in which whosoever fails must fail through want of ability, and not through the imperfections of our language." He also wrote to Lord Lonsdale in that same year, "It was my wish and labour that my translation should have far more of the *genuine* ornaments of Virgil than my predecessors. Dryden has been very careful of these, and profuse of his own, which seems to me very rarely to harmonize with those of Virgil. . . . I feel it, however, to be too probable that my translation is deficient in ornament, because I must unavoidably have lost many of Virgil's and have never without reluctance attempted a compensation of my own. Had I taken the liberties of my predecessors, Dryden especially, I could have translated nine books with the labour that three have cost me."[36] Not only had Wordsworth pondered Virgil's style and the difficulties of translating the *Aeneid* but he was ever conscious of Dryden's version, usually finding fault with it, to be sure, but never really forgetting it.[37]

Table 5 lists the more important uses of poetic diction in Wordsworth's translations from the *Aeneid* and their identical or close counterparts in Dryden's *Virgil* and in the Pitt-Warton *Virgil;* Pope's *Iliad* and *Odyssey* appear as other possible sources for some of the diction. Book and line numbers are to the *Aeneid* and the *Iliad* and mean that the phrases are identical to those listed under Wordsworth; when they are close, I quote the pertinent phrase in Pope or Dryden. Under Dryden and Pitt-Warton G stands for *Georgics* and P for *Pastorals.*

198

TABLE 5

Poetic Diction in Wordsworth's *Aeneid* Translations Compared with Dryden, Pitt-Warton and Pope

Wordsworth's *Aeneid*	Dryden's *Virgil*	Pitt-Warton	Pope's *Iliad*
1. 6 new abodes	1. 736; 3. 618	2. 811	
1. 506 belov'd abode	4. 964 lov'd abodes		
1. 503 an adverse blast [of wind]			*Odyssey* 9. 90; 10. 19, adverse winds
2. 968 adverse Greeks	10. 716 adverse foes	1. 286²; 2. 145, 441	*Odyssey* 22. 233, adverse host
1. 291 flames aspire	G. 4. 554¹		1. 608; 2. 205; 23. 271; *Odyssey* 3. 88
1. 594 the aspiring town		1. 450 aspiring walls³	12. 368 th' aspiring wall
2. 459 an auxiliar train			2. 987, auxiliar troops; 7. 444, auxiliar bands; 10. 491, auxiliar forces; 13. 574, auxiliar force; *Odyssey* 4. 553, auxiliar force; 19. 147, auxiliar troops; 20. 51, auxiliar aid, 22. 123, auxiliar shafts
1. 408 azure region [sea]			13. 442 azure main; *Odyssey* 5. 70 azure wave
1. 95 beauteous progeny			3. 530
3. 546 the bristly kind [pig]	G. 4. 589 a bristly boar	3. 521	16. 994 a bristly boar; *Odyssey* 14. 128, the bristly kind
1. 800 the circumambient cloud	1. 813 ambient cloud		*Odyssey* 7. 187, an ambient cloud
3. 801 confound the sky			21. 374 confound the place

1. 108 congregated power			2. 1006 congregated troops
1. 1001–2 many a blazing light / Depends	1. 1015 From gilded roofs depending lamps display[4]		
2. 212 devoted [doomed] head	2. 132; 5. 908; 11. 275; P. 8. 103	2. 163, 209; 5. 1090	24. 50[5]
2. 13 dewy night	11. 306	11. 277	2. 372; 4. 102
1. 42 the dire Achilles			5. 447; 6. 335; 13. 499; 16. 597
3. 36 dire portent			15. 99[6]
2. 296 distain'd with gore	2. 322; 4. 655; 5. 689	5. 535; 10.583	14. 510 flow'ry ground
1. 174 fields of air	11. 56 distain'd with purple gore	4. 331, 349; 5. 683	
1. 583 flowery grounds	1. 196; G. 4. 103		
1. 151 Headlong the pilot falls	6. 888 flow'ry ground	1. 158 [the pilot] shot headlong	
	5. 1118 Headlong he ["the pilot" of 1. 1112] fell[7]		
1. 334 headlong sea			Odyssey 24. 613, headlong tyde
1. 429 headlong course		9. 727 headlong speed	18. 186
2. 272–73 o'er the tranquil main / incumbent		2. 277 incumbent on the glassy tide	Odyssey 5. 63, incumbent on the rolling deep
2. 913 the lambent flame	2. 931[8]	2. 924 lambent glory	Odyssey 11. 178, the latent cause
3. 44 the latent causes		3. 40	18. 441
2. 1017; 3. 504 and 642 massy gold	9. 55	2. 1027; 3. 471	Odyssey 7. 112, massy brass
3. 344 fowls obscene			19. 30 worms obscene
3. 374 obscene birds	3. 341 and G. 1. 635 birds obscene[9]		Odyssey 24. 10, birds obscene
3. 344 fowls obscene[9] [10]			Odyssey 3. 322
1. 419 the pendent grove			21. 522 the pendent groves
			Odyssey 3. 97, pendent woods
3. 795 a pitchy cloud	3. 748; 4. 170		
1. 152 the gulph profound		1. 145 the dark profound	21. 229 gulphs profound

2. 999 refulgent arms	6. 660; 8. 697; 11. 1238	7. 1006	2. 698; 4. 254; 6. 661; 13. 38; 18. 173, 592; 23. 160
3. 181 a sable sheep	6. 230 two sable sheep[11]		Odyssey 10. 628, sable sheep
3. 164 the lofty steep			14. 263 Athos' lofty steep
1. 670 swarthy Memnon	1. 686 and 1052	1. 661	Odyssey 4. 256 (by Fenton)
1. 223 sylvan shade		7. 509 sylvan shades	21. 546 sylvan shades Odyssey 12. 396 and 16. 255 (both Broome)
1. 314 eternal sway		1. 308	
1. 653 Supinely stretch'd		1. 640 Supine	
2. 57 a numerous throng	12. 200; P. 6. 42		
3. 489 a numerous train	1. 697; 3. 445; 5. 380; 6. 549; 12. 654		2. 805; 3. 301; 18. 577; Odyssey 17. 163; 24. 491
2. 421 vocal cries		3. 609 vocal accents	
1. 40 the watery waste			Odyssey 5. 497

[1] Sheets of fire "aspire," 2. 1031; a blaze "aspires," 11. 318.

[2] Note here and elsewhere that identical passages, in this case identical to Pitt, are involved.

[3] aspiring mountain, 7. 893; aspiring bulwarks, 9. 688.

[4] Pope, Thebaid, 1. 610, "depending lamps."

[5] Dryden uses dire as an epithet for Ulysses 2. 341 and 3. 354; for Celaeno in 3. 469 and 938; and for Tisiphone in 6. 749. Pitt has "dire Orion" (1. 720), "dire Ulysses" (2. 135; 3. 366; 6. 729), "dire Avernius" (6. 609), "dire Scylla" (7. 377), "dire Alecto" (7. 412, "dire Hecate" (4. 877), as well as 20 other uses of the word. It is used as an epithet for Scylla, Charybdis, and Polypheme in the Odyssey: 12. 280, 506; and 20. 27.

[6] At least five times in the Odyssey: 5. 58; 6. 19; 8. 8; 13. 510; 16. 169.

[7] Also Aeneid 16. 908, "falls headlong," and Iliad 5. 357; 8. 381; 16. 370 for "headlong" falls; Pitt uses the word 20 more times.

[8] From Virgil's lambere flamma, Aeneid 2. 684.

[9] Pope has "birds obscene" in his Statius His Thebaid, 1. 735.

[10] Cowley, Davideis 2. 304, in Waller's edition of the poems, states that the word obscene was used by the "Augures" to signify ill-fortune and quotes Virgil's Aeneid and Ovid in illustration.

[11] Pope has "a sable ewe" and "a sable lamkin" in 10. 255–56 and "sable oxen" in 13. 205; black animals were sacrificed to the infernal powers, but then Wordsworth could have used "black" instead of "sable."

Some similarities are not so easily fitted into Table 5. Thus, Wordsworth joins goblets and wine in a coronation figure, one of the oldest: "Huge goblets are brought forth; they crown the wine" (1. 998). The same combination of these three elements appears four times in Dryden's *Virgil* and eight times in Pope's *Iliad*.[38] Wordsworth writes of the "hoary-headed Priam," hardly a daring epithet, as Pope almost invariably refers to Priam as the hoary monarch, king, or sire, or simply as "hoary Priam" (21. 613); once he refers to "Priam's hoary hairs" (6. 576). Pitt describes Priam as "the hoary sage" at 2. 681. When Wordsworth describes men as "within that cloud involved" (1. 707) he has precedent for the "cloud-involved" phrase in eight uses in Dryden's *Virgil,* three in Pitt, and five in the *Iliad*.[39] Even Wordsworth's "wafted o'er" (3. 571) may recall Dryden's four uses of the words together; Pitt couples them five times.[40] One of the lines Wordsworth may have modeled closely on Dryden is "Made manifest by copious streams of light" (3. 228) for the latter has "With radiant beams and manifest to sight" (4. 513), and manifest is not too common in this sense. Indeed, there is no use of manifest in any sense in Pope's *Iliad*. And then there are other items of poetic diction in Wordsworth's translation that might have been suggested by Dryden or Pitt or Pope; even if they were not, it is still true that they were there in the *Virgil* and the *Iliad* to which he would seem to have been indebted. In this group are "liquid produce" (honey, 1. 586), analogous to Pope's "liquid harvest" (wine, 14. 139); "luxuriant wood" (3. 384), the adjective being used as Pitt uses it in "luxuriant leaves" at 12. 577 and as Pope uses it in "luxuriant harvests" (1. 205); the verbs scud and skim, used to describe movement through or over water, as in "scud along the main" (3. 188) and "skim the foaming surge" and "skim the waves" (3. 382 and 304), used, respectively, four and five times in Dryden's *Virgil*. Pitt so uses the verb skim four times. Further, there are other words and phrases of poetic diction which were so common that it would be rash indeed to claim that Wordsworth remembered them from the *Virgil* or the *Iliad*. Among these would be: kind, vocal, watery, briny, to deck, foamy, oozy, scaly, steep (noun), sway (noun), flood (noun), dome, craggy, impend. But Wordsworth availed himself of some of the older diction not to be found in these two sources (billowy, welkin) and included some that was almost surely of later date. His dependence upon or possibly his sense of the fitness for epic of Latinate words can be seen in the following, none of which is in the *Virgil* or the *Iliad:* agglomerate, circumambient, conflagrant, docile, flexile,[41] gratulant, lenient,[42] prevenient, ululation. His description of how the serpents that killed Laccoon sweep "In folds voluminous and vast, the deep" (2. 278) comes from Milton's description of Sin whose body below the waist "ended foul in many a scaly fold / Voluminous and vast, a serpent . . ." (*Paradise Lost* 2. 651–52). Worth noting is the fact that the rhyme words in five couplets of the first 72 lines of Wordsworth's version of the *Aeneid* are to be found in the first 81 lines of Dryden's version of that book, but it hardly seems profitable to carry this line of investigation further here.

Perhaps it would not be amiss to conclude the matter of poetic diction in Wordsworth's poetry with a relatively bare catalogue of those words and phrases in *Lyrical Ballads* which are held to be part of that diction. One observes initially that while the Lane Cooper concordance lists eleven uses of sat in Wordsworth's poetry, the five that are listed for poems in *Lyrical Ballads* appear as sate in the 1798 edition and only one is marked as revised to sat in a later edition.[43] Even if the other six uses of sat are correct they are to be opposed to the 96 occurrences of sate listed in the concordance. But Dorothy Wordsworth wrote in her journal that "William sate beside me" (Dec. 21, 1801). Sate, as has been remarked before, is almost invariably used in epic of sublime contexts in earlier poetry, with Milton as an exception to the general rule. Pope does not use sat anywhere in his translation of the *Iliad;* Dryden uses it but once in his translation of Virgil.[44] Wordsworth, to go on to other matters, was rather fond of verdant and vernal, both appearing five times in *Lyrical Ballads.* Sylvan and headlong appear thrice each; and ruddy twice. Winds curl the waves and the silent sea. There is a craggy steep, embowering hollies, a mossy network, pearly white tints, and a gulph profound. Surprisingly enough, Wordsworth reaches back in time for delicious, meaning pleasing, in the line, "That intermixture of delicious hues" (*Poems on the Naming of Places,* 2. 1. 47). His most original bit of diction is in his description of green stones "fleec'd with moss" in *Nutting* (1. 34); the *OED* gives only one figurative use of "to fleece," and that in a work of prose, "Waterhouse *Fire Lond*" (1667), "Thrifty Oaks, though fleeced of under boughs, yet if not headed, may thrive." I have come upon one use in Giles Fletcher's *Christ's Triumph* (1610), in which the morning star is likened to a shepherd chasing the "bright drove, fleec't all in gold" (st. 12) and another in Thomson's *Seasons:* "a sober calm / Fleeces unbounded either" (*Autumn,* 11. 957–58, 1746 edition).

From this incomplete analysis one can only draw tentative and restricted conclusions. While Wordsworth's definition of poetic diction has very little in common with the poetic diction defined in this study, he was aware of the commonplace quality of a number of poetic words and phrases and was at some pains to omit part of them in his revisions of some of his longest and most important poems. But, it must also be said, he kept some of the poetic diction in the earliest versions of those poems and even added some in revision. The break with eighteenth-century poetry was far from a cataclysmic one. What is more, Wordsworth, in his translations from Virgil, was either acutely conscious of the special vocabularies demanded by particular genres or he quite unashamedly borrowed with both hands from Dryden and Pope and from their predecessors and successors, good, bad, and indifferent. Indeed, considering both his original poetry and his translations, Wordsworth, because of the amount and variety of poetic diction to which he had recourse, was as much a conservative in the practice of his poetic theory—the language of poetry should not materially differ from "the real language of men in *any* situation"—as he once seemed a revolutionary in his formulation of it.

NOTES AND REFERENCES

1. *Literary Criticism of William Wordsworth,* ed. Paul M. Zall (Lincoln, Neb.: University of Nebraska Press, 1966), pp. 63 and 54–55.

2. In the first manuscript version of *Guilt and Sorrow,* Wordsworth had written of "the church-visiting bells' delightful chime," revised to "the sabbath bells" for *Lyrical Ballads,* and eventually to just "the church bells."

3. For Tillotson's observations on Wordsworth's Appendix, see *APD,* pp. 87–92, especially p. 91 n. 1 on the epithet "church-going" in Cowper's lines.

4. Respectively, *The Early Life of William Wordsworth, 1770–1798 . . . ,* translated by J. W. Matthews (London: J. M. Dent and Sons, 1921), pp. 133–47, and *Wordsworthian and Other Sketches,* ed. Helen Darbishire (Oxford: Clarendon Press, 1947), p. 20.

5. *Critical Opinions,* p. 390.

6. Lines 105–14 of the 1850, revised version.

7. Edited in 1905 by Harold Littledale as *Poems and Extracts Chosen by William Wordsworth For an Album Presented to Lady Mary Lowther, Christmas 1819.*

8. Quoted in *Critical Opinions,* respectively, pp. 298, 369, 250, and 381.

9. *Critical Opinions,* pp. 237 and 251, and see the following note.

10. Havens, *The Influence of Milton,* p. 253.

11. C. M. Maclean, "Lewesdon Hill and its Poet," *Essays and Studies by Members of the English Association,* vol. 27 (1941, published in 1942), p. 32; the authority for Wordsworth's reading of the poem is a letter quoted by Maclean, p. 30.

12. *Monthly Review* 78 (Jan.-June 1788):306–8.

13. Quoted in *Poetical Words,* ed. E. de Selincourt (Oxford: Clarendon Press, 1940), vol. 1, p. 333–34. Page and line references in the text are to this edition.

14. But there is a "gulph profound" elsewhere in *Lyrical Ballads;* see *The Idle Shepherd-Boys,* 1. 70.

15. There are "curling waves" elsewhere in *Lyrical Ballads;* see 1. 5 of *Lines Left Upon a Seat* . . .

16. This is particularly interesting in light of Wordsworth's much later remarks on the verb "to hang" in the Preface to the edition of 1815. See de Selincourt, *Poems,* vol. 2, pp. 436–37.

17. Wyld, *Some Aspects of the Diction of English Poetry,* pp. 60–61.

18. Mayo, "The Contemporaneity of Lyrical Ballads," *PMLA* 69 (1954):486–522.

19. *Wordsworth's Theory of Poetic Diction,* p. 62.

20. Ernest de Selincourt (ed.), *The Prelude or Growth of a Poet's Mind,* 2nd ed. revised by Helen Darbishire (Oxford: Clarendon Press, 1959), p. lv.

21. *The Poet Wordsworth* (Oxford: Clarendon Press, 1950), pp. 120–21.

22. De Selincourt, *The Prelude,* pp. lx and lxi.

23. Mary Burton, *The One Wordsworth,* pp. 144–46.

24. Ibid., p. 145.

25. The only use of sagacious in the old sense in the canon.

26. They may do for a footnote. Both contain sylvan combs and dewy grass, massy, pile (a building), vocal (streams in *The Prelude* 14. 146 and utterance in *The Excursion* 4. 653), sedentary, servile, delicious (pleasing), correspondent, starry, and the coronation figure (two in *The Prelude,* but some twelve or thirteen in *The Excursion*).

27. Lyon, *"The Excursion": A Study* (New Haven: Yale University Press, 1959), pp. 120–30, passim.

28. Burton, *The One Wordsworth,* p. 123.

29. Reynolds, *Treatment of Nature.*

30. *Wordsworth's Theory of Poetic Diction,* pp. 44, 45.

31. See *The River Duddon* 28. 6.

32. Quoted in *Critical Opinions,* pp. 245 and 247. Compare Coleridge in *Biographia Literaria:* Pope's *Homer* "which I do not stand alone in regarding as the main source of our pseudo-poetic diction."

33. Line 16 in Wordsworth, *Poetical Works,* vol. 1, p. 283; line 684 in Dryden, who appends a note acknowledging that he took the line from the Marquess of Normandy's translation. Wordsworth has "And" for "The."

34. This information is documented in a yet unpublished study of "Wordsworth's Translations from Virgil."

35. I establish both points in the unpublished article cited in the preceding note.

36. *Critical Opinions,* pp. 372, 436, and 437; see also p. 117 for his praise of "the first paragraph of the *Aeneid.*"

37. See *Critical Opinions,* pp. 247–48.

38. *Aeneid* 7. 181; P. 5. 108; G. 2. 771 and 3. 584; in Pitt's *Aeneid,* goblets and bowls are crowned, almost invariably with wine at 1. 949, 972, 977, 997–98; 3. 470, 713; 8. 239, 367. *Iliad* 1. 616; 4. 4, 299; 9. 229, 771; 10. 680; 15. 94; 18. 632.

39. *Aeneid* 1. 571; 3. 766; 4. 403; 10. 896; 12. 615, 976, 1180; G. 4. 614; Pitt, 1. 587; 2. 477; 4. 189; and *Iliad* 5. 236, 446, 932; 14. 168; 15. 349.

40. 6. 452, 504, 560; 9. 114; only once in Pope's *Iliad* 24. 920. See also Pope, *Sapho to Phaon,* 1. 210, and eight occurrences of the two words together in the Odyssey: 2. 242,

334, 446; 4. 490; 11. 36; 14. 423; 17. 616; 24. 480. Pitt's uses are at 1. 487; 3. 501, 586, 933; 6. 576.

41. He may have recollected Thomson's "flexile wave" (*Summer*, 1. 980), although there are other earlier uses of the word.

42. But there is one use in the *Odyssey*, Fenton's "lenient of grief," 4. 731.

43. The Cooper concordance is based on the Oxford *Wordsworth;* I have used the edition of *Lyrical Ballads* edited by R. L. Brett and A. R. Jones (London: Clarendon Press, 1963.) See p. 206 for the revision.

44. "Sate" is worth a further note. It is Spenser's preferred spelling, if one can trust the concordance, for he has "sate" 63 times as opposed to a scattering of "sat." Herrick has only "sate." William Collins writes "sat" twice in the *Popular Superstitions* ode (11. 196, 212) but "sate" twice in the *Ode on the Poetical Character* (11. 31, 43) and once in both the *Ode on the Passions* (1. 58) and the first of his Persian *Eclogues* (1. 17). Gray, in a poem about an imprudent cat, writes that "(Malignant Fate *sat* by, and smil'd)," but when he treats of Odin he writes "By the moss-grown pile he *sate,*" and when he translates Dante he had Count Ugolino say "That day and yet another, mute we *sate.*" What is more, Gray could make fun of the dignity of "sate" as in the line in his humorous poem, *A Long Story,* where one reads that "the Court was sate."

Index

Shakespeare, William, 69–85; *All's Well that Ends Well,* 78; *Antony and Cleopatra,* 75; Coleridge on, 74; *Comedy of Errors,* 70; Groom on, 70, 73; *Hamlet,* 76, 80, 127; Havens on, 52; *2 Henry IV,* 71, 77; *Henry V,* 73; *1 Henry VI,* 60, 70; Johnson on, 69; *King Lear,* 70; language of, 60; Latinisms in, 61, 62, 80–81; *Measure for Measure,* 78; *Midsummer-Night's Dream,* 71–72, 73, 75, 76, 77, 99; *Othello,* 3–4, 71; periphrases in, 77–78; Pope's edition of, 83; *Richard II,* 77; *Richard III,* 80; *Romeo and Juliet,* 70, 78; Rowe's edition of, 83; *The Tempest,* 70, 73; *Timon of Athens,* 70, 77, 81; *Titus Adronicus,* 60, 75; *Troilus and Cressida,* 79; *Twelfth Night,* 73; *Two Gentlemen of Verona,* 78; *-y* adjectives in, 71–72, 75–76, 79–80, 110
Shelley, Percy Bysshe, 31, 61
Shepherd's Calendar, 48, 49, 50, 54, 73
Sherburne, Sir Edward, 101, 113–14
Shirley, James, 51
Sidney, Sir Philip, 110, 111
Sigismonda and Guiscardo, 118, 119
Silius Italicus, 31, 32, 34–36, 126
Smollett, Tobias, 6
Spacks, Patricia Meyer, 158, 160, 162
Spanish Friar, The, 55
Spectator 27
Spence, Joseph, 5, 55, 133, 151
Spenser, Edmund: *Daphnaida,* 60; *The Faerie Queene,* 46, 57, 60–61, 62, 64, 79, 99; favorite or semi-favorite words of, 53; Groom on, 53, 60, 73; Havens on, 52; *An Hymne of Heavenly Love,* 63; influence of DuBartas on, 55–56; influence of, on later English poets, 62; influence of, on Milton, 99; influence of Sylvester on, 55–56; influence on Fenton of, 97–98; Latinisms in, 49, 58–59, 60–62; *Mother Hubbard's Tale,* 60; periphrases in, 59, 65; and poetic diction, 52, 54; *Ruins of Rome,* 55–56; and Sackville, 46; *Shepherd's Calendar,* 48, 49, 50, 54, 73; and transmission of poetic diction, 88–89; Wyld on, 56–59; *-y* adjectives in, 49, 59, 71; *Virgil's Gnat,* 34
Spleen, The, 13–14, 16
Stafford, John, 124, 125
Stanyhurst, Richard, 46
Staplyton, Robert, 108
Statius, 21, 22, 31, 139
Statius his Thebais, 120, 139–41

Stephens, Thomas, 139, 140
Stock diction, 10, 11
Summer (Pope), 26, 39
Surrey, Henry Howard, Earl of, 45, 46, 90
Sutherland, James R., 17
Swift, Jonathan, 15, 58
Sylvae (Pope), 107, 108, 113
Sylvester, Joshua, 65, 90; *Du Bartas* translation, 46, 47, 52, 53, 66, 77, 93, 110, 114, 127, 128; influence of, on Spenser, 55, 56; periphrases in, 65; poetic diction of, 52; and Sackville, 46; Tillotson on, 132

Taming of the Shrew, 78
Tasso: *Aminta,* 36; *Gierusalemme Liberata,* 36; Pope on, 36, 37
Tasso (Fairfax), 32, 33, 37
Tate, Nahum, 22
Tempest, The, 70, 73
Temple of Fame, The, 36, 39
Thebaid, 21, 22
Theocritus: Dryden's opinion of, 114; and Dryden's *Idyllia* translation, 112; *Idyllia,* 113–14; influence of, 24; pastoral poems of, 21; translations of, 112–16; and his debt to Virgil, 116
Thomson, James, 158–80; *Autumn,* 160–61; favorite words of, 164–65; Havens on, 163; Hazlitt on, 159; Johnson on, 158–59; Latinisms in, 9, 160, 163–64; and Milton, 165; periphrases in, 160; and revision of *Winter,* 165–76; *The Seasons,* 158–80; *Spring,* 102; *Winter,* 9, 17, 165–76; Wordsworth on, 185; *-y* adjectives in, 164
Timon of Athens, 70, 77, 81
Tillotson, Geoffrey, 39; *Augustan Poetic Diction,* 12, 19 n. 47, 109; and definition of poetic diction, 8; on favorite words, 25; on Milton, 53, 99; on poetic diction, 8, 14–15, 17; on Sandys, 132, 138; on Spenser's favorite words, 53; on Sylvester, 52, 132
Tillyard, E. M. W., 22
Titus Adronicus, 60, 75
"To ***," 190
To His Coy Mistress, 136
Tonson's *Miscellanies,* 146
Tooke, Charles, 147
"To the Primrose," 191
Tottel, Richard, 45
Tottel's *Miscellany,* 45, 46
Troilus and Cressida, 79
Turberville, George, 29–30, 49